While suffering is not sought by any person, Bry
a theological perspective on the subject. This b
Bible, counsellors, teachers, pastors and especia..,
are a part of human existence, Arthur encourages the believer witn ᴛᴜᴇ ...
stance that suffering is a process that increases meaning in life. The suffering of great
men of the Bible, the suffering of Paul and early church leaders, as well as the suffering
of Christ himself, are all shown as ways in which spiritual healing is promoted and
grace is given from God to mankind. While suffering is never sought, Arthur creates
a balm with his theological stance that begets an increased capacity to know the
glory of God.

Rev Azar Ajaj
Principal,
Nazareth Theological College, Israel

Dr Arthur profitably probes the nature of suffering and offers guidance on how faithful
Christians, like those before us in biblical times, are called to respond in situations of
personal suffering. He guides us by these theological mediations to think biblically
about our suffering and to encourage us onward towards even rejoicing in our suffering.
This book is a helpful guide for every believer who wants to reflect theologically about
this subject, and who needs the reassurance of God's gracious purpose in allowing
us to suffer.

Rev Brian DeVries, PhD
Principal,
Mukhanyo Theological College, KwaMhlanga, South Africa

Bryson Arthur has written what will be the standard work on suffering for theological
thinkers. It is learned, deep and profound. It is also passionate about biblical truth and
spiritual realities. This book is pure gold, towering over the many books on this subject.

Rev Phil Hill
Baptist Pastor and Professional Counsellor
Former Pastoral Dean, Union School of Theology, UK

Reading *A Theology of Suffering* reminded me of Dietrich Bonhoeffer's book *Cost of
Discipleship*. In that book Bonhoeffer emphatically says, "When Christ calls a man,
He bids him come and die." This is a rallying call which is almost seen or implied in
nearly every page of *A Theology of Suffering* by Dr Bryson Arthur. In this book one sees
not so much the triumph of the individual Christian but the triumph of God in the
context of his suffering for the sake of errant humanity. The individual Christian stays
on the pilgrimage because of faith and hope of the eventual completion of the journey.

Dr Arthur gives us a theology of hope which highlights the importance of a biblical, theocentric thinking because it does not culminate in the Christ-event but in the actualization of God's sovereignty and triumph. We are aware of God's pathos (pain and suffering) as we observe his action in Christ – the sovereignty of sin and death is replaced by the solidarity of the "new creation." Consequently, Christians are called upon to embody their hope in God's coming triumph in "worldly" acts of solidarity and companion. The praxis of solidarity in acts of compassion and stewardship necessarily involves the Christian in another dimension of solidarity, a solidarity-in-suffering. For "we know that the whole creation has been groaning together in the pains of childbirth until now" (Rom 8:22 ESV).

Dr Arthur writes with rigour and passion. Here we have a theologian who takes seriously the words of Christ: "If anyone would come after me, let him deny himself and take up his cross daily and follow me" (Luke 9:23 ESV).

Rev Gerishon M. Kirika, PhD
Professor of Theology in Old Testament,
The Presbyterian University of East Africa, Kenya

This is a thought-provoking book on one of the most difficult topics to ever have concerned the church universal – suffering. Arthur ably draws on theological and biblical resources to provide new insights which will be of interest to many.

Rev Duane Alexander Miller, PhD
Associate Professor, Facultad de Teología,
Unión Evangélica Bautista de España, Madrid, Spain

Bryson Arthur has understood that although the theology of suffering is not an amusing topic or discipline to teach or share, to every living person including Christians, suffering is an unavoidable condition and inseparable from the Christian life. Clearly this book explores various meanings, nature, and types of suffering, noting that God uses deserved suffering, undeserved suffering and inner suffering to convict us of our sins, to refine us, to reposition us and to lead us to another level and direction of physical and spiritual life.

I wholeheartedly recommend this book to you. Certainly, reading it will give you comfort in your situation and assist you to understand the purpose of suffering. More importantly, the fact that you are following our Lord Jesus's footsteps and those of heroes of faith in the Bible, why should you not read this book?

Rev Willie Zeze, DTh
Head of BTh Programme and Ecclesiastical Science Lecturer,
Mukhanyo Theological College, KwaMhlanga, South Africa

A Theology of Suffering

A Theology of Suffering

J. Bryson Arthur

© 2020 J. Bryson Arthur

Published 2020 by Langham Global Library
An imprint of Langham Publishing
www.langhampublishing.org

Langham Publishing and its imprints are a ministry of Langham Partnership

Langham Partnership
PO Box 296, Carlisle, Cumbria, CA3 9WZ, UK
www.langham.org

ISBNs:
978-1-78368-782-4 Print
978-1-78368-796-1 ePub
978-1-78368-797-8 Mobi
978-1-78368-798-5 PDF

J. Bryson Arthur has asserted his right under the Copyright, Designs and Patents Act, 1988 to be identified as the Author of this work.

All rights reserved. No part of this publication may be reproduced, stored in a retrieval system or transmitted, in any form or by any means, electronic, mechanical, photocopying, recording or otherwise, without the prior written permission of the publisher or the Copyright Licensing Agency.

Requests to reuse content from Langham Publishing are processed through PLSclear. Please visit www.plsclear.com to complete your request.

Scripture quotations are from The Holy Bible, English Standard Version® (ESV®), copyright © 2001 by Crossway, a publishing ministry of Good News Publishers. Used by permission. All rights reserved.

Scripture quotations marked (NIV) are taken from the Holy Bible, New International Version®, NIV®. Copyright © 1973, 1978, 1984, 2011 by Biblica, Inc.™ Used by permission of Zondervan.

British Library Cataloguing-in-Publication Data
A catalogue record for this book is available from the British Library

ISBN: 978-1-78368-782-4

Cover & Book Design: projectluz.com

Langham Partnership actively supports theological dialogue and an author's right to publish but does not necessarily endorse the views and opinions set forth here or in works referenced within this publication, nor can we guarantee technical and grammatical correctness. Langham Partnership does not accept any responsibility or liability to persons or property as a consequence of the reading, use or interpretation of its published content.

I dedicate this book to my wife, May

I am also very grateful to Isobel Stevenson, Langham's Senior Editor, for her wonderful help in shaping the structure of this book and acquiescing with concepts. She artfully took "deep pools and transformed them into a flowing river." To my friend Pieter Kwant who inspired me to write the book when he was staying with us in Amman, Jordan. And to Morag Stenhouse and Martin Smith who read portions of the text and offered valuable comments.

Contents

Foreword xi
Preface xiii
1 Introduction 1

Part 1: The Nature of Suffering 3
2 The Fall and Human Suffering 5
3 Creation and Human Suffering 13
4 Types of Suffering. 31
5 Undeserved Suffering; Meaning, Hope, Healing and Forgiveness . . . 43
6 The Inner Pain of Angst. 53
7 The Solution to Angst 69

Part 2: The Suffering of Biblical Figures 79
8 The Suffering of Job 81
9 The Suffering of Jesus. 101
10 The Suffering of God 117
11 The Suffering of the Apostle Paul. 137
12 The Suffering of the Church: Persecution. 155

Part 3: Trauma and Triumph 177
13 The Roots of Human Conflict. 179
14 The Dialectic of Difference and Similarity 195
15 The Triumph of Faith and Glory 209

Recommended Further Reading 219
Bibliography 221
Index 225

Foreword

All human beings experience suffering at some point in their lives. For some people, the suffering they endure may be relatively minor and occasional in relation to the whole course of their lives. For other people, the suffering they endure may be that which defines their lives. Whether suffering is great and constant or minor and occasional, however, it is inescapable. The question is not whether we shall suffer but rather how we shall respond to suffering. Will it crush us and lead us into despair, or will it prove to be character-building and positive? All of us have met people whose suffering was such that we could not imagine ourselves in their shoes and doubt whether we would have survived as they did. My father was a prisoner of war of the Japanese, an experience of which he never spoke but which was clearly an intense period of suffering which killed and crushed many, although others survived and appeared to go on to live productive lives. We will never know what that suffering did to them, what angst they suffered throughout their lives as they remembered.

If we are Christians, suffering raises particular problems. I have often been with a bereaved family, particularly in cases of traumatic loss such as the death of a child and been asked, "Why did God allow this?" For some people, the idea that there is an all-powerful God who could have prevented the death, but did not, is enough to drive them away from God and from the church. On the other hand, I knew a man who lost both of his children in fairly quick unrelated deaths and who was asked why he still went to church. He replied that it was his faith which carried him through the suffering and that without it, he would have no hope, either for his children or himself.

Given the seriousness and complexity of the subject, it is encouraging to see a Christian theologian turn his attention to the problems surrounding the theology of suffering, seeking to understand the subject from the perspective of faith. Dr Arthur is well-equipped to engage with this theme because, although he is a Scottish theologian in the evangelical tradition, he has also worked in both Israel and South Africa, where much suffering has taken place and where communities have been divided against one another.

In the first part of the book, Dr Arthur engages with the primary question as to the nature of suffering. These early chapters are profoundly theological and philosophical, engaging with a wide range of topics. He explores the question as to whether or not there was pain before the fall and goes on to ask important questions, such as whether or not pain is always a bad thing. He examines the true nature of human life in relation to God and points out the futility of disobedience and the search for human autonomy. He explains that this search for autonomy and the attempt to live a human life apart from God leads to angst, whereby we find ourselves unable to live as we ought. In doing this, he explores different kinds of suffering and analyzes each one in the light of his core theology of creation and the fall. He does so in dialogue with a number of significant theologians and philosophers.

In the second part of the book, Dr Arthur considers the suffering experienced by various biblical figures, including Job, Jesus and the apostle Paul. He also takes us into the depths of perhaps the most difficult question of all, as to whether or not God himself suffers. In exploring the suffering of God, we are led into a significant meditation upon the nature of the suffering of the God-man on the cross. This part of the book concludes with an examination of the suffering of the persecuted church and the way in which Christians are called to respond to suffering on behalf of Christ. He concludes that suffering is in the will of God, part of his gracious providential dealings with his creatures.

In the third and final part of the book, there are three chapters of particular depth, in which Dr Arthur seeks to draw the whole book together. He explores the roots of human conflict, the dialectic of similarity and difference, and the triumph of faith and glory. He recognizes that suffering is, in some ways, a mystery but concludes that suffering is ultimately spiritual and is the pathway, through faith, to glory.

This is a book which draws the reader into an intense and insightful reflection on some of the most weighty issues in Christian theology, but it does so in ways which are accessible. I consider it an honour to have been asked to write this foreword, having known Bryson for a long time, and I trust that it will lead many people into a deeper understanding of their own and other people's suffering, when viewed from the standpoint of the resurrection and faith.

Rev Professor Andrew T. B. McGowan
Director, Rutherford Centre for Reformed Theology, Scotland

Preface

The genesis of the present book can be traced back to an invitation to attend a conference in Cairo, Egypt, and present a paper on the suffering of the Apostle Paul. Later, I was asked to give another paper elsewhere in Cairo on the topic of persecution and risk, and still later I was asked to give a five-day conference in Adelaide and Melbourne, Australia, on the theology of suffering. The research and writing I did in preparation for these conferences grew into a course on the theology of suffering which I taught to masters' students at the Jordan Evangelical Theological Seminary (JETS) in Amman, Jordan. And that, in turn, led to my writing the book that you now hold. Whilst I hope that the book is accessible to a wider readership than theology students and academics, it is essentially a theological text about Christian suffering.

I think I could safely say that all people, including Christians, want to avoid suffering and when it comes upon them, similarly to the great and good man Job, they want to escape from it. Job, as so many, misunderstood his suffering and what it was all about. And yet the effect of his struggle for the meaning of his suffering and the painful depths of his suffering itself led to the greatest effect in Job's life. Job's suffering, physical, mental, emotional and spiritual, had great purpose in a phenomenally, great increase in his faith and being and, we might say, all aspects of his life to follow; supremely the increase in value of his service to others.

The lesson is that suffering is not a destructive evil but a great good. It is a purposeful trial from God. We ought never to take suffering as a singular infliction but always as a couplet such as suffering and healing, suffering and knowledge, suffering and being and suffering and faith. We suffer to be healed, we suffer to be attuned to grow in the (revelation) knowledge of God, we suffer to become bigger persons and we suffer to increase in faith and so forth. All Christian suffering is a bearer of God's gift, even suffering and punishment. Seen in Christian perspective, the function of punishment is repentance and turning of the will back to peace and love and, of course, essentially God.

Suffering is never the end but always the beginning of a journey leading to abundant, or authentic, life. It is often held that suffering produces sanctification. Sanctification is surely the fruit of suffering, but suffering does not produce sanctification it is simply the appropriate approach to it. Suffering is always triumphant in the end as it is rewarded by the glory and majesty of the grace of God in salvation and eternal life in the glory of heaven in the majesty of the eternal presence of God.

This is why James the brother of Jesus was able to write:

> Count it all joy my brothers when you meet trials of various kinds, for you know that the testing of your faith produces steadfastness. And let Steadfastness have its full effect, that you may be perfect and complete, lacking in nothing (James 1:2–4)

Suffering is surely one of these kinds of trials and indeed it is reasonable to concede that there is an element of suffering in all trials from God. James then is exhorting the early Christians to accept suffering as a gift from God and to rejoice in it.[1]

> Blessed is the man who remains steadfast (resolute, solid, a rock) under trial for when he has stood the test, he will receive the crown of life… (James 1:12)

Suffering is a crown of thorns which morphs into the crown of eternal life.

---

1. We should not consider suffering in merely physical terms. If we consider one of the trials as "temptation," yielding to temptation produces terrible anguish in believers; even the Apostle Paul himself.

1

Introduction

Suffering is seldom seen as a good thing. Indeed, for most people it is not. That is why Christian love should move us to alleviate the suffering of others and to seek to promote justice and freedom from oppression and evil.

Yet it is also true that there is a special quality to the suffering of Christian believers that makes it both positive and essential for spiritual life and growth. It eliminates mediocrity and hypocrisy and forces us to focus on the love of God and the glory of God shining on the cross of Jesus. This type of suffering, with all its pain, is never outside the plan and will of God. We see this clearly in the case of the Lord Jesus, the Apostle Paul, the other apostles and Job. God himself is the author of this suffering and uses it to achieve his great and glorious purposes. Such suffering can be described as "suffering to be healed" and to be restored tenfold in an environment in which the lamb can lie down at peace with the lion.

No one should seek this suffering; to be sought is not its nature. Nor is there cause and effect in it; it is beyond what is "deserved." When in its grasp, the suffering has the appearance of hell, but beauty arises from the ashes. The suffering involved in the death of the ego, the self, is not in itself joyous, but the flowers of this death are a sweet fragrance to God.

James Dunn says that "suffering now is a necessary preparation for and complement to future glory . . . Only when death has had its full say, only when mortality has corrupted to death, only then will the believer escape the clutches of death."[1] Believers are reborn of the spirit. But their rebirth requires the death of their old nature and their old identity in the present as well as ultimately in physical death. The newborn spirit may enter the kingdom of heaven, but not

---

1. James D. G. Dunn, *The Theology of Paul the Apostle* (Grand Rapids: Eerdmans, 2006), 483.

in its fallen tension with the old body (the flesh). The old body remains and continues only as the seed or the physical principle of the new eternal body. In the drawing together of the reborn spirit and the new heavenly body, we have a new and glorious human unity of being and absolute peace of identity.

What you have just read may be hard to hear and hard to understand. That is why we need to take time to reflect on it, as we do in the three parts to this book. The first part (chs. 1–7) is a reflection on the nature and origins of suffering. The second part (chs. 8–12) looks at how suffering operates in the lives of people in the Bible, presented in chronological sequence so that we learn from Job, Jesus, Paul, and persecuted believers. Part 2 also includes a chapter on the suffering of God, the ultimate Person in the Scriptures. Finally, in part 3 (chs.13–15) we show how the understanding of suffering we have received in the first two sections plays out in relation to conflict and difference in particular contexts. These chapters help readers to understand and apply this theology to the world around them, while chapter 15 sounds a clarion call to rejoice in our suffering.

Part 1

The Nature of Suffering

*"Suffering is permanent, obscure and dark,
And has the nature of infinity"*

— William Wordsworth in "The White Doe of Rylstone"

We begin our theological exploration of the nature of suffering by looking at the root causes of suffering and the elements that contribute to it, and then we identify five different types or categories of suffering that we may (or must) endure. These categories are illustrated with reference to the life of the apostle Paul, whose suffering will be studied in more depth in part 2 of this book.

We then take a closer look at aspects of two of these categories, namely undeserved suffering and the inner suffering of angst. In relation to undeserved suffering, we begin our consideration by focusing on social aspects involving offences against our personhood, whether inflicted by others or arising from our own internal disunity. We reflect on the appropriate responses to this type of suffering by positing the superiority of forgiveness over retribution and condemnation when it comes to the restoration of social harmony and of a "self" in society. We reflect on the ultimate meaning of suffering, seeing this as a key element in hope and healing.

In relation to angst, we discuss its roots in our fear of non-being and our sense of impotence and aloneness and then show how the Christian faith addresses each of these sources of angst.

2

The Fall and Human Suffering

God's warning that Adam and Eve would die if they disobeyed him meant that the consequence of disobedience would be that their being would be towards death. Through some impulse like individuation, they turned from the truth to take up power, fuelled by a great delusion (which at heart is Satan's lie). They thus lost access to the resources of paradise, and all human beings now live in the knowledge of good and evil. In this chapter we consider their original sin and show how the roots of suffering in the world are outlined in the curses God pronounced on them.

In Genesis 1:31 we read that God surveyed everything that he had made and saw that all of creation was "very good." Adam and Eve, the first human community, were placed in the garden of Eden or "paradise," the ultimate human utopia where they lived in blissful unity with God and with each other. The key to life in this perfect state of peace and joy was continual obedience and loving submission to the will of God.

The Knowledge of Good and Evil

Human beings were free to come and go in Eden. They could remain in obedience, but they were also free to disobey. The latter was the real test of their freedom. The act that would constitute disobedience was defined by God when he declared that the tree of the knowledge of good and evil was unconditionally forbidden to them. Human beings ought not to know the opposite poles of reality that this knowledge would reveal.

In seeking the knowledge that God had forbidden them, Adam and Eve sought to grasp equality with God. They thought that this knowledge was the source of God's power. But their disobedience resulted in disunity with God and brought catastrophe on their descendants. Their choice contrasts with that of Jesus, "who, though he was in the form of God, did not count equality with God a thing to be grasped" (Phil 2:6). When free to act, Jesus obeyed; in the same situation, Adam disobeyed.

Adam and Eve's act of eating the forbidden fruit is referred to as the original sin that brought suffering into the world. But we need to note that their disobedience began in their hearts before they took action. In a step of radical individuation they made the rebellious choice to replace living in communion with the infinite, unlimited, transcendent being of God with living in reliance on their own limited being. They thus cut themselves off from God's infinite resources, for they were expelled from Eden. By grasping equality with God, Adam led the human race into the state of hamartia[1] and the suffering that flows from it.

All other sin flows from the original sin in Eden. It opened the gate for evil to enter the world and corrupt human nature. Suffering resulted from disunity and division as we began to know and experience both good and evil.

In disobeying God, Adam and Eve turned away from him as their source of life to live in a qualitatively different state of creatureliness. That was the tragic result of their free choice. The reality of creation remained, but with the knowledge of good and evil came judgement and the loss of eternal life. As God had warned them, they would now die. But before death signalled their expulsion from this world, they would have to live with the other part of the judgement, namely the curses God pronounced on them in Genesis 3:16–19. Death and the effects of the curses were the inheritance of all people from then on.[2]

The curse pronounced on Adam in Genesis 3:17–19 declared that the environment would become alien and in opposition to humanity. The satisfaction of bodily needs would involve painful struggle. The whole of human life would be permeated with toil and misery. At the very genesis of the human story, we are thus shown a picture of great physical suffering.

In addition, death now looms large, "for you are dust, and to dust you shall return." Every human person has to live with the knowledge that they will collapse into nothingness, into mere general physicality, "dust." Our expectation is not life but coming death. That is why the existentialist philosopher Heidegger

---

1. Hamartia is the sinful state or lifestyle that falls short of the mark, failing to fulfil the perfection of the design of creation. This state or lifestyle is the realm of evil, suffering and death.

2. Here I am upholding the standard Augustinian interpretation of original sin.

speaks of human existence as "Being-towards-death" and argues that authentic life involves coming to terms with the prospect of death. He reminds us that "as soon as a man comes to life, he is at once old enough to die."[3] Death is our way of being after birth. Human beings must be aware of and come to an understanding of their finitude and temporality, and awareness and acceptance of death is the beginning of this understanding. As Christians, we would argue, of course, that while Heidegger may perceive the truth of the curse of death, the solution does not lie in coming to terms with and facing this truth alone but in turning away from self-determination and back to the infinite resource of God. The solution to death lies with God alone.

In the brief seventy years of the human lifespan,[4] the chief concerns of Adam's descendants are coming death and the supply of their physical needs. We have been condemned to a negative and alien economy. Having rejected the infinite God in whom Adam had his whole being, we have been left to operate within the limits of human finitude. Adam's sin sets the stage for the inevitability of universal poverty, which is the consequence of radical self-life apart from God.

Rejection of the infinite being of God in favour of finite human being is not merely ignorant; it is also absurd. As our own lords and masters, we are spiritually bankrupt, emotionally unstable, and intellectually incoherent. Materialism cannot satisfy the human soul.

The curse on Eve in Genesis 3:16 also affects human society as a whole. The imposition of pain in childbearing means that the entry of human beings into the world becomes a channel of pain. Moreover, the profound unity that characterized the primary society of husband and wife is broken and replaced by the oppression of one group by another. Human equality is lost, and the concept of superior and inferior categories of human beings appears.

As the biblical story unfolds, we see the spread of sin in the generations born into the new but fallen world. The judgement on humankind is clearly defined and limited, but its effects are disastrous. Alienation from God brings suffering in the form of physical, emotional and spiritual pain. The resources of Eden are gone and disconnection from God who is the creator and sustainer of all being is the continuing reality. Human beings now live out their lives in profound insecurity, at enmity with God, in conflict with human society, and divided within themselves.

---

3. Heidegger, *Being and Time*, 236.
4. See Psalm 90:10, where "seventy" is symbolic of the limits on the human lifespan.

Death is at the core of all curses. God's warning in Genesis 2:16–17, which we may term the law of death, has been seen to be absolutely true. There is a very real sense in which in turning from God to serve self, Adam and Eve proclaimed death upon themselves. They had the capacity to obey God; there was no need to disobey him other than the rising hubris within their hearts. Through bowing to pride and to Satan, they brought immense physical, mental, emotional and spiritual suffering upon the generations to come. And after this suffering, the finale is death.

The Analogy of Individuation

Looking further into the nature of the turning away from reliance on God to self-reliance by our first parents, it might be helpful to consider the kind of individuation we see with children as they mature to what is termed the age of reason. When children are very young, they live in a kind of sphere of perfection where they are utterly reliant on their parents, whom they almost worship as gods.[5] But as children gain knowledge, true or false, of the world outside the home, they begin to engage in an early form of critical thinking that produces a major change in their disposition towards their parents.[6] Their whole desire turns to being free from the constraints and influence of their parents and to making their own way in the world. Their parents are now judged and found wanting.

Karl Jung defines individuation as "a process of differentiation having for its goal the development of the individual personality."[7] In other words, individuation is the process by which individuals in society become differentiated from one another and establish themselves as distinct from the group. It involves the individual's will towards self-determination.

We may ask whether there is an analogy between the process of individuation and the original sin of Adam and Eve. There do appear to be similarities. Adam and Eve were created as very good. This goodness would have been seen in their loving, obedient and submissive service of God and each other. The perfection of paradise would mean that there was no logical need for them to assert their individual wills. So why did they assert their finite human wills in opposition to the transcendent and infinite God? The answer

---

5. I am talking about children with good and loving parents; for those who are abused, it is another matter.

6. Generally termed the age of rebellion or teenage rebellion.

7. Karl Jung, "Definitions," in *Psychological Types*, para. 757.

may be what Friedrich Nietzsche calls the "the will to power."[8] This desire for power lies at the root of profound suffering in the world.

Is the will to power essential to individuation? Listen to Jung again: "As the individual is not just a single, separate being, but by his very existence presupposes a collective relationship, it follows that the process of individuation must lead to more intense and broader collective relationships and not to isolation."[9] Thus the process of seeking to understand oneself as a different unique being need not necessarily involve the desire for power. Individuation may be an exploration of our unique personhood within a community of other equal persons.

In Adam and Eve's case, they were together in the presence of God. They were differentiated from each other by their sex as man and woman. As human beings they would necessarily have had the capacity to reason, but theirs would have been a pure and holy reasoning imbued with love and loving service. Their reason would be employed fully and joyfully in growing in the knowledge of God and his wonderful creation, or in what we may term "knowledge of good."

If humanity had continued in its unfallen state, people would have come to understand themselves as unique individuals in loving community in God; their purpose being to live to worship him. The process of individuation that is normal for human psychology, and indeed for identity, should have resulted in the celebration of each person's unique personhood within the unity of God. The essential identity question, "Who am I?" would have been answered joyfully and satisfyingly in the wonderful security of Eden.

But something else was going on in the individuation of Adam and Eve. Like fallen human children, their desire was to be free from their parents – in their case, from God himself. Their individuation involved seeking self-determination through profound disobedience. Theirs was an act of absolute rebellion. They sought to usurp the position of God as Lord, rejecting his transcendence and grasping at the knowledge that was his alone, namely "the knowledge of good and evil." They perceived this knowledge as power, and they sought the power of God for themselves. In this dark desire to gain God's power, Adam and Eve set the pattern for the fallen human behaviour that is a major source of suffering in the world. The desire for power and the determination to gain and wield power at any cost (ironically, often in the name of God) are the roots of war.

---

8. Nietzsche, *Will to Power*. The will to power is a major element in his concept of the overman (*Übermensch*) in *Thus Spoke Zarathustra*.

9. Jung, "Definitions," para. 758.

I would argue that the search for power by certain men and women is similar to that of Adam and Eve. Leaders seek to claim and exercise the power of God and to set themselves up as gods and lords of the world. From tribal leaders to Roman emperors to despotic national leaders like Adolf Hitler, Benito Mussolini, Joseph Stalin and Saddam Hussein, to terrorist leaders like Osama bin Laden and the leaders of the Islamic State of Iraq and the Levant (ISIL), all sought or seek the ultimate power of God.

The very idea of finite human creatures seeking infinite power is logically absurd. No wonder God laughs at them:

> The kings of the earth set themselves,
> and the rulers take counsel together,
> against the Lord and against his Anointed, saying,
> "Let us burst their bonds apart,
> and cast away their cords from us."
> He who sits in the heavens laughs:
> the Lord holds them in derision. (Ps 2:2–4)

Limited beings do not have the capacity to wield infinite power. Their destiny is perhaps to be forever delimited.[10] In seeking such power, they brought death upon themselves. In effect, they committed suicide, but they were allowed to live in the world outside Eden for a number of years in the great purpose of God.

Adam and Eve's rebellion broke the unity they enjoyed with God, with each other, and with creation. The conviction that they would be "like God" and equal with God gave way to a different reality. With their new knowledge came an awareness of their nakedness. Their different genitalia were now a source of shame and so were covered. This action and the entry of the sense of shame into their consciousness are evidence of profound disunity. They sought to understand and perhaps exploit their difference from God and from each other, but the reality that engulfed them was rejection and shame that would soon move to enmity and conflict.

The Great Delusion

The serpent's lie was that Adam and Eve would not die but their eyes would be opened, and they would become like God, gaining his knowledge and power. This lie is at the root of the great human delusion, developed through a vast

---

10. For more on the concept of delimitation, see Karl Rahner, *Hearers of the Word*.

array of more or less sophisticated belief systems. Our security is grounded on holding the delusion to be true.

Although Western philosophy and psychology do not grasp the profound root of human delusion, they acknowledge that it is there. Existentialists refer to the delusion as "inauthentic life." The reality is that given the limitations of human life, human beings cannot be fulfilled; they cannot ever fully realize their potential. To be human in the fullest sense we have to be fulfilled, but the limitations of human finitude make this impossible. This being the case, human life is seen to be absurd. Sartre even describes it as nausea.[11]

If finite human being believes in itself as its own lord and provider, then it is proclaiming to itself that it is infinite. This fallen perspective grounded in lies and delusion is the chariot that has sped the seed of human suffering from its origin to every quarter of the globe in every age.

Writing about natural revelation in Romans, Paul speaks of the delusion as the suppression of the truth, in fact the exchange of the truth about God for a lie, which renders all human thinking futile. God's power and deity have been revealed in the things he has made, but although human beings "knew God, they did not honour him as God or give thanks to him, but they became futile in their thinking, and their foolish hearts were darkened. Claiming to be wise, they became fools, and exchanged the glory of the immortal God for images resembling mortal man and birds and animals and creeping things" (Rom 1:21–23).

Being and having our being in God in whom we live and move, along with the confession of God's lordship over us, are the only ground of coherence and authenticity for human life and knowledge. Without this, death is the ultimate horizon, and on the way to death we endure guilt, meaninglessness, profound insecurity and angst, producing extensive, deep-reaching incoherence.

The essential dynamic of fallen human life is a continual turning away from and denial of God. This deluded life in the finitude apart from God is inauthentic and truly fruitless; it is both futile and nihilistic. The truth of the knowledge of the existence of God and his power, available to all through the revelation of nature, is continually suppressed by the vast majority, aided by human science. Inauthentic life is suffering life in which the harsh reality of suffering is the frustration of self-glory.

By contrast, beholding the glory of God with the whole mind, soul, and heart renders suffering impotent. His glorious light purges human suffering as the heart is taken up in transcendent majesty. Such a vision points powerfully

---

11. Sartre, *Nausea*.

back to the transcendence whence humanity came. Yet, ironically, this glory is revealed to fallen humanity through triumph over suffering.

3

Creation and Human Suffering

The fall may not be the only root of human suffering, for it is a fallacy to believe that human life and happiness require us to be completely free from pain. Pain may have existed before the fall and may thus be an attribute of a creation that is essentially good and of a different order to the suffering caused by sin. The insight that love, too, is associated with suffering helps us to redefine the value of both physical and spiritual suffering.

In the previous chapter we saw that original sin is the root of suffering in this world. But is that the full explanation, or is there possibly a more primordial root of suffering inherent in the very nature of creation? In other words, might Adam and Eve have experienced some degree of pain before their fall into sin? If so, then some suffering is intrinsic to creation itself and must be a gift like the other creation gifts God bestows on us.

Such thinking involves a radical shift in our way of thinking about suffering. It is a perspective that we need to explore together, rather than merely dismissing out of hand.

The starting point for any argument that pain predates the fall must be rooted in what the Bible tells us about creation itself, and so we turn again to the creation narrative. There we read that "God said, 'Let us make man in our image, after our likeness.' . . . So God created man in his own image, in the image of God he created him; male and female he created them" (Gen 1:26–27). We are told more about this act of creation in Genesis 2:7, where we see God forming the first man from "dust from the ground," or more accurately, from the earth (Latin *humus* – hence the word "human"). Adam was given a physical body. Then God breathed "the breath of life" into the formed, inanimate matter. In Hebrew, the word used is *ruach* (*pneuma* in Greek). This word refers to both breath and wind, but in Genesis it refers specifically to the breath of God or God's spirit. The union of matter and breath produced "a living creature" (ESV).

The image of God in human beings is associated with God's Spirit being breathed into them. It is through the infusion of the Spirit that the first man awoke to consciousness with the capacity to know God and to love. I am proposing that from that point on human beings had the capacity to feel both physical and spiritual pain. They also had the capacity to do evil, but they could feel pain before they actually did evil. Pain may be an essential element in the human constitution, but evil is not.

Physical Pain Before the Fall

God designed the human body with the senses of sight, hearing, taste, smell and touch and a nervous system that can convey feelings that range from intense pleasure to intense pain. Pain is experienced though the more than three million pain receptors spread throughout the body – in our skin, muscles, bones, blood vessels, and some organs. These receptors can detect mechanical stimuli (cuts or scrapes), thermal stimuli (burns), or chemical stimuli (insect stings). The sharp pain signal sent by a pain receptor encourages us to move away quickly from a harmful stimulus such as a piece of broken glass or a hot stove. The receptors can also cause a dull pain in an area that has been injured to encourage us not to use or touch that limb or body part until it has healed.

The technical name for these pain receptors is nociceptors. The Latin prefix *noci* means "injurious" or "hurting," reminding us that these receptors detect pain or stimuli that can cause damage to the skin and other tissues of the body. They play an important role in keeping the body safe from serious injury or damage by sending early warning signals to the brain.

Did the unfallen bodies of Adam and Eve have nociceptors? Or were they miraculously added to the human body after the fall? If the latter were true, this would mean that before the fall Adam and Eve had bodies that did not feel and that sin and the curse radically changed the physical nature of the human body.

But Adam and Eve were not unfeeling. We are told that they saw that the fruit of the tree of the knowledge of good and evil was good to eat (Gen 3:6), which implies that they had vision and could taste food. So should we say that they were able to feel pleasure in bodily functions before the fall, but not pain?

The problem with this view is that Adam and Eve's bodies came from the dust, implying that they shared the same chemical and biological constitution as animals. And we know that animals feel pain. So the question is, would animals in the unfallen world have felt pain, or did their physical constitution also change as a result of Adam and Eve's disobedience? For if animals had the capacity to feel pain before the fall, then we can say that pain was normal to at least part of the animate creation.

Given that there is no mention of Adam and Eve's bodies being remade after the fall, it seems likely that the physical constitution of the created human body was similar both before and after the fall, which would mean that Adam and Eve had the capacity to experience pain.

Of course there is the possibility that the pre-fall human body had a similar nervous system to ours and included pain receptors, but that somehow Adam and Eve never felt pain because there was no effective cause of pain. In that case, the human capacity to feel pain, while present, would only come into effect after the fall. The pain receptors and the nervous system sending messages to the brain that are interpreted as pain was, in effect, a latent mechanism for punishment after the fall.

That seems to be as far as we can go on this line of argument.

But when we start to think more deeply about the nature of creation itself, another perspective on the possibility of pain in a pre-fall scenario comes into view. God's creation, while good, includes potential dangers embedded in it by natural laws.[1] For example, any instance of height or depth has the potential for a fall. So if Adam had explored the garden and climbed a tree, he could have fallen and injured himself. The pain he would have experienced would have served both a teaching and healing purpose. He would have learned to be careful about heights and the pain would have reminded him not to move the injured part before it had healed. Even the heat of the sun could present a danger. If Adam and Eve stayed out in the open for a long time, they would have suffered from sunburn or sunstroke. But their pain sensors would have alerted them to the developing discomfort and prompted them to seek shade. Similarly, the sun can heat up stone and sand enough to burn exposed feet. Pain would warn them that damage was being done, and they would learn when it was safe to be exposed to the sun and when not.

All the above scenarios show that physical pain has a teaching function (warning us of potential harm to our bodies) and a healing function (reminding us to rest certain parts of our bodies). If we say that Adam and Eve felt no physical pain before the fall, then really we are saying that they never moved around the garden or explored the world God had given them. In that case, how were they obeying his command to subdue the earth (Gen 1:28)? God

---

1. Karl Barth refers to these laws as "the shadow side of creation" in his *Church Dogmatics*, 3.3, 349–350.

did not create them to sit idle; they were given great purpose. Thus, pain and the suffering of pain could be seen to be necessary. As Adam and Eve moved through and lived in the physical world God had created, pain would teach them how to live in and relate to nature. They would have experienced this type of pain even though they were still sinless. So it may be that this pain would have been experienced more as discomfort than as suffering. This is all the more possible given that they lived with the immediate presence of God.

We would also do well to point to the exact words used when God spoke to Eve:

> I will surely multiply your pain in childbearing;
> in pain you shall bring forth children. (Gen 3:16)

The word "multiply" implies increasing pain. That which does not exist cannot be increased, and so this too is an argument for pain before the fall. Had Eve given birth before the fall, she might have experienced some discomfort, possibly even pain, during childbirth. But as a result of God's curse, this minor pain grows far worse than it would otherwise have been.

Note that in making this argument for the existence of pain in Eden, I am not denying that Adam and Eve had a higher order of being than our own. What was possible in Eden would not be possible in the fallen world in which we live. If there was pre-fall pain, it should be thought of as different from the pain we experience in our fallenness.

Spiritual Pain Before the Fall

While we may accept that physical pain before the fall was a blessing and a creation gift, can the same be said of the mental anguish of spiritual pain? How can soul pain or spiritual pain possibly be a blessing?

Well, consider the human conscience, the psychological and moral mechanism that equips us to distinguish between right and wrong. While it is true that it was in eating the fruit of the forbidden tree that Adam and Eve gained knowledge of good and evil, they must already have had some rudimentary knowledge of the difference between right and wrong because they were made in the image of God. Moreover, if they had no concept of right and wrong, how could God have given them an instruction to obey? How could they have known that it was wrong to eat of the fruit of that tree if they did not know that it was wrong to disobey God's command? Thus, we can argue that God had already implanted the substance of conscience and that Adam and Eve, being morally perfect, would have responded to even its gentlest pricks.

They would only know the full pain of being racked by pangs of conscience after the fall, but their consciences must have been uneasy as they took the fruit. Since then, however, we have needed strong goads of conscience because our consciences have been damaged by the fall and dulled by sin.

Another element of spiritual pain that must have existed before the fall was the pain of aloneness or loneliness. Why else would God have said, "It is not good that the man should be alone; I will make him a helper fit for him" (Gen 2:18)? Before the creation of Eve, Adam's radical aloneness was spiritually and emotionally painful. This aloneness, which we may think of as incompleteness, is a reflection of the reality that God made us for community and for love. The aloneness of Adam was the only "it was not good" in all creation. God cannot create something that is not good, and so creation was not complete until Eve was created as the soulmate and wife of Adam. With Eve and with God, Adam was complete, as also was Eve.

I would argue that the pain of Adam's aloneness is profoundly creational. Such pain is an essential element in the cohesion of human society after the fall and of the perfection and completion of human being before the fall.[2]

Suffering Embedded in Creation

The types of physical and spiritual suffering we have spoken of so far occurred before the fall because of the basic constitution of human bodies and human nature. But I would argue that there are also elements of spiritual suffering deeply embedded in the structure of God's perfect creation.

Meaninglessness

The opening words of Ecclesiastes are both shocking and poignant. Shocking because they are not what we expect to find in Scripture inspired by God and poignant because they seem to fit with our experience of life, especially for those who are older and no longer very excited by the world. What are we to make of them?

> "Meaningless! Meaningless!"
>   says the Teacher.
>   "Utterly meaningless!

---

2. The pain of aloneness continues in fallen human beings. This problem is to some extent, although not perfectly, healed and so resolved in a true marriage of one man and one woman (J. Bryson Arthur, *A Theology of Sexuality and Marriage*, 9–11).

Everything is meaningless." (Eccl 1:2 NIV)

The Teacher goes on to speak of life as a meaningless cycle, with nothing new under the sun. Everything appears to be an eternal, pointless repetition.[3] If there were something new, it would show that it is possible to break out of this bleak cycle, but alas there is nothing new. The answer to the question, "Is there anything of which one can say, 'Look! This is something new'?" (Eccl 1:10 NIV) is clearly, no, there is nothing new.

Greek mythology tells of Sisyphus, a king whom the gods punished by making him push a huge boulder up a steep hill. Whenever he got the boulder near the top, it would break free and roll back down the hill. Wearily, Sisyphus would have to start pushing it up the hill again. This eternal cycle became a symbol for futility and meaninglessness. The French philosopher Albert Camus used it to illustrate the absurdity and meaningless of life, which causes profound human suffering.[4] Even Christians sometimes find their faith challenged by the meaninglessness and apparent incoherence of human life and being.

Do we dare ask whether this kind of suffering derives from the nature of creation? Does it also have primordial roots, so that it existed before the fall? Surely God's creation was perfect, and as such must have immutable and sustainable meaning? So why are the opening words in the book of Ecclesiastes set in the context of creation?

> The sun rises, and the sun goes down,
> and hastens to the place where it rises.
> The wind blows to the south
> and goes round to the north;
> around and around goes the wind,
> and on its circuits the wind returns.
> All streams run to the sea,
> but the sea is not full;
> to the place where the streams flow,
> there they flow again. (Eccl 1:5–7)

For the writer of Ecclesiastes, as well as for Camus, meaninglessness appears to have its root in the eternal repetition in creation. The sun rises and goes down, apparently for ever. Round and round goes the wind and all streams flow to the sea. The writer uses these as illustrations of meaninglessness and

---

3. Not all repetition is bad. There can be a repetition of a choice to do good and day by day to remain in obedience. The structure of human finitude orients itself in terms of blessed and creative repetitions.

4. Camus, *Myth of Sisyphus and Other Essays*.

futility. Throughout the book, explicitly and implicitly, repetition is seen to be meaningless and purposeless. The writer is weary with all things. Again there is nothing new under the sun.

But this repetition is not a result of a curse, as it was in the case of Sisyphus, but is embedded in the very nature of creation. It is both a component of creation's and our finitude and a spur to look beyond it. We are constantly reminded by creation itself that what is finite is not as an end in itself and cannot be complete in itself.

Were it not for the fall, we would not see these cycles as meaningless. The meaning of creation would be self-evident, not something we needed to search for. Today, science and the laws of physics do find logical patterns of cause and effect in the structures of creation, but the creation itself is silent. In terms of meaningful language, all of creation, inanimate and animate (apart from human beings) is silent and appears to be meaninglessness. This produces a profound and painful dissonance that acts on the soul rather like indigestion acts on the body.

The gospel message is that we will only find real meaning by going beyond our finitude to the infinite being of a loving God. This is effectively the denial of self and the wholehearted following of Christ. Through the wonderful journey back into God in Christ, we are ultimately set free from a profound and deathly boredom. We are set free from a pointless repetitive cycle in which there is no love, only eternal waiting.

The writer of Ecclesiastes concludes his book with these words:

> The end of the matter; all has been heard. Fear God and keep his commandments, for this is the whole duty of man. For God will bring every deed into judgement, with every secret thing, whether good or evil. (Eccl 12:13–14)

Jesus restated this message like this:

> You shall love the Lord your God with all your heart and with all your soul and with all your mind. This is the great and first commandment. And a second is like it: You shall love your neighbour as yourself. On these two commandments depend all the Law and the Prophets. (Matt 22: 37–40)

The truth that meaning must be sought in the infinite love of God and not in his finite creation is embedded in creation itself.

Finitude

All human religions involve belief in a power or being that transcends the known universe. In worship, finite human beings reach out to this infinite transcendent being. They are seeking release from a mundane and apparently pointless existence by reaching out to something greater, clinging to the hope that this entity, which most religions understand to be God, will make sense of it all. Worshippers seek to connect their finite (limited) being with the infinite (boundless) transcendent being of God, which offers authentic meaning and purpose for their lives. This reaching out to God is right because human beings were created in the image of God to be in relationship with him, and not to seek meaning in their finitude, which breaks down into a sterile futility.

It is also true to say that we often find the supernatural much more exciting than the natural simply because it opens up possibilities that exceed our present ontological limitations. The countless movies and television shows that involve some element of the supernatural are a witness to this reality.

Both of these phenomena indicate that human beings have a deep longing to connect their finite being with the infinite being of God. This primary relationship provides the spiritual infrastructure for meaningful human life. The true meaning and purpose of human life is spiritual and not material and is absolutely dependent on having a relationship with the true God. This follows because God created the finite physical world to shower his infinite love on it – to give that which was limited an unlimited resource. This is the raison d'être of creation, and so any division between the finite and the infinite source of life fractures the structure of creation.

The matter of the knowledge of good and evil is also grounded in this finite/infinite dialectic. Adam and Eve sought God's knowledge, which is transcendent, infinite and far beyond what a finite human being can bear. As a result, their finite eyes were opened to see their own nakedness.[5]

But our nakedness is more than we can bear. So human beings who turn to self and away from God seek to be complete in themselves. We could use Sartre's term "being-for-itself" to describe this condition.[6] Being-for-itself is life entirely in terms of an individual self, with no perceived lack. An example of such a life would be a tree that has roots, a trunk, branches, twigs, leaves, flowers, and some form of fruit. It is complete in itself, even as regards procreation. Yet it needs soil, water, sunlight and specific environmental conditions to survive.

---

5. God's plan was to open the eyes of finite human beings through spiritual birth, through which they would be able to see the kingdom of God and enter it.

6. "Being-for-itself" is the heading of part 2 in Jean-Paul Sartre, *Being and Nothingness*, 119.

In the same way, what is finite is not as an end in itself and cannot be complete in itself. To worship what is finite (as fallen human nature prompts us to do) is the essence of idolatry. The Roman emperors who proclaimed themselves gods are a good example of the idolatry of worshipping the finite as infinite. In the Bible, we see similar idolatry in the Pentateuch. While Moses was seeking God on Mount Sinai, the Hebrew people gathered golden items, melted them down and forged a golden calf, which was a tangible image that they bowed down to and worshipped. They were asking this inanimate object for help with their needs and problems, even though it was vastly more limited than the people who created it! To have faith in the calf to help them and give them prosperity was to have faith in nothing. Instead of turning to the infinite transcendent God, they bowed down to and worshipped their own finite creation. Such behaviour appears ridiculous!

Some may argue that the Israelites were not really worshipping the image as such. It may be that the calf was merely the form they gave to beautiful gold that comes from the ground, and that the calf was thus merely a symbol of creation or nature itself. In that case, in worshipping the calf they were worshipping nature. This may be better than worshipping a specific inanimate object, yet it is still inadequate. Nature, even when it takes the form of something as seemingly infinite as the sea, is finite with respect to the world and the universe.

As finite beings who come from infinite being, the experience of being thrown into fallen existence produces profound insecurity. Our finitude imposes a radical vulnerability that we immediately try to hide from or seek to flee. We construct more or less elaborate systems of delusion to disguise our vulnerability. Some turn to drugs, other to heroes or national leaders, Roman emperors, political leaders like Adolf Hitler and Joseph Stalin and even the beloved Nelson Mandela, film stars and sports legends, and many others who are exalted virtually, as gods. Others turn to false religions, ideologies and cults, including the worship of Mother Earth and of nature itself.

A common tendency is to seek security through material wealth. Being rich is seen as conferring the blessed peace of being secure. I have heard it said that "the rich have no worries." The great American dream is that with hard work one can rise from poverty and become rich and famous. Riches and greatness are usually understood in numerical terms; the greater the number, the greater the owner. Somehow or other, virtue is also linked to riches; the quantity of dollars a man or woman has is an indication of their virtue. The rich are worshipped like royalty, with Bill Gates or Jeff Bezos of Amazon as the king of kings.[7] Film stars and celebrities who are enormously rich appear to define royalty in the USA.

It is worth pausing here to consider the parable of the rich fool in Luke 12:16–21:

> And he told them a parable, saying, "The land of a rich man produced plentifully, and he thought to himself, 'What shall I do, for I have nowhere to store my crops?' And he said, 'I will do this: I will tear down my barns and build larger ones, and there I will store all my grain and my goods. And I will say to my soul, "Soul, you have ample goods laid up for many years; relax, eat, drink, be merry." But God said to him, 'Fool! This night your soul is required of you, and the things you have prepared, whose will they be?' So is the one who lays up treasure for himself and is not rich toward God."

In this parable Jesus teaches that such a person is a fool because they do not take God into account in their reckoning of the security of their soul. They substitute material wealth, which becomes an idol, for God. They now trust in their idol not knowing that disaster is at the door and that urgency with respect to the presence and coming of the kingdom of God is required, not complacency. Believing that finite riches give them infinite security, they put their feet up, trusting in worldly wealth. Their attitude immediately strikes a reasonable mind as crazy; the rich fool was greatly deluded!

In all the examples we have discussed, we have seen people substituting various forms of finitude for the infinite being of God. All such substitutions are "lies." Worshipping and defining human being and life in terms of the idols of delusion enslaves the human spirit and is thus profoundly dehumanizing. Finite being was set free from infinite being to find its cohesion, meaning and purpose in terms of and "in" the infinite being, who is God. The finitude within an unfallen, non-sinful reality would turn to the infinite being of God for its raison d'être and its absolute security. But in this fallen world, what we see is a perpetual turning away from God and a turning to self, which produces a malady of the soul that manifests as a perpetual pain. This is the inner pain we know as angst.[8] Angst is not the same as fear. Fear has to do with some experience in the world; angst, by contrast, has to do with our essential

---

7. The richest man in the world in 2008, and the third richest in 2018.
8. Angst is dealt with at more length in chapter 6.

nature. Fear has an object, while angst is intrinsic to being, or at least to finite human being.

Angst can also be called insecurity. Insecurity is a great threat to us – to our being. It is angst that makes human beings reach beyond themselves, seeking for some greater being who will somehow watch over them keeping them safe. This is the root of many pseudo-religions and ideologies.

Pain as the Cost of Creation Love

So far, we have been considering pain, suffering and creation primarily from the human perspective. Now it is time to lift our eyes higher and consider also the pain of God.

Adam and Eve were made to know true human love because God is love and his motive for creating the world was love. We can rightly call his love "creation love". It may be helpful to begin by distinguishing this love from agape love.

Self-love (which is not true love) focuses on the self, whereas agape love is focused on the other. It moves us to unconditional service of the other. It is the highest form of finite human love. Because we are finite, our experience of agape love tends to function on an individual basis – we are called to love one another. But agape love is also general and unconditional, and so can be extended to all others. That is how Jesus can command us to love our neighbour, no matter who or what they may be (as modelled in the parable of the Good Samaritan).

Because we think in human categories, we tend to assume that the love of God is like agape love. But unconditional love between human beings cannot be compared to the transcendent creation love of God. While human agape love is analogous to the love of God, it is by no means the same. We cannot sum up the nature of God using the concept of human agape love.

Human agape love is existential, meaning that it must be experienced, acted out, to be love. By contrast, the creation love of God is ontological, meaning that it is God's essential nature. When God breathed his spirit into human beings and made them in his own image, that love became an essential element of human being. Our true being is in the creation love of God. That is why such love is at the heart of the dual command to love given by Jesus: "You shall love the Lord your God with all your heart and with all your soul and with all your strength and with all your mind, and your neighbour as yourself" (Luke 10:27). When Jesus gives this dual command, he is pointing out that God's love is the real source, power and joy of our being. We must receive this love to be our true selves and live abundantly, and it is this love that we must draw on when loving others, as John reminds us when he says, "We love because he first loved us" (1 John 4:19). We love with God's love, which we are "in" if we are in Christ.

The analogy of agape love is, however, useful when it comes to thinking about the cost of creation to God. There is a cost in agape love. True and wholehearted service of the other is costly to the being of the one showing love. The Good Samaritan endured a cost to serve the man who was robbed and beaten and left for dead. Similarly, when God through and in his love creates beings other than himself, there is a cost to that creation love. The cost is that while God was under no necessity to create the world of human beings, once he had created it, he was bound to maintain it and bring it to fulfilment. God's integrity demands that he be faithful to his creation. This faithfulness appears to us as God's promise. The obligation accepted by God, which could appear to us as a limitation on his freedom, is the real cost of God's love. Later, I will argue that the cost of God's love is also the pain of his showing grace to human beings. Without this pain, God's love would not be felt as substantial, and therefore it would not be perceived as true.

Adam and Eve were made in the image of God, into whom he breathed his spirit. They must thus also have had the capacity to experience the pain of true love. Their love for each other, and indeed for God, must have included a cost, and a cost implies pain. The love of God is as deep as the universe, and this depth becomes evident in the pain of God's creation love. Adam and Eve's love is similarly revealed through the pain of their love although this pre-fall pain was of a different order than pain after the fall.

As I have argued, God's love meant that he accepted responsibility for his creation, and thus accepted a limitation on his freedom. Adam and Eve's love of God, too, involved a limitation on their freedom. They were given great power over the creation that they were to subdue (Gen 1:26, 28), but they had to obey God's prohibition of the fruit of the tree of the knowledge of good and evil.[9] The cost of their love was that they had to obey God and respect his knowledge and power. In other words, they had to remain in their proper place as created beings. The acceptance of this limitation was the cost of their love of God.

Sadly, through their disobedience Adam and Eve turned from the love of God to the glorification of self. In so doing, they betrayed and rejected God's love. Much later, Judas Iscariot would do the same to the Son of God.

---

9. What was prohibited was the knowledge of God, and therefore the power of God. They were, however, not physically prevented from eating the fruit of this tree; in other words, they were free to choose to disobey God.

I would argue that just as there was nothing arbitrary about the cross of Calvary, so there was nothing arbitrary in the fall of Adam and Eve. Both profound events were in the providence and decree of God from before the foundation of the earth (Eph 1:4–5). When we take this perspective, we come to recognize that through the cross of Christ, God is re-creating or redeeming the original fallen, creation (2 Cor 5:17; Rom 8:19–22). His goal is to bring forth a new and glorious creation, which we may term the eternal kingdom of God for redeemed human beings. There is a sense in which we can say that God created the world for his Son to die a sacrificial, vicarious death as the efficacious means of re-creation, and indeed the great and glorious ultimate creation, of the new heavens and the new earth.

As we will later discuss in more depth, the sacrifice of the Son of God is the greatest expression of the eternal love of God for humankind. In a sense, God's love is indistinguishable from the pain of Christ. The very love of God that was the motivation for creation included within it the roots of the pain of the cross. This pain is the essence of God's love and vice versa. This pain, of an infinitely higher order than human pain, we can call the pain of grace.

Given that the fall and the means of re-creation were already in the mind of God before he created the world, no arbitrary cause and effect applies in relation to God's lordship over the world. His lordship is absolute, and his providence is revealed in the history of the world.

I have now laid the base for my claim that the ultimate love of, and the great pain suffered by, Christ are of the very nature of creation itself. The love and the pain of grace, though shadowed in the immanence of God in creation, are manifestly, explicitly and gloriously revealed through the cross, which is in the same moment the greatest good and the greatest evil ever to happen in the world.

The synthesis of love and pain in the passion of Christ demonstrates that there is no enmity between God and pain, as there is between him and sin. I am arguing that pain is a corollary of his love. The pain of grace is the source of our greatest blessing. What greater proof could there be that pain and suffering are not evil in themselves, and that the suffering of pain is not, in itself, a futile burden but a fruitful good, than the cross of Christ.

In saying this, we must be careful to avoid anthropomorphism. The possibility of the pain of grace as the cost of the love of God should be understood as utterly transcending human pain, just as the love of God utterly transcends human love. What is important is that pain is the most intense form of emotion, and as such is a vital element of creation.

Pain as the Cost of Freedom

The question of where suffering comes from is closely related to the question of where evil comes from, for in general suffering follows evil of some kind. This much seems clear from our discussion of the link between suffering and original sin. However, evil itself seems in some way to be a creation principle. In the garden of Eden there was already a tree whose fruit was the source of the knowledge of good and evil. Even if we take the tree and its fruit as symbolic, the concept and the possibility of evil were real. It appears that the knowledge of evil existed before the fall, as did human pride (hubris). Adam and Eve had already sinned in their hearts before they ate the fruit. That act of disobedience did not flow from a pure heart but from a heart that had already been corrupted. Sin mysteriously entered the world before Adam and Eve actually did the forbidden act.

How can this be true when God had declared that all of creation, including Adam and Eve, was "very good"? Augustine taught that evil is a corruption of the good, but does this imply that the good is not absolute as it is capable of being corrupted? This capability itself could be considered to be the root of evil, even if it had never been acted on and evil had not come into the world.

The question that succinctly sums up the problem of evil in the world is this: If God is perfectly good, and a God of love, and has absolute power, why does he permit evil and suffering in his world? This question must be answered. Theologians through the ages have wrestled with it, and it has even become a subject of study, known as "theodicy." Augustine offers the most compelling theodicy, which is known as the "free will defence." Real human freedom (or to put it better, free will) requires that humans be able to make a real, free, choice between good and evil actions. Evil, or at least the potential for evil that we call unrealized evil, must exist because evil is necessary for freedom. It must be something that human beings can actually choose. If they have no choice, they are not free.

Adam and Eve were not pre-programmed to obey God: they were confronted by a real moral choice. Would they choose to disobey or choose to remain in obedience? Both possibilities were open to them. Sadly, they chose to disobey.

To take the argument a step further, we can say that the integrity of human freedom demands not only that evil be potentially present in the world but also that the infrastructure of evil exists. This argument parallels the argument above, where we posed that God's providence from before the beginning of creation included the cross as the major mechanism of the structure of grace and the greatest revelation of that grace to humankind.

It is time now to return to our previous argument: Must suffering always be a direct product or result of evil? We have already challenged that idea. At this stage, the point that needs to be made is that if evil is the opposite of good and is destructive to human beings in creational and actual terms, and to the being of God's creation itself, then it follows that the product of evil is suffering, even the suffering of death itself. If evil is a corruption of the good, then the corruption itself is evil.

Irenaeus took this argument as proof of why Christ could not suffer corruption.[10] Human beings and apparently angels are corruptible and can lose the perfection of goodness. Their corruption involves a rotting of the spirit, which causes intense spiritual pain. Human beings try to escape this pain through delusion, drugs and the false promises of materialism. All of this suffering is the manifestation of the curse of the presence and actualization of evil in the world. Yet, as was shown above, even unfallen human life may have involved physical pain as a means of protection and safety. Moreover, even that intensity of being which we may term "abundant life" may involve pain – the pain of being brought closer to God and so to truth. Truth about the world is painful for our (still) fallen human nature to bear, for we prefer to deny responsibility.

We have argued above that the principle and potential of evil must exist in the created world if human beings are to be truly free. We have also stated that the motive for creation is God's love. The expression of this love is God's setting human persons free. In creating the world, God set it free from himself. Essentially this freedom was freedom to sin or not to sin. Adam and Eve exercised or tested their freedom by choosing disobedience, bringing captivity and God's curse upon themselves and all of humankind. By not choosing to remain with God in obedience to his love and glory, they rendered themselves impotent when it comes to choosing the good, although they continued to be free to choose evil.

> My contention is that freedom is not only at the heart of redemption and recreation: it is the original gift of God given in and through the act of creation itself. My view is that in the very making of the creatures of the world, God set them free. He set free that which was other than himself; those beings whose nature included a difference to God. The creation is a freed reality. All beings are

---

10. Irenaeus, *Against Heresies* 3.18–3.22, 4.4 under "Recapitulation and Incorruption."

given freedom to the limit of their nature. Such freedom is both wonderful and terrible. It is wonderful when it is not abused but when it is abused it is terrible. The abuse of freedom leads to inevitable captivity.... This captivity is the captivity of persons.[11]

The freedom to love God and each other and ultimately to share in the glory of God eternally is the purpose and truth of human being, and so the purpose of creation. It is infinitely costly. The lie of Satan leads human beings to glory in themselves, which is the essence of captivity. The truth of the gospel of Christ sets us free from the lie of Satan and so from captivity itself. Christ's death on the cross atones for our sin and so, along with the proclaimed truth, sets us free into the glorious freedom of the children of God.

Prior to the cross, the creation itself, with its wonderful provision for human life, was the first revelation of God's love, in which Adam and Eve were created free. They were royal persons who had dominion over all the world (Gen 1:28). Sadly, they were corrupted and despised the freedom they had been given, grasping after the knowledge and power of God himself. It appears that they were no longer content with freedom as defined by the love of God but rather desired to be free "from" God. Through this corrupt, proud desire they led all their descendants into the pseudo-freedom of the world, which is captivity.

As the corrupter of the good, original sin (which we can term moral evil) destroys human freedom. And the destruction of human freedom is the destruction of the essence of the human spirit. Such destruction involves profound pain. Captivity is the murder of the human spirit in the world. That is why Jesus proclaimed that he had come to set the human spirit free, "to proclaim liberty to the captives ... to set at liberty those who are oppressed" (Luke 4:18).[12]

Evil and suffering are thus intrinsically related to freedom, both as regards the reality of freedom itself and as regards the existential destruction of freedom. The battle between good and evil is fundamental to the human story and to the story of our lives. God determines what is the good way, but because of true human freedom, it must be possible not to follow that way.

Suffering related to freedom is a necessary element of the best of all worlds. Understood in this way, the suffering of pain that is not a result of sin is seen in positive terms, for it is in some sense related to the nature of God. We love because God loves. Can we then say that we have pain because God has pain?

---

11. Bryson, *A Theology of Sexuality and Marriage*, 27.
12. Note that in the immediate *sitz im leben* of Jesus, Luke 4:18 relates to the Year of Jubilee.

Neither pain nor suffering are evil in themselves. The suffering of pain is not in itself a futile burden but a fruitful good. Thus, there is no enmity between God and pain. Pain is normal to being in this created world. And if the pain of grace is the cost of creation and re-creation and is intimately linked to God's love and freedom, then God's pain is our very great good.

4

Types of Suffering

In looking at the roots of suffering, we have used the broad categories of physical and spiritual suffering, which reflect the medium of the suffering. Now it is time to consider a categorization into five types of suffering based on the perceived reason for the suffering. Each type is illustrated with reference to the experience of the apostle Paul.

Not all suffering is the same. It is possible to identify five types, or categories, of suffering, each of which has its own quality. They are deserved suffering, undeserved suffering, suffering for others, suffering for God (persecution), and inner or ontological suffering, which we can also term the suffering of being. These types of suffering are often interwoven, and except for persecution, they are part of the universal human experience.

Deserved Suffering

In chapter 2 we saw that human suffering is a consequence of the original sin of Adam and Eve, which St Augustine argued is passed on to all of humankind since we were all in some sense seminally present in Adam. Thus, like the psalmist David, we are both conceived and born in sin (see Ps 51:5). At birth we already have a fallen human nature, and so in some sense we deserve punishment and the suffering associated with it.

But there is more to the concept of deserved suffering than this. The Old Testament framework of righteousness held that if we do right and obey the law, we will prosper; but if we sin, disaster will come upon us. It also taught that the penalty for parents' sin would be passed on to the children (Exod 34:6–7; Deut 5:8–10). This way of thinking prompted Jesus's disciples to ask whether a man was blind because of his own sin or because his parents had sinned (John 9:2). While in that case Jesus denied this chain of causation, it is still true that sin has consequences and that we reap what we sow (Gal 6:7). This holds true even when we are forgiven in Christ – his forgiveness does not annul all earthly consequences of our actions.

This is the basis of deserved suffering. When we suffer because of ongoing sin or because of criminal acts, we deserve to suffer. We know what we have done and we understand that what we suffer is a result of our actions. If we commit theft and go to prison, we immediately know the cause of our suffering. We agree, if we are realistic, that this suffering is deserved; there is no mystery to its origin or its meaning.

We are dealing here with justice – getting what we deserve – our just deserts. Christians in these circumstances know that they have sinned and that there is a price to pay. If they ponder the subject of forgiveness, they acknowledge that they are eternally forgiven by God but not by the state or society. We may question the proportion of pain exacted to meet the requirement of justice, but the meaning of this suffering is clear. There is nothing profound or mystical going on.

If we look for an example of deserved suffering in the New Testament, we might want to consider the case of Saul/Paul. We know Paul for his profound and intense Christian life, but before that new life began Paul was Saul the Pharisee, who vigorously persecuted the young church until stopped in his tracks by a vision of the risen Christ who chose Paul for what may be described as the most remarkable ministry of all the apostles.

Let us be clear. Paul was involved in leading the vicious and ruthless persecution and murder of Christians. He was present when Stephen, the first martyr, was murdered. We might even dare to say that Paul, like Moses before him, began his life in God's ministry in the spirit of murder. If we had met him at that stage in his life, we would have categorized him as a radical extremist, an activist for what he believed in. He was determined to exterminate the Jewish sect that worshipped a man called Jesus, whom he hated passionately. The mystical power of the new sect presented a profound threat to Paul. While arising from within Judaism, it presented itself as being essentially different from and so threatening to the Judaism Paul knew and loved. Deeply concerned for the purity of the Jewish people, he sought to retain this purity by the persecution and destruction of the sect in the name of God and in accordance with the law of Moses.

In the twenty-first century, we have witnessed the ethnic cleansing of Shia Muslims and Christians by the so-called Islamic State (ISIL). In the twentieth century we saw the ethnic cleansing of six million Jews by the Nazis, and the

Rwandan genocide in which a million Tutsis were killed by Hutus. I give these examples to illustrate not the proportion but the intensity of Paul's religious campaign, which would have been similar in essence and character. Members of the young church rightly feared Paul. When told to go to him by God, Ananias objected, saying "Lord, I have heard from many about this man, how much evil he has done" (Acts 9:13). Even after his conversion, suspicions lingered and many Christians wanted nothing to do with him (Acts 9:26).

But God was already at work in Saul the persecutor. When telling King Agrippa the story of his conversion Paul states that in the vision Jesus told him, "It is hard for you to kick against the goads" (Acts 26:14). Goads were sharp metal-tipped sticks used to prick bullocks, forcing them into submission. The goads pricking Paul must have been the pangs of conscience which Jesus was imposing. Paul had already begun to suffer before the point of his conversion. He had heard the gospel message from Stephen, and the process of regeneration had begun.

In his encounter with the risen Lord, Paul was confronted by the presence of God and compelled to believe. The mark that this encounter put upon him was blindness. We have here the opposite of the miracle of sight given to the man born blind (John 9:1–14). That man was given sight by the one who is the light of the world; Paul, by contrast, was given temporary blindness. Yet both immediately believed.

Paul's dramatic encounter with Christ must have thrown him into a deep spiritual and psychological crisis, producing suffering that included emotional, mental, spiritual, and physical elements. He was left to deal with the crisis while, for a short time, enduring the condition, or indeed the punishment, of blindness. His profound evil must have echoed on every side of his stricken mind, contrasting starkly with his new fear of God. Like Job, he could have said, "I am terrified at his [God's] presence; when I consider, I am in dread of him" (Job 23:15). Like Job, he must have loathed his life (10:1). Isaiah, too, had been filled with dread when he encountered God. "Woe is me! For I am lost; for I am a man of unclean lips, and I dwell in the midst of a people of unclean lips" (Isa 6:4–5). Isaiah had seen the Lord, and so had Paul. Through his supernaturally imposed introspection, Paul would see something of the extent of his evil acts and his hamartia lifestyle. For all his zeal, he had been missing the mark.

Profound anguish and pervasive pain marked Paul's beginning. It is hard to see how he could ever recover from such depths of despair and from such great shame. And his awareness of what he had done did not fade, for many years later he described himself as "the least of the apostles, unworthy to be called an apostle, because I persecuted the church of God" (1 Cor 15:9). He was acutely aware that it was only by God's grace that he had been called to suffer and to serve.

Paul's deserved suffering was relieved by grace, but there can be no doubt that it was intense. His acute awareness of the suffering he had inflicted on the young church would have been sharpened as he himself endured the same type of persecution he had inflicted on others.

Undeserved Suffering

Underserved suffering comes in many forms; bereavement, job loss, illness, rejection, or some other personal tragedy that is no fault of the sufferer. Oppression, injustice, persecution, abuse, neglect, etc. are also members of this category. So are disappointment in marriage or not being married when one strongly desires to be so, childlessness and other forms of impotence. This category also includes the suffering of refugees who have lost possessions, home, relatives and friends and endure a profound identity confusion. The list could go on and on.

All these forms of suffering are profoundly difficult to understand. The sufferer, perhaps aided by others, struggles to know the meaning of his or her plight. This struggle, if in the Lord, is essentially theological, and in the end, it produces both revelation and ontological growth, that is, growth as a person and as a being in Christ. The meaning comes through great confusion and a dire need for vindication, and through great anguish of soul. Such suffering is a test of faith and has the result of increasing and strengthening faith and personal growth through revelation and a higher knowledge of God.

This is the type of suffering that we will be looking at in detail when we examine the experience of Job. But it is worth noting that this type of suffering also manifested itself in the life of Paul.

After his encounter with Christ, Paul's lifestyle was utterly different from what it had been before. Whereas he had once enjoyed high social status and great respect as a Jewish leader, a Pharisee of the Pharisees, he lived a life of utter humiliation. Later he would describe himself and the other apostles as having become "like the scum of the world, the refuse of all things" (1 Cor 4:13).

Paul was dedicated to the cause of Christ and to preaching him, and so some might expect God's blessing to shine upon him. Yet in the course of carrying out his ministry as an apostle, he suffered greatly. He lists some of these sufferings in 2 Corinthians:

> Three times I was shipwrecked; a night and a day I was adrift at sea; on frequent journeys, in danger from rivers, danger from robbers, danger from my own people, danger from Gentiles, danger in the city, danger in the wilderness, danger at sea, danger from false brothers; in toil and hardship, through many a sleepless night, in hunger and thirst, often without food, in cold and exposure. (2 Cor 11:25–27)

Besides the dangers mentioned above, many of which were inevitable given Paul's itinerant ministry, Paul also endured a unique form of suffering that he referred to as "a thorn . . . in the flesh" (2 Cor 12:7). We do not know the exact nature of this thorn, but it appears to have been some form of physical disability. The fact that Paul refers to it as "a messenger of Satan" implies that it was severe enough to be discouraging, and even depressing. It induced not only physical pain but also spiritual and emotional anguish.

Paul pleaded with God three times to remove this painful disability, but God would not take it away. Paul had to learn to trust in God's grace in undeserved physical suffering.

Paul comes to speak of this undeserved suffering as a balancing pain given to him by God to keep him humble after the great revelation he speaks of in 2 Corinthians 12:1–5. It served to keep his feet on the ground, so to speak, and prevent his becoming conceited. The mere fact that such a risk existed is an eloquent testimony to Paul's humanity.

There is an irony in the fact that something that Paul referred to as a messenger of Satan was actually working for God's goodness and overall purpose. The same may be true of other examples of undeserved suffering. The blessing has the appearance of a curse. We are reminded of Jesus's words in the Sermon on the Mount. "Blessed are the poor in spirit . . . Blessed are those who mourn . . . Blessed are the meek" (Matt 5:3–5). The thorn in the flesh ensured Paul's continuing weakness through which he had the strength of Christ, because "my grace is sufficient for you, for my power is made perfect in weakness" (2 Cor 12:9).

Inner Suffering (Angst)

The inner suffering known as angst occurs within the other four types of suffering, but unlike them it is not related primarily to experiential factors. Rather, it is mental and emotional suffering at the centre of our being.

It is important that we distinguish angst from fear. While both Paul and Job experienced angst, neither of them showed fear. Angst is not fear. Fear is existential in that it involves something external to us. When whatever is causing the fear is removed, the fear vanishes. Angst, however, is not directed at a specific external circumstance (although it may be provoked by it). Angst has to do with our essential being. Angst simply is. It is a nagging thing, an inner disease, a primordial threat, a deep sense of inner turmoil. It is the burning heartache of the soul and the anguish of tortured being. Angst is the suffering of profound pain at the very centre of being, along with a nagging insecurity, an all-pervasive sense of meaninglessness, and guilt. It exists as a radical and ultimate reality in our mind and emotions. It cannot ultimately be avoided and it cannot be totally removed.

We begin our discussion on angst in this chapter, and continue at more length in chapters 6 and 7. At this point we focus on the reality that angst is related to the curse on Adam and Eve ("for you are dust and to dust you shall return" – Gen 3:19) and to their newfound knowledge of good and evil. Angst therefore concerns our future return to the dust, which we perceive as ceasing to exist or non-being.

Angst and non-being

Adam and Eve were raised from the dust and received the life-giving *ruach* (the breath of God). This was a rising to paradise in perfection and harmony, in immediate relationship with God. The fall came through a second rising, prompted by hubris, namely the rising of the self, seeking security in the self and under the lordship of the self. Ultimately this second rising results in a return to nothing in physical death. Angst arises as we glimpse the reality of the ultimate return to non-existence (das *Nichtige*).[1] Awareness of this threat to being results in profound inner suffering and even the nihilism that drove the French philosopher Albert Camus to accept absurdity and meaninglessness and live in a world devoid of meaning or purpose. He illustrates this by describing an exchange he had with his mother, who was looking out a window above a busy street in Paris. When he asked her what she was looking at, she said "Nothing." All the activity she could see had no meaning or purpose to her, and nor has life. Our only options are suicide, acceptance of the meaningless absurdity of staring out a window and seeing nothing (inauthentic life), or taking a leap of faith and trusting God.

Christians have taken the leap of faith, but they discover that this leap is not a way to escape all angst. As believers we too return to nothing, for we

---

1. Barth's use of this term will be discussed in more detail in the next chapter.

have to begin with *metanoia*, repentance and a commitment to obey Jesus's command to die to self (Luke 9:23). That is why Paul speaks of dying to self (Gal 2:20; 5:24). The death of our old self throws us into the world naked once again, and without the (pseudo) power of hubris. We must face our limited being in its raw nakedness and experience deep vulnerability. In and through this terrible experience, however long it lasts, our angst is dealt a deathly blow.

But after suffering the collapse of the delusion of the ego and the perceived return to nothing of personal identity, our need for personal identity is satisfied through the gift of a new identity in Christ and a new power of being in the Holy Spirit. We are new creatures, the old has gone and the new has come (Eph 4:20–24).

We see this transition in Paul, who went from being a powerful and influential Pharisee to a humiliated and lowly weakling who considered himself the least of the apostles and the scum of the earth. He became nothing, and from this nullity a phoenix arose – but this rising was in the life of Christ and not in the human ego. We see in Paul then, as we must see in all true Christians, a condition of dying to live.[2]

Angst and the knowledge of evil

The inner suffering of angst is also related to the primary creational dialectic of the knowledge of good and evil. This knowledge produces experience of the reality and nature of evil in human consciousness. Such suffering is existential in that it is rooted in human experience, but the experience is integral to being in the world. The knowledge of the good alone cannot bring suffering, but the knowledge of good and evil produces profound cognitive dissonance and turmoil. We are continually confronted by the need to make ethical choices between good and evil. Indeed, the great dramas of the world involve the triumph of good over evil. Human consciousness is necessarily concerned with the questions such as "What is the highest good?" and "What is right?"

In democratic governments, systems of law and the work of the police are, at least in theory, focused on justice and on upholding what is right and good over what is wrong or evil. Human laws define what is deemed to be right. But laws differ from country to country, and in some cases between different states or provinces within a country. The spectrum of legal systems and laws mean that justice comes to be seen as an expression of great relativism. There

---

2. This is the essence of the dynamic of the cross: Life through death; indeed resurrection and eternal life through death.

are no absolutes, and so the highest good and that which is absolutely right evades the fallen, human ethical capacity. The absence of any absolute values in the human distinction of good and evil is, I contend, a great source of the pain of the soul.

According to the theologian Dietrich Bonhoeffer, the absolute is the command of God, which he describes as follows: "The commandment of God . . . embraces the whole of life. It is not only unconditional; it is also total. It does not only forbid and command; it also permits. It does not only bind; it also sets free; . . . God's commandment is the only warrant for ethical discourse."[3] But Adam and Eve disobeyed, and so discarded God's command. In this intention and this act, they entered on a path of cognitive, emotional and spiritual pain. They were removed from their origin, which was their infinite source of peace.

Bonhoeffer again: "Already in the possibility of the knowledge of good and evil Christian ethics discerns a falling away from the origin. Man at his origin knows only one thing: God . . . He knows all things only in God, and God in all things. The knowledge of good and evil shows that he is no longer at one with his origin."[4] We are now disunited from God and so also from ourselves. This terrible disunity within us tears at our hearts.

The command of God in Christ was the restorative dual command of love – we are to love God, the origin and source of being, with all of our heart, mind and soul, and we are to love our neighbour as much as we love ourselves. In this command Jesus directs us to be reconciled with our origin and to serve others, not only our selves. In this repentant love the law is fulfilled and peace is restored.

Under the old covenant, God's commandment was given in the Ten Commandments. Ethics relied on God's revelation of the law, certainly as far as the Pharisees were concerned. They had apparently worked out a sophisticated ethical system of laws and rules for human conduct. In an intriguing passage, Bonhoeffer comments, "It is in Jesus' meeting with the Pharisee that the old and the new are most clearly contrasted." Bonhoeffer interprets the whole concern of the Pharisee for the law as rooted in the disunity of the knowledge of good and evil. The Pharisee is dedicated to the contemplation of the good and to contrasting it with evil and uses this knowledge to condemn others and himself. He sees life as evil and is thus a disunited man.

---

3. Bonhoeffer, *Ethics*, 272.
4. Bonhoeffer, 272.

> In the knowledge of good and evil man does not understand himself in the reality of the destiny appointed in his origin, but rather in his own possibilities, his possibility of being good or evil. He knows himself now as something apart from God, outside God, and this means that he knows only himself and no longer knows God at all. . . . The knowledge of good and evil is therefore separation from God.[5]

Bonhoeffer argues that because of the fall we now see ourselves as the origin of good and evil, and so we act as if we are the lord of our own creation in terms of our potential for good and evil. Such thinking lays the basis for self-righteousness: "the man who has become like God has forgotten how he was at his origin and has made himself his own creator and judge."[6]

If it were not for the awful reality of sin, we would claim great dignity and honour. Indeed, we still think of ourselves as the origin of the good, with the right to decide for ourselves what constitutes moral conduct. But because we are mistaken about this, we experience angst, guilt and shame.

Suffering for Others

We next come to suffering for others, the type of suffering seen in the lives of Jesus and Paul.[7] Such suffering is profoundly meaningful, for through it God is seen and grace is given entry. The essence of grace is being willing to suffer for another who does not deserve the gift. Suffering and dying for an enemy reveals the truth of God, and so reveals God. God is in such suffering, sharing the suffering of the beneficent sufferer.

I would argue that suffering for others, even to the extent of dying in another's place, is the highest good and the highest virtue in the world. It spreads the sweet fragrance of life through sacrificial death. It confers life as it conquers death and so it is utterly compelling. All sacrifice sincerely offered has the force of softening hearts and restoring the balance of love, which is the spiritual infrastructure of creation. Vicarious suffering, especially of the good for the bad, thus has immediate power that calls for repentance. The cross is the supreme example of this power at work. It led the Roman soldier at the cross to declare "Truly this man was the Son of God!" (Mark 15:39).

---

5. Bonhoeffer, 272.
6. Bonhoeffer, 22.
7. Note that although I mention Jesus and Paul in the same breath in regard to the categories of suffering they endured, they are far apart with respect to the extent of their suffering.

In the perhaps rare instances of the bad suffering for the good, the heart is drawn to the scenario of the reformation of the bad and profoundly warmed towards the previously bad person. We find ourselves drawn to the belief that good is greater than bad and will ultimately overcome and prevail. This is well illustrated in Charles Dickens's novel *A Tale of Two Cities*. The two cities are London and Paris and the setting is the French Revolution. In this story a bad man dies sacrificially in the place of a good man, and as he goes to the scaffold, he says, "It is a far, far better thing that I do, than I have ever done; it is a far, far better rest that I go to than I have ever known."

When it comes to Paul, we can say that his ministry in itself necessitated suffering for others. His ministry and his physical suffering were an extension of the ministry and suffering of Christ towards the Gentiles. Through his suffering, Christ was revealed to them, and so was the true and compelling nature of the cross.

Note that I am not saying that Paul is in any sense on a par with Christ. All that is being said is that the witness and language of Paul's suffering shows that his ministry is an extension of the ministry of Christ. Thus his undeserved suffering came upon him by virtue of God's providence.

The suffering Paul endured for others was not just physical but included "the daily pressure on me of my anxiety for all the churches. Who is weak, and I am not weak? Who is made to fall, and I am not indignant?" (2 Cor 11:28–29).

Suffering for God – Persecution

We will look at persecution in more detail in a later chapter. At this stage, we can simply say that when persecution results in death, the sufferer's fate is termed martyrdom, which is noble and truly heroic. The apparent meaning of this suffering is that it has a heavenly, and so eternal, reward. However, perhaps the greater meaning is that laying down one's life for Christ and in the name of Christ vividly demonstrates the veracity of faith in him. It sends a loud signal that what Christians believe is true. Jesus is indeed the Son of God.

The suffering that came upon Paul from external sources was largely the suffering of persecution. From 2 Corinthians 11:23–28 we learn that he was imprisoned on a number of occasions and was often beaten until nearly dead: he received thirty-nine lashes five times, was beaten with a rod three times, and stoned once. All this in addition to the other forms of suffering and danger we noted under the heading of undeserved suffering.

The list of imprisonments and beatings is explicit evidence of intense persecution. Paul's enemies, who were many and diverse, wanted rid of him.

Paul was sharing in the suffering of Christ and at the same time, through persecution, he was suffering for God.

In Paul's confession of his sufferings, he is almost claiming martyrdom while still alive, given how often he was persecuted nearly to death, but continued to live. In his letter to the Philippian church, he states that in many ways he would prefer to die, for that would mean that he would be with Christ, but he remains alive for the sake of the church:

> For to me to live is Christ, and to die is gain. If I am to live in the flesh, that means fruitful labour for me. Yet which I shall choose I cannot tell. I am hard pressed between the two. My desire is to depart and be with Christ, for that is far better. But to remain in the flesh is more necessary on your account. (Phil 1:21–24)

In this response to persecution, Paul's desire to die and be present with Christ is weighed against his service of the churches. Dying is gain for Paul not only because it unites him with Christ but also because it would mean escape from great suffering. Yet Paul remains, as he also remained in the Philippian prison on the occasion when he could have easily escaped and gone free. On that occasion, his willingness to remain and suffer led to the conversion of his jailer (Acts 16:25–31). Paul's ministry is his triumph over suffering and death, and his life is his triumph over humiliation.

Paul would continue to suffer for Christ until his martyrdom at the hands of Nero and his being raised with Christ in glory. He had proved worthy of the reward promised to those in Smyrna who were enduring persecution: "Be faithful unto death, and I will give you the crown of life" (Rev 2:10).

5

Undeserved Suffering; Meaning, Hope, Healing and Forgiveness

In this chapter we consider the issue of the meaning of life and the relationship of suffering and healing in God's plan of salvation. We also consider the suffering of offence, which results in social breakdown and a call for justice through retribution. We pose the superiority of forgiveness over justice as the only basis for peace and social harmony.

Suffering produces a crisis of meaning as sufferers struggle with the burning question, "What does this suffering mean?" This question is intimately related to the bigger question of the meaning of human life itself, so that the question "What does this suffering mean?" merges with the question "What is the meaning of such a life?" In suffering, our past answers to those questions tend to sink into an overwhelming sense of incoherence. That incoherence is a black ribbon that runs through the entire history of human suffering. It is a great confusion of darkness compounded by lies and delusion.

Over the centuries many ideologies, philosophies and religions have been developed to answer metaphysical questions about the meaning of life in general and of an individual life. Their prophets have sought to offer messages of assurance and peace. But all these belief systems tend to break down when intense undeserved suffering comes upon persons and communities. The only way to resolve this crisis of meaning is through recognizing the authentic ground of meaning that is rooted in the Bible and especially in the gospel of Jesus Christ.

Essentially, the church should be the guardian of the true meaning of life. But in Europe and America in the seventeenth and eighteenth centuries, the Enlightenment sought to remove the ground of meaning from the control of the church and place it firmly with human reason and human science. We soon entered the period known as modernity during which it was believed that science would answer all questions and alleviate human suffering, paving the way to a glorious future for humankind, who had now "come of age." But modernity failed. Science did not achieve what it promised, and so we entered the new age of postmodernity, which stresses the radical relativism of all truth and has led us to the utter meaninglessness of all being. Meaninglessness itself became the new basis for meaning! The result has been a total loss of value and tradition in developed societies throughout the world.

Meanwhile, intense undeserved suffering has been inflicted on the peoples of the Middle East, and has been spread to Europe, the USA and Africa by the rising and enduring phenomenon of terrorism. The task of terrorism is to create confusion, chaos and incoherence in the societies it hates and seeks to destroy.

A great deal of undeserved suffering is also imposed by the oppression of corrupt governments. Officials misappropriate funds to line their own pockets while the populace endure the misery of dire poverty. Yet there remains a universal quest for meaning, although it cannot be denied that the immediate concern is to escape the suffering.

Christians are not immune to this suffering. While we may not struggle with the meaning of life, we do struggle with the meaning of suffering. The concern of this chapter, and of this book as a whole, is to show that there is great meaning in Christian suffering. There is nothing arbitrary or negative about it, nor is it in any way shameful; rather it is noble. Indeed Christian suffering defines meaning and reveals God. It is the front line in the battle for authentic life in this fallen world and also in the church.

Suffering and Hope

Undeserved suffering and suffering for God (persecution) are profoundly difficult to understand. When speaking to a Christian who is enduring undeserved suffering such as that of terminal cancer, all we can say is that the meaning of this suffering lies outside of everyday life and thought. We are being directed in and through this suffering and its great struggle towards a higher knowledge of God. It is in this knowledge that meaning is possible. Through the struggle in our being and personhood and the revelation that follows, meaning is achievable. In other words, we will go deeper into the infinity of God, and in this new depth we find new and wonderful meaning.

While the undeserved suffering of believers appears to be destructive, in the reality of God it is eternally creative. The key to enduring undeserved suffering is thus hope through faith. This hope is not unfruitful, and so the faith that hangs on increases until we have victory and triumph. Triumph over suffering is the rock upon which the church is built.[1] Undeserved suffering, and indeed suffering for God, is community suffering, and the suffering of the church throughout history is the source of the true and substantive vitality of the church. While deserved suffering is endured alone, undeserved suffering is endured by the loving community. It is the community's pain and also the community's healing and profound comfort.

Suffering and Healing

The paradox of dying to live can be expressed in different ways: death and resurrection; losing life to save it; living is Christ and dying is gain. In the context of this book, we can speak of it in terms of suffering to be healed. Suffering defines and is defined by the opposite pole of healing, which is the root of lasting comfort. In this book, I want to hold both realities together as one.

Christians engage with the physical and spiritual universe through suffering and healing. In other words, our worldly relations in the different spheres of being – physical, spiritual, cognitive, emotional and volitional – all derive from the couplet of suffering and healing. The precise tension of our suffering and our being healed connects us and constitutes the sanctifying dynamic that is the essence of Christian living. This is the way of the cross.

The primary and glorious example of suffering to be healed is the ministry and passion of Jesus. Jesus suffered for others of every nation so that they could be spiritually and eternally healed. His ministry was surely a healing ministry.

All human beings are disconnected by the fall – disconnected from God, from each other and from ourselves. We are even disunited in our own beings. The same is true of the physical universe: the ground itself has been cursed.

---

1. Peter, whose name means "rock," was declared by Jesus to be the rock upon which the church would be built. He actually becomes the rock, along with other disciples, through triumphing over the suffering of denial and restoration. Ultimately, we believe, he was martyred.

All this disconnection is a profound source of suffering. Men and women live in angst and pain, insecurity, guilt, and meaninglessness.[2]

Speaking generally of all human beings, outside of Christ, those who are disconnected experience utter aloneness. They may be part of a human community, but such communities are aggregate gatherings. We might do better to speak of them as a "crowd" rather than as a connected, relational community. A crowd is an aggregate of disconnected beings. "World being" is aggregate: it is non-connected existence, not formed by personal relationships.

Human marriage represents an attempt at establishing a connection that dispels aloneness and insecurity. It is a real and sincere attempt to be "in" a one-flesh-sharing intimacy. Yet many marriages, even Christian marriages, break down completely as the attempt at connection fails.

People yearn to be "in." They yearn to be accepted, to be recognized and to be loved unconditionally. They yearn for physical and spiritual intimacy in a community that is true and loyal to them. But at the same time they yearn to be fulfilled – and this yearning is the expression of the self, the individual ego. To be fulfilled, they must act as radical individuals, and when they do so, the community reacts against them. Community by its very nature opposes individuals and individualism. The way to live in true community is to die to self, forgive and not judge, but these qualities are foreign to the natural man and woman.

Those who are outside of authentic community can never reach "in" and they cannot be "in." Reconnection in the authentic and not the pseudo sense requires the reversal of the curse of disconnection resulting from original sin. Reversal of the curse brings true and absolute healing, and the only way to it is by repentance and being changed through conversion. The only way is through suffering the death of the self. Those who come to the utter end of themselves in terms of their old nature are attuned to receive the power and strength of God and can now step "in," so that they are utterly out of themselves and utterly "in Christ." To be in him is to be comforted and to be healed. It is to be reconnected with God, who is the only source of total security. To be in Christ is also to be in the authentic community known as the body of Christ or the church.

To be in Christ means that Christ is at our side. We are not alone. The Holy Spirit is the Paraclete, the Comforter. He is Christ at our side. He is our strength to be. But the courage to be must be ours.

---

2. In his *Principles of Christian Theology*, John Macquarrie discusses the human quest as a search to be free from guilt and a quest for meaning.

Christians do endure loss and mourning. But Jesus's promise reassures us: "Blessed are those who mourn, for they shall be comforted" (Matt 5:4).

Suffering and Offences Against Our Personhood

The suffering caused by offences against our personhood is a form of undeserved suffering, for it involves being sinned against, either by others or even by our own selves.[3] It also falls within the broad category of inner suffering for it involves personal loss and threat and produces psychological pain and confusion.

Offences against out personhood include insulting our dignity, compromising our integrity, accusing us falsely, robbing us of dearly held status, and shaming us. While they may involve physical loss, they generally present as a threat to our being, for such offences always result in some form of loss of personhood. They rob us of who we believe we are and what we have. They attack and question our ownership physically, cognitively and emotionally. The pain that such offences induce involves various forms:

- *The pain of poverty* – We experience grief when we are robbed, whether what is lost is a material object, our reputation, a potential future, our freedom, or a family member or friend. The loss of harmony and balance results in a sense of poverty, vulnerability and insecurity. We feel downcast and even rejected.
- *The pain of being demeaned* – When we are demeaned, we are made to feel less than a person. Robbing us of our self-worth is an attack on our identity.
- *The pain of unfairness (injustice)* – If those who caused the offence are not punished, they benefit from what they have stolen from us, leading to a strong sense of unfairness, which essentially is injustice, which in turn generates fear and a desire for revenge.
- *The pain of being shamed* – The one who has shamed us has made us look and feel a fool. It may seem that the only way to restore our honour is to exact retribution by making a fool of the one who made us seem like fools.
- *The pain of rejection* – Rejection is perhaps the greatest human fear. We fear not being accepted, being shut out, having doors closed in our faces and hearts turned away.

---

3. In saying this, I am not denying that all sin is ultimately against God, but it may take different routes to get there.

- *The pain of confusion and frustration* – All the above emotions associated with offences against personhood produce confusion and frustrate our desire for happiness, joy and peace.

Offences come in many forms, but often they take the form of slanderous lies that seek to destroy our reputation. Such offences, which transgress the ninth commandment against bearing false witness (Exod 20:16), are particularly insidious as we care desperately what others think of us. Our standing in society and in our community of friends and supporters and even our occupation depend on our good reputation.

If what is being said about us is true, we may perceive it as an offence although no real injustice is involved. The truth can rightly offend, especially when brought to bear on a deluded psyche, that is, a life constructed, to a greater or lesser extent, on lies. But the truth cannot offend in the real sense as it ultimately does us good by setting us free from the delusions that hold us captive (compare John 8:32). That said, the way we express the truth, which is different from the truth itself, can be offensive and sinful.

There are two dynamic options open to those who have endured offences against their personhood: to take revenge or to forgive.

Revenge is sweet, and the greater the retribution, the sweeter the revenge. Why? Because despite the fall, we still have a sense of justice and fairness, and revenge seems to indicate that things are coming right and that justice is being done. We feel that it is only right that the offending person suffer the pain of a punishment equal to the pain we have endured. This type of retaliation or retributive justice is defined by the Old Testament *lex talionis* ("eye for eye, tooth for tooth" – Exod 21:22–25).[4] The deserved suffering of the offender, if precisely equivalent to the offence, is held to be a positive thing.

Revenge may thus be understood as the cleansing fire that consumes the painful feelings associated with offences against our personhood. If these feelings and emotions are not adequately channelled, deep resentment can take root in the hearts of the victims and hatred towards the offenders will solidify. Retribution has the effect of making victims feel better. This "feeling better" is deemed closure, and closure is posited to be the end of the matter and to signal a return to normality and equanimity.

But is this the case? Is justice truly served by revenge? Does it restore the heart to peace? We could argue that this might be the case if perfect justice, full

---

4. Note that this law actually served as a restraint on retribution, ensuring that the legal punishment corresponded in kind and degree to the injury.

and exact, were meted out. But is such justice attainable on earth? Here justice is always only approximate because something is always missing.

Moreover, in taking revenge against those who sin against us, we may sin ourselves. If the punishment does not exactly fit the crime, then we, the offended, are guilty of offence – this is what *lex talionis* is about. In that case, our opponents need to take revenge on us for causing them more suffering than they caused us.

The problem is that for justice to be justice, it must be exact and complete. The punishment must be exactly equivalent to the offence. But an offended heart cannot know with certainty that the exact cost is paid. Shakespeare's play *The Merchant of Venice* illustrates this dilemma of exactitude. Shylock has the right to take a pound of flesh from Antonio, but he is told that he may only take flesh, and not a drop of blood, because the contract specified only flesh. If he takes more, he will be punished. Similarly, it is impossible for us as human beings to know the exact cost of any offence, and so it is impossible to be certain that exact justice is done.

Moreover, retribution does not provide peace of mind because that which is lost is not restored. Revenge has no lasting power for that which is lost is still lost. The offence and the memory of the offence remain. The actuality of the offence happening and the memory of its happening are embedded in the mind, even if there is also a memory of retribution. The ghost of the offence remains, and the heart cannot return fully to peace, love and beauty.

Happiness, joy and peace are grounded on realities far deeper and more profound than emotions. That is why what is needed is not revenge but a complete change of heart. The offence turned the heart away from love, and so what is needed is repentance – *metanoia* – a complete ontological change of being so that the heart can love again and forgive the offender.

Forgiveness is paying the full price of the offence against you and returning to love of the offender. It is repenting yourself for your neighbour's sin against you. It is the repentance of the victim, not the offender. Some may find this idea repugnant and say that it is the offender who must repent. That is undeniably true, but how are they to be brought to this point? The exaction of retribution seldom results in repentance. Moreover, if an offender does not repent, must the victim live with the desire for revenge for the rest of their life? Must they live in fear that the offender will offend again, or will take revenge for any retribution exacted?

Our goal here is not to deal with healing the heart of the offender but with healing the heart of the victim. When offences are committed against our persons, we must be the ones whose hearts are changed. The reuniting dynamic of offender and victim takes place within the being of the victim alone. This is grace that is modelled on the grace of God to those who offend him. He has shown us that grace is greater than justice. Indeed, grace is the only true justice.

Jesus's command to love our enemies (Matt 5:44) is key to loving those who hate us. This act of love to those who have offended us means that we retain full control of our disposition upon which our freedom rests. No offence can destroy us, although it can cast us down for a while.

God paid the cost of our sin and for our forgiveness himself (compare John 3:16), and similarly we must pay the cost of offences against us ourselves and so secure the basis for our own forgiving. Indeed this forgiveness is commanded by God (Matt 6:14–15).

Suffering and Offences by Ourselves Against Ourselves

Sin not only divides persons and societies, but it also divides persons from themselves. We suffer from the disunity of our own being. Sin disunites us in our own being and affects our identity, the way we talk to ourselves about ourselves.

The disunity shows itself in many different ways. We both love and respect ourselves as heroes pure and strong, and we despise ourselves as weak sinners. There is a kind of schizophrenia within all of us that can cause us to despise ourselves, and even in extreme cases, loathe ourselves.

I would argue that it is the noble ideal self that despises the weak sinner who continues to do sinful things. The weak sinner, the shameful one, does not despise himself or herself for he or she is consumed by and at one with his or her sin. It is the noble self that despises the shameful self. This duality of the self is well depicted in Robert Louis Stevenson's novel about Dr Jekyll and Mr Hyde,[5] in which the same man has both a good and an evil self and, as is inevitable in the world of fallen human nature, the bad overcomes the good.

To retain a positive self-image, we have to hide and deny the bad. We have to delude ourselves and deceive others by hiding our shame from them. Thus we live in fear that we are going to be found out in the end and punished by being consigned to our proper place with the dregs of society. We know our own guilt and know that each of us in the end is a Judas.

This covering up of our shame is the primary purpose of clothing. Clothes cover our shame at least symbolically, but also actually because it is shameful

---

5. Robert Louis Stevenson, The *Strange Case of Dr. Jekyll and Mr. Hyde* (London: Longmans, Green & Co., 1886).

to have our private parts uncovered in public. Naturists who shed their clothes to expose their whole body claim that public nudity is liberating. But liberating from what? It is liberating because it is both a denial of and a facing up to their shame. By uncovering themselves, they are declaring to themselves and their fellows that they are not shameful. They then put their clothes back on to join the greater public back in regular life.

In covering up our sin, which is our shame, we are effectively judging ourselves. We are making a statement to our noble self, which needs no cover, that we want to be accepted. But we never can be accepted because the noble self is the enemy of the shameful self. The human self becomes its own enemy. This leads to self-loathing, low self-esteem, self-judgement and condemnation, and for some even to suicide. The physical act of suicide is simply an enactment of the inner suicide that is the real tragedy of a fallen humanity.

The law of God as expressed in the Ten Commandments is a light to show us the true reality about ourselves. Either we accept this light as true, or we have to, in some way and to some extent, reject God. We know the commandments are right. Our noble self embraces them and even loves them, but our sinful self forgets them or seeks a rigorous dynamic of self-justification. Thus I would argue that the rejection of God is also self-rejection. The ultimate form of the rejection of the self by the self is suicide. For many, I believe, there is an inner suicide, an inner hopelessness and despair.

The forgiveness of God is the covering of our shame and the removal of our guilt. This forgiveness comes with a promise that we will not have our shame uncovered except to ourselves. The uncovering of our sin to ourselves lets us behold the truth, and this truth creates in us a new nature. The split dissolves and we become one with ourselves. We cease being duplicitous and become one in our dealings with people.

Since God has forgiven us in Christ and through the atonement, we are absolutely justified; our noble self must forgive our shameful self. This is an application of Jesus's parable about the unforgiving servant (Matt 18:21–35). When the master has forgiven his servant, the servant must extend that same forgiveness to others. In the same way, we must forgive ourselves. The restoration of personal unity requires that we forgive ourselves if we are to experience inner healing.

Self-forgiveness requires us to let go of the judgement and condemnation of the shameful self by the noble self. The enmity within has to die. The shameful self is justified by the grace of God, and its history and continuing (hopefully, diminishing) presence is completely covered. There is therefore, for those born by the Spirit of God, no shame.

Self-forgiveness in Christ is the means and power of the new unity of a self. Gone are the inner lies and deceit, replaced by the self-honesty and self-integrity of the growing new nature of the united self, and by an identity at peace with itself.

6

The Inner Pain of Angst

Philosophers speak of inner, ontological suffering using terms like anxiety, dread and angst, the latter being the term I prefer. It is an inescapable part of the human condition; it cannot ultimately be avoided and it cannot be totally removed. It is rooted in our fear of non-being, our sense of impotence, and our aloneness.

People may vary in their awareness of angst, for not all people think or reflect very deeply. Some rarely enter the door of introspection or even contemplate death, and some have no interest in spiritual things. Such people may not be aware of angst, but still angst breaks in on them from time to time, as ultimate reality breaks in on them, possibly through some substantial loss.

We had nothing to do with our creation. We are all thrown into being in this world, and we all live with the knowledge that sooner or later we will die, peacefully or violently, due to age, illness, accident, suicide or even murder. To repeat the quotation from Martin Heidegger, "As soon as a man comes to life, he is at once old enough to die."[1] God himself confirmed this reality: "You are dust, and to dust you shall return" (Gen 3:19). All human beings experience the journey towards the cessation of existence in this world.

Adam, of course, was different from us because he was not born into a fallen world and became vibrantly and perfectly alive, in harmony with God. He was not born of a woman but created from dust into which God breathed his spirit. His body came from the earth (or the dust) and his spirit came from God. He was a unity of body and spirit and he was born into the immediate fellowship and presence of God. But he had the possibility of looking into the

---
1. Heidegger, *Being and Time*, 226.

abyss, for the warning "for in the day that you eat of it you shall surely die" (Gen 2:17) must have rung in his ears.

After Adam and Eve's disobedience, the curse of death became a reality. Adam was immediately expelled from Eden, and ultimately he would be expelled from the created world. The return to the dust from which he came was the symbol of his return to non-being. Adam was thrown back whence he came.

This looming prospect of return to non-being appears to be the primary root of angst. But why is this so, and what exactly do we mean when we talk of *non-being* and *nothingness*, terms that I treat as synonyms?

Barth and das Nichtige

The German theologian Karl Barth taught that nothingness or nullity (*das Nichtige*) is the essence of evil. To get to this point, he argues that God created a good universe out of nothing. In choosing to create being from nothingness, God rejected nothingness, and as something that God has rejected, nothingness is evil. Nothingness is the enemy of created being and is dedicated to its destruction – which it accomplishes when we return to nothingness.

> Nothingness is the "reality" which opposes and resists God, which is itself subjected to and overcome by his resistance and opposition. Nothingness . . . is totally distinct from Him.[2]

This nothingness is not the same as the shadow side of creation, the dark aspects of this world. This shadow side is the dialectical opposite pole of all essential aspects of creation, but it does not oppose creation.

> In creation there is not only a Yes but also a No; not only a height but also an abyss; not only clarity but also obscurity; not only progress and continuation but also impediment and limitation; not only growth but also decay; not only opulence but also indigence; not only beauty but also ashes.[3]

This shadow side of creation may account for such things as natural disasters, but it remains an essential part of God's good creation. It is not to be confused with *das Nichtige*, which is entirely evil, resisting and opposing God. It is the absolute antithesis of good.

---

2. Barth, *Church Dogmatics* 3.1, 305.
3. Barth, 296–297.

There is a paradox in Barth's understanding of God's election of a good creation and consequent rejection of *das Nichtige* as evil. It implies that in creating "being," which had not existed before, God simultaneously created non-being, *das Nichtige*, which seeks to effect the collapse of the good being.

Some, like the philosopher John Hick, reject this line of thinking as merely playing with concepts. They claim that Barth's argument about the existence of *das Nichtige* involves only meontic necessity, that is, a necessity imposed only by thought or language, with no referent in the real world:

> From the point of view of twentieth-century logic, the notion of meontic non-being is an example of the inveterate tendency of the human mind to hypostasize or reify language. The term "being" generates the cognate term "non-being"; but it does not follow that there in any sense is or exists anything of which this is the name.[4]

Barth counters that *das Nichtige* is more than merely an abstraction, and that we can see it most clearly when we look at it through the lens of Jesus Christ:

> Only from the standpoint of Jesus Christ, His birth, death and resurrection, do we see it in reality and truth, without the temptation to treat it as something inclusive or relative, or to conceive it dialectically and render it innocuous. From this standpoint we see it with fear and trembling as the adversary with which God and God alone can cope.[5]

Barth insists that sin is real, and so are death, the devil and hell, all of which are manifestations of *das Nichtige*. There is a concrete referent to *das Nichtige*. He argues that Hick is approaching the problem from the wrong viewpoint, and not in "fear and trembling" from the standpoint of Jesus Christ.[6]

Non-being can also be conceived as the state of being after death, which for those who have not received Christ is Gehenna or hell. Non-being, in fear and trembling, is the eternal state of death, which is beyond or outside the world. It is the spiritual state of the absence of God. It is the state of absolute moral negation.

Barth's understanding of *das Nichtige* throws light on the concept of angst. When we are born physically, we are given being in the world. We then seek to

---

4. Hick, *Evil and the God of Love*, 186.
5. Barth, *Church Dogmatics* 3.1, 305.
6. "Fear and trembling" is a spiritual category used also by Søren Kierkegaard in his book of the same name.

grow in being, materially through amassing possessions and in our reputation and standing as defined by our knowledge and achievements. We form an identity, which can be described as a perpetual conversation with ourselves about who we are. All of this we may ontologically term our "being." Our being is what we perceive it to be in our own minds and hearts. To a greater or lesser degree, this perception involves the delusion that enables us to believe we are who we think we are; an opinion confirmed by our family and friends and those who admire us and hold us in good standing and so boost our ego.

Barth would say that we are unable to see the *das Nichtige* in our own being for nothingness threatens our ego. It wants to win us back to itself from whence we came. When nothingness attacks us through insults, lies, slander, theft and physical danger, as it constantly does, our being is threatened. We perceive an attack that threatens to demote our being, moving us in the direction of nothingness, and this threat produces furious anger. The anger comes in two forms, anger at injustice, which is right and good, and ego anger, which is bad and sinful. This ego anger is the evidence of the reality of nothingness, the negative element in our lives. Threats to our being produce profound and intense angst.

Nothingness is the greatest human problem, symbolized for Adam and all his descendants by the dust from whence we came. The dust itself is not nothingness, but its origin is nothingness (it was created *ex nihilo*) and so Adam's return to the dust is being's return to nothing. A human being comes into the world through birth and leaves the world through death.

Death is the great problem for human being. Because it is the means of the utter destruction of life, the cessation of being in the world, we perceive it as a great evil and the root of insecurity. Death and nothingness are bedfellows and constitute the primal cause of angst in those who are to die. The anticipation of the cessation of being in the world, which we know awaits us, causes a profound nagging insecurity at the centre of our being. This feeling of insecurity, the looming loss of all that produces our identity, is primordial angst. The prospect of the cessation of "I" or "me" and all of my effects fills me with horror. Human beings flee from this horror and seek a hiding place from it. Angst, at root, is facing the horror of non-being-in-the-world. It is evidence of how our fallenness affects the actuality of our lives and being.

Sartre and suicide

Jean-Paul Sartre would disagree with Barth, arguing that nothingness does not exist apart from the negative possibilities of our free choices. He would argue,

"Man is the being through whom nothingness comes to the world."[7] That is why Sartre's associate Albert Camus argues that we can seek nothingness through suicide: "There is but one truly serious philosophical problem, and that is suicide. Judging whether life is or is not worth living amounts to answering the fundamental question of philosophy."[8] In other words, the first question we must answer, before answering any others, is whether life is worth living. Should we live in hope or die in absurdity?

Thoughts of suicide can arise at a fairly early age – even children have committed suicide, and many teenagers have contemplated it.[9] Camus states that, "All healthy men have thought of their own suicide."[10] We are born with physical beauty and perfection but spiritually we are born dead, and so life appears to be meaningless and absurd. Awareness of this absurdity and futility causes us to face the question "Should I commit suicide?" Almost all answer no; but many live as if they had answered yes.[11] Or they hide in the delusion of pride as the driving force to realize their selfhood. This we foolishly term "personal fulfilment," and it forms part of the great delusion.

Non-being and the Bible

The Bible teaches that nothingness as non-being-in-the-world through the gateway of death does exist as the reality of the curse of God. It is the outworking of his statement that we shall "surely die" and "return to the dust." It is true that this nothingness, which lies before us and comes upon each of us, is the result of the free choice of Adam. This choice was a representative choice that he made in freedom. It was made once only, and so it is not now our choice. Adam's negative choice lost us our freedom of choice.

Angst is evidence of this reality in human being and human consciousness. But we should never forget that the very possibility of nothingness is the remains of freedom. While living in a fallen sinful state, we choose to sin. We love sin and to us it appears falsely to be our true home. Somehow we believe

---

7. Sartre, *Being and Nothingness*, 36–69.

8. Camus, *Myth of Sisyphus and Other Essays*, 3.

9. While giving a talk to some two hundred fifteen-year-olds at a school in Scotland, I spoke of my own teenage depression and mentioned that I had thought about suicide. So many students responded to this idea that a 30-minute session ended up lasting for two hours, while the students poured out their own thoughts about suicide.

10. Camus, *Myth of Sisyphus and Other Essays*, 6.

11. Camus, 7.

that if we deny this home, we cease to be a special self in the world. Our sin defines us to ourselves.

Genesis is not the only place where the Bible refers to non-being and returning to dust. Consider Psalm 104:29:

> When you hide your face, they are dismayed;
>> when you take away their breath, they die
>> and return to their dust.

In Genesis 2:7, God is said to have breathed "the breath of life" into Adam. Death comes when God takes away that breath, removing the Spirit of God which is the essential principal of human life, leaving behind a human body that decomposes into dust.

It is worth noting that the most essential aspect of this descent into non-being is not the return to dust as such but the removal of the Spirit of God. Breath is a symbol of the Holy Spirit, and the Spirit of God is the essential element in all being. Non-being, then, is primarily the absence of God from being. All being has its being in God, who is the one in whom "we live and move and have our being" (Acts 17:28). The return to dust is simply a consequence of the removal of his Spirit. When the divine essence is removed, the human body returns to amorphous dust and all traces of its existence vanish, except for images in fading photographs and eroding inscriptions on tombstones.

The author of Ecclesiastes was well aware of this: "For the living know that they will die, but the dead know nothing, and they have no more reward, for the memory of them is forgotten. Their love and their hate and their envy have already perished, and forever they have no more share in all that is done under the sun" (Eccl 9:5–6).

Being is aware of non-being, "for the living know that they will die." To live as a human being involves an ongoing struggle against non-being in our soul, for God "has put eternity into man's heart" (Eccl 3:11). The struggle against non-being within is the eternal, internal pain of the division of our original unity with God. Angst is like the eternal gnawing of a bone by an eternal dog.

Angst is the state in which we are aware that we will return to non-being. We perceive we are going to die. Our end is coming closer and we perceive we will return to the dust, ceasing to exist. Non-being looms large in our thoughts.

It is interesting that the serpent's "You will not surely die" (Gen 3:4) is the first recorded lie in Scripture. The import of this lie is that human beings have infinite and eternal being. But the truth is we have finite and temporal being.[12] Satan's lie holds out the delusion of an infinite possibility to a finite human being. If there were no death, human beings would be immortal and they could think of themselves as infinite.

Angst is the reality of the awareness that we are finite. It is the experience of the finitude as one's own finitude, as the truth comes into view that I myself will die. It is terrifying to face our own finitude in its naked rawness. It is the place of demons. The hellish darkness that this angst engenders penetrates our whole being.

The lie that we will not die throws men and women into delusion, and so does another lie that plagues Western thought, namely the lie of atheism grounded on the theory of evolution. A large part of humanity has abandoned the belief that the universe was created by a loving God and now believes that it began by chance, that human life arose from single-celled organisms that emerged from nowhere, and that life is governed by chance and survival of the fittest. The new lie states that there is no good news (no gospel) and no loving God, and that when we die we return to non-being and that is that.

This new lie, ironically, follows from the first lie. What is radically missing is faith and love. Where there is no faith, there is no hope. As the author of Ecclesiastes says, all that remains is to eat, drink, and be merry for tomorrow we die (Eccl 8:15; see also Isa 22:13; 1 Cor 15:32).

But the Bible teaches that the Creator loves his creation and especially the human beings who bear his image. In the person of his Son he came into the world, incarnate in a human body. He came to heal the many illnesses, maladies, and disorders that flow from the great delusion and to destroy the demonic regime that perpetuates it. The metaphors Jesus used when speaking of that delusion is spiritual blindness and captivity. The Son of God came to give sight to the blind and freedom to the captives (Luke 4:18). The gospel is the good news that God came to save his people through putting non-being to death on the cross. The real truth is that for those who have faith in the Son of God, non-being has died, and so they no longer need to be anxious. It is non-being that has ceased to exist.[13] The death of non-being, referred to in some places as the negation of the negation, finds its glorious hope in resurrection.

---

12. Those who are in Christ have eternal life, but not in this world.

13. This is a very difficult concept to grasp. How can that which does not exist cease to exist? If we think of it as the negative element in the human heart and consciousness, it can cease to exist by a complete change of hearts and minds (which we will term *metanoia* or repentance). The problem is more difficult to resolve from a metaphysical (Barthian) approach, in which "nothingness" takes on the character of an existing entity that we may term evil. And so, in some sense, while logically impossible, non-existence exists as a negative deadly entity; and as such it can be negated by good.

Our Sense of Impotence

Angst is a non-directional emotion. Our awareness of it may be triggered by some event in our lives, but unlike fear it has a relationship with our experiential lives and our essential being. Our sinful existence oppresses our essential selves, producing the inner turmoil which we have to live with. During our time in this world, we are expected to live productively and authentically, but we fail to do this. Our lives are often impotent and inauthentic, and our failure to live as we ought produces profound angst, which often manifests itself as spiritual depression.[14]

Bonhoeffer ascribes this state to our fundamental loss of unity. Adam was united in his own being because all his knowledge was in God. However, through Adam's disobedience, human beings gained the knowledge of good and evil but lost unity with their origin. We are thus disunited both from God and from ourselves and torn by terrible disunity as we live "apart from God, outside God."[15]

From the ground of our inauthentic existence, we reach out to authentic being through seeking fulfilment. We seek to realize our essential selves through an inauthentic sinful state and of course we fail. This is the whole tenor of the book of Ecclesiastes, and indeed echoes the other wisdom literature in the Old Testament.

Responsibility and inability

Paul's cry of inability and incapacity in Romans 7:19–24 rings true not just for Christians but for all human beings. We may want to do what is right and good; but we end up doing what is wrong and evil. Meanwhile those who actively seek to do evil try to justify themselves by relabelling what they do as good.

It is true that in God's common grace there are many who do seek to do good, and some good is done in the world. But this good ultimately fails and is conquered by evil. Human beings in themselves cannot persevere in goodness; they cannot reverse their fallen state. The words of the writer of Ecclesiastes are apt, "I have seen everything that is done under the sun, and behold, all is vanity and a striving after wind. What is crooked cannot be made straight, and what is lacking cannot be counted" (Eccl 1:14–15).

---

14. I use the term "spiritual depression" to distinguish this from clinical depression, which springs from other causes.

15. Bonhoeffer, *Ethics*, 21–22.

We acknowledge that human beings who seek to realize their full potential and to be fulfilled must be completely responsible in every situation. We must do as we ought. We must do what is right, which means that we must be truly righteous. But the problem is, as John Macquarrie put it:

> It is well known that while the summons of conscience may be clear enough, the will to obey this summons may be too weak. We recognise responsibility and even the "oughtness" of a situation, yet we cannot bring ourselves to do what is demanded . . . such impotence seems to make no sense of the moral life (where "ought" must imply "can") and challenges the value of any aspirations.[16]

The horrible and terrible truth is that we cannot be completely responsible. We all fall short of the mark. We remain unrighteous sinners and really should pray like the tax-collector, "God, be merciful to me, a sinner!" (Luke 18:13). Indeed we fail to rise up very far from the depths of our sin.

The essential dialectic is that of responsibility (doing what we ought to do) and impotence. We *must* do as we ought, but we *cannot* do as we ought. We are free to do as we ought, but we cannot do it. In terms of what we ought to do, we are impotent, and the demands of our freedom show up our impotence and incapability. The history of our personal lives is a history of this incapability.

Angst is the felt awareness of this reality. Every morning on awaking we once again stand before the possibility of our being and in the great infinitude all things are possible, only to be crushed by our history of impotence. The mornings of those who are spiritually aware can be times of profound angst, producing, albeit momentarily, depression and despair. The awful reality of our impotence weighed against our failed, responsibility confronts us when we awake from slumber. This inner pain of the spirit and soul always haunts us to some degree.

Added to our inability to be responsible is our guilt about our past failures. This guilt is an anguish of soul. Morally we have fallen short of the mark (hamartia). We keep doing what we ought not to do. Because of our inability to do what we ought to do, human life appears to be absurd.[17] Those of us who are Christians know that our sins are forgiven, but from time to time our history of sin can flood our consciousness and overwhelm us. Perhaps this humbling experience is important for our new Christian identity, but nonetheless it adds additional weight to our stark awareness of our impotence. Meanwhile

---

16. Macquarrie, *Principles of Christian Theology*, 63–64.

17. I am talking here about human life in general, and in particular about human existence without God. The way out of the absurdity is to believe in and follow Christ.

our continuing sin, which we desire not to do, disgusts us. It echoes our past life before conversion and we struggle to grasp the meaning of it all. Angst is the distress or agony we feel at the disjunction between our intentions and our actions.

Freedom and responsibility

All human beings are called to live responsibly before God. Doing so is a prerequisite for a fulfilled life. Yet as we have argued above, none of us can live responsibly before God. Strangely enough, it is our very freedom that undermines our responsibility.

We could think of freedom and responsibility as being at opposite poles. If we are completely responsible, we cannot be free. The constraints of our responsibility take away our freedom. Responsibility seems to imprison us. It makes demands that we must obey. Take God's demand that Adam continually obey the prohibition on eating fruit from a specified tree. Adam was confronted with the choice of obedience or disobedience. In choosing to keep obeying God, Adam's freedom was swallowed up by his responsibility. Yet Adam was free to disobey. Disobedience was the great and terrifying possibility of his freedom.

Every day Adam faced the choice to be responsible or to be free. It must have been like standing at the top of a great height or at the edge of an abyss. He must have had an urge to exercise his freedom, yet doing so involved leaping into the abyss and dying. We know from Genesis that, encouraged by the lies of the serpent, Adam and Eve did make that leap and fell into the infinite darkness, the bottomless abyss.

As Adam acted to fulfil the possibility of his freedom, he utterly failed in his responsibility to God and, although he did not know it, to the vast multitudes of human beings who would follow. The representative of the human race led these multitudes like lemmings over the cliff of utter destruction.

Every man and woman today is subject to the same conditions. We know that we ought to be responsible to God, but we also have the strong urge to be free of the responsibility, and so all of us, without exception, leap from the great height into the abyss of sin. We have inherited fallen human nature; we inherit the legacy of original sin and act out the pattern and act of original sin in our own lives. We are born fallen, but we confirm this state by our own choice to act in freedom and rebel.

Kierkegaard refers to this dialectic of freedom and responsibility as "the dizziness of freedom."[18] He describes a man standing on the edge of a tall building or cliff. On looking over the edge, he experiences two sensations: extreme fear of falling and a terrifying urge to throw himself over. He has freedom to do either, and so he experiences dread, or what we here refer to as angst. If, however, he was standing in the same position but was surrounded by a strong steel frame, making it impossible to fall or jump, he would lose both his freedom and his angst.

Think of yourself as standing on the roof of the Burj Khalifa skyscraper in Dubai or the Petronas Towers in Kuala Lumpur, outside the safety railing, and gazing down, and you will know that shudder of fear as you see the ground far below. Clearly your responsibility is to move away from the edge and go inside. Yet you will also be aware of a strong urge to jump, and know that doing so is a real possibility. The sensation of dizziness that we experience in such circumstances is known as vertigo, and is a manifestation of angst. We may say that angst is the dizziness of our freedom in the face of substantial responsibility.

> Anxiety may be compared with dizziness. He whose eye happens to look down into the yawning abyss becomes dizzy. But what is the reason for this? It is just as much in his own eye as in the abyss, for suppose he had not looked down. It is in this way that anxiety is the dizziness of freedom, which emerges when the spirit wants to posit the synthesis and freedom looks down into its own possibility, laying hold of finiteness to support itself. Freedom succumbs in this dizziness. Further than this, psychology cannot and will not go. In that very moment everything is changed, and freedom, when it again rises, sees that it is guilty. Between these two moments lies the leap, which no science has explained and which no science can explain.[19]

Kierkegaard insists that angst itself is not wrong. The unfallen Adam experienced angst in the garden of Eden as he contemplated his freedom to disobey by eating the forbidden fruit, but he only became guilty when he took the leap into the abyss.[20] That leap was taken in opposition to the law and will of God, and like every such leap, it resulted in guilt. Not to leap is our responsibility to God, but we are unable to refuse to leap, and so the exercise of our freedom, the choosing of the negative, is guilt.

---

18. Kierkegaard, *Concept of Anxiety*, 61.
19. Kierkegaard, 75.
20. Kierkegaard, 62.

Kierkegaard held that the freedom given to people leaves them in constant fear of failing in their responsibilities to God. I think we can go further and say that the reality of human freedom produces the fear of failing to meet our responsibilities in general. Sartre agrees with Kierkegaard.

> First we must acknowledge that Kierkegaard is right; anguish [angst] is distinguished from fear in that fear is a fear of beings in the world whereas anguish is anguish before myself. Vertigo is anguish to the extent that I am afraid not of falling over the precipice, but of throwing myself over. A situation provokes fear if there is a possibility of my life being changed from without; my being provokes anguish to the extent that I distrust myself and my own reaction in that situation.[21]

After some disaster or catastrophe comes upon us, angst is experienced as we cry out,

> "But what am I going to do?" In this sense fear and anguish are exclusive of one another since fear is unreflective apprehension of the transcendent and anguish is reflective apprehension of the self ... The normal process in the case that I have just cited is a constant transition from one to the other. But there exist also situations where anguish appears pure; that is, without ever being preceded or followed by fear. If, for example, I have been raised to a new dignity and charged with a delicate and flattering mission, I can feel anguish that I will not be capable perhaps of fulfilling it.[22]

Sartre, too, considers the issue of responsibility. The purest form of angst arises from our inability to do what we know we ought to do. In saying that angst is "reflective apprehension of the self," Sartre is saying that a thinking being cannot exist without thinking about itself. Animals do not experience angst because they do not reflect; animals think about what they see, whereas human beings think about the fact that they see. Animals fear only known danger; when the cause of danger is gone, the fear disappears. For example, an antelope fears and takes immediate evasive action in the presence of a hunting lion; but in the absence of the lion, the antelope grazes peacefully as if the danger had never been.

---

21. Sartre, *Being and Nothingness*, 65.
22. Sartre, 66.

Kierkegaard agrees with this view on animals who cannot experience "freedom's actuality as the possibility of possibility."[23] They cannot respond to God. They are not created in his image and so they cannot have knowledge of God. Choices involving freedom do not trouble them. They simply follow their instincts in satisfying their appetites.

Humans, however, have freedom to exercise their responsibility to God, and this freedom gives rise to angst. It is the experience of all thinking, reflecting human beings.

Our Aloneness

Daniel Defoe's famous novel *Robinson Crusoe* tells of a man who is shipwrecked on a desert island, where he is utterly alone. This awful aloneness permeates the story until after some years a band of cannibals land on the island. Robinson manages to free the man they are planning to kill, and this man, whom Robinson later calls Friday, becomes his servant. Yet Robinson is still very much alone until he trains Friday to speak English and conform to the norms of British culture. What discerning readers experience in reading this book is the angst of aloneness.

A more recent exploration of this theme is the film *Gravity*, in which two astronauts marooned in space struggle to return to earth. For much of the time, each of them is on their own and has to face their own mortality and extreme isolation. The ultimate moment of horror is when the two astronauts lose all contact and seem to have no hope of reconnecting. The female astronaut is utterly alone in deep space, and this aloneness is a terrible force that reaches out to grip the audience and engages their angst.

Our need for community

Human beings are afraid, even terrified, of being alone. The source of this angst is that we were created to be in community by God who is himself a community. Adam was created as an individual, but God proclaimed, "It is not good that the man should be alone" (Gen 2:18). This is the only "not good" of creation. It becomes clear that there are two stages in the creation of human beings: first, the creation of the man from the dust, and then the creation of woman from the man's body. The man and the woman together with God are complete human beings and the primary community.

---

23. Kierkegaard, *Concept of Anxiety*, 51.

The union of the man and the woman produces children who extend the created community of God, giving us the family as the ground of society. Families together make a village, villages together make towns and cities, and towns and cities together make nations. Part of the image of God in human beings is their capacity to love the others in their community. In so doing, they represent the creation love of God to all other beings, most especially human beings.

After the fall, human nature turned away from the love of God to love of self and the pursuit of self-glory. The potential for completion in community was lost and the aloneness of Adam, in the absolute sense, returned. Radical love of the self replaced a community filled with the love of God. Now, the community is used by the self for self-gratification and fulfilment.

Of course, community by its very nature resists the fulfilment of individuals who in using it are not serving its best interest. Those who deny themselves and serve the community are accepted by the community, but those who abuse it are rejected by it. To be fulfilled, human beings need the community, but to be fulfilled as individuals they abuse the community and must leave it. This negative dialectic makes for the angst of aloneness.

The pain of aloneness

The pain of aloneness is termed loneliness. Loneliness is a dreadful malady of the soul, an aching of the heart and an intense yearning to be complete in another human being. It is the yearning for Eve or the yearning for Adam, and the yearning is a continual inner pain that drugs cannot alleviate. This yearning is the angst of the soul that touches the most intimate aspects of our inner being. This is the "not good" proclaimed by God.

Adam's aloneness was the denial of his sexuality and his most powerful need to be one with another human being equal to himself. Adam needed to be married to be complete. He needed to be part of a community and not a radical individual. Being the one man in the universe is not human being. Human beings are not gods; we need to be human in the same way that angels need to be angels. The pain of denied human identity is the pain of being incomplete.

True, we have our being in God. But this being is plural, we have *our* being and not *my* being in God. In Africa, there is a famous saying, "I am because we are."[24] In the West, however, we tend to say, "I am because I am

---

24. This is the famous saying of the Kenyan Christian philosopher John Mbiti, which reads in full, "I am because we are; and since we are, therefore I am." From *African Religions & Philosophy* (2nd ed. Oxford: Heinemann, 1989), 106.

me." This "me" is both deluded about human identity and enduring the pain of aloneness of being.

The intimate relation of marriage (which can never be perfect in a fallen world) does offer a vestige of community, but the angst of aloneness remains beneath all human relations. Marriage, which solved the problem of aloneness for Adam, now often becomes the problem, for in the intimacy of marriage our sin is uncovered. Physical nakedness is a symbol of spiritual nakedness, and spiritual nakedness is often an awful reality. Few married couples know what it is to "live happily ever after," as the divorce statistics testify.

The pain and angst of aloneness is well captured in John Fowles's novel *The French Lieutenant's Woman*. The main character spends much of her time over the years standing at the end of a quay staring out to sea, waiting for the French naval officer who promised to return and marry her. She lives only in the expectation of reunion with her lover, whom we learn has taken a wife in France. The lonely woman's life is consumed by the angst of yearning.

7

The Solution to Angst

The principal root of angst is the recognition that we will return to non-being and the utter destruction of our personhood. The desolation that accompanies this recognition is countered by the concept and reality of resurrection. Death itself dies through the atonement of Christ. The sacrifice of the atonement removes our inability to be responsible to God and sets us free – not free to sin as Adam was, but free to obey the will of God and please God. Christians know that they are no longer alone in the universe; they have joined the vast multitude of the redeemed as the adopted children of God. As such, they enjoy a life that is real, true and ultimate. From this perspective, angst is a continual reminder that we should be seeking our temporal and eternal security in God alone rather than in material things. The pain of angst thus becomes a blessing rather than a curse.

Men and women use many ways to escape the profound pain of angst. Some resort to drugs, workaholism, promiscuous sex, or an obsession with food. Others strive to control everything and everyone in their orbit. We love to flee from the truth about our real selves and prefer to massage our egos. We do not see who we are or how others see us.

When our attempts at evading angst fail, we may sink into depression, into utter hopelessness and negativity, feeling that there is no point to life. Even the simplest action can present a terrifying prospect. To be depressed is to be at the bottom of everything and the end of everything. The depression arising from angst cancels out all trace of peace. It is the place of zero peace, the place of utter desolation of the soul and person.

Such depression is very close, just next door, to non-being. Yet even this despair can be positive rather than negative for those who believe. Consider the case of Elijah. He raised the widow of Zarephath's son, he executed 450 of the prophets of Baal, he ran before Ahab's chariot . . . and finally his fear of Jezebel led him to flee into the wilderness where he sat down and prayed for death: "It is enough; now, O Lord, take away my life; for I am no better than my fathers" (1 Kgs 19:4), Elijah had had enough. He had come to the end of himself. He had recently killed 450 human beings, and cannot have been unaffected by this awful reality. He had acted zealously for God, but his actions must have been at great personal cost.

Now, like Job, he wants to die – but not at Jezebel's hands. That prospect leads him to fear Jezebel more than he fears God and results in his utter collapse. Elijah's powerful witness at Mount Carmel is followed by a sense of utter impotence, but God does not leave him. Angels come to serve him and Elijah goes on with his ministry as one of the greatest Old Testament prophets. When we come to the end of ourselves, we are at the beginning with God. He is the one who offers solutions for the pain of angst.

Non-Being and Resurrection

Christian's thinking about death, and their remembering that they are going to die, is framed by their regular remembrance of Christ's death in the celebration of the Lord's Supper (Luke 22:19; 1 Cor 11:23–26). His death on the cross is the negation of negation. It is where death dies, with the logical corollary that life must then continue. This it does through resurrection – first, the resurrection of Christ, and then the resurrection of believers. Resurrection is the antithesis of non-being and so it is the solution to angst, or the healing of angst.

Resurrection, of course, follows physical death. Life in the fallen world ends and eternal life, outside of the world, begins. The regenerate spirit is united with a glorified body that cannot be corrupted. In this union of spirit and body there is total compatibility of spirit and matter. The resurrected man or woman is totally one – at unity with himself or herself, with others in the heavenly community, and with God. There is now no antithesis and no synthesis; only the pure and absolute thesis of perfect, unified being. The whole meaning of being comes through resurrection.

Resurrection being must be utterly free and utterly creative. In this unity there can be no tree of the fruit of the knowledge of good and evil. And so our knowledge must also be of the higher order that we associate with heaven. The humanness we currently know includes the great history of human suffering, dwarfed by and including the suffering of Christ, in a complex of fallenness that is an essential element of being human. But this humanness will pass away, and we will know complete humanness in the presence of God.

When we are reborn in Christ, the Spirit returns to our being as the principle of eternal life (breath). When we are resurrected, we are re-formed as the true men and women who are the ultimate creation of God, higher even than the angels (Heb 2:7; see also 1 Cor 6:3). This full transformation cannot take place while we are still in our earthly bodies, for sin is still present with us. However, the resurrected man or woman is the true man or woman because their sinful nature died when they died. They are now brothers and sisters of the true man who was and is God with us in Christ. Jesus of Nazareth is the ground and essence of our heavenly being. There is now no negation of being; there is only "yes" and not "no." Death, the negation of being, has been put to death, and so there is now no death. The negation of the negation renders the incoherence of being coherent, so that being is full of glorious meaning, which is the truth, and wears the white robe of peace and joy.

The Word, which is eternal truth, is still in the flesh as the first fruit. The new heavenly life is the truth, a resurrected human life which is utterly "in" Christ, the true man, the eternal God and the Prince of Peace and so the angst of worldly life has passed away.

Just as we did not chose life in this world, so we do not choose life in heaven, which is life in the truth or true life. This resurrection life is the antithesis of inauthentic life in the world, which is life in the lie. This authentic life has been won and cannot be lost as the earthly powers of the lie are destroyed, and so the earth also is resurrected: "Then comes the end, when he delivers the kingdom to God the Father after destroying every rule and every authority and power. For he must reign until he has put all his enemies under his feet. The last enemy to be destroyed is death" (1 Cor 15:24–26).

Non-being ceases; it is now utterly and eternally at an end. Being is set free from non-being as the transcendent God is all in all (1 Cor 15:28). Resurrection opens the way to absolute free being in God, which is the state of infinite peace. Angst in resurrection is redundant, superfluous. It has no space to be and no history to indwell.

Impotence and Atonement

As stated above, we are free to be responsible, but we cannot be responsible before God. It is doubtful if we can be responsible in the completely authentic sense at all. Ultimately we fail miserably; we cannot do as we ought. Being responsible is most essentially being responsible to God; indeed, responsibility can be defined as responding to God in a way that is acceptable to him. Our own response is always unacceptable. It becomes acceptable only through the atonement made by Christ. We may desire to do good and please God – we are free to choose to do this – but we cannot carry out this choice. So we cannot do what we ought; we are impotent. Attempts at responsibility serve only to produce evidence of our impotence. Awareness of this impotence is also a factor in angst.

Our failure to be responsible before God is the reason why atonement is needed. This inability is the product of our fallen nature. Since the fall of Adam, human beings have been free to sin and to live in sin, but unless they can responsibly and perfectly obey the law of God, they are lost. They live a deficient lifestyle in a deluded identity that they are free to continue but not to abandon.[1] Yet to gain the transformation from inauthentic life to authentic, abundant and eternal life, the fallen lifestyle must be abandoned. This *must* is an absolute constraint.

How are we to deal authentically and adequately with this "must"? This is the question the Philippian jailer asks: "What must I do to be saved?" (Acts 16:30). The jailer was asking about what he must do, but the answer given was "believe in the Lord Jesus, and you will be saved." In dealing with the "must" we are directed away from good works and towards believing in Jesus, who is both God and God's provision for salvation. In believing, or having faith in, Christ, we are appropriating his atonement for ourselves.

The rich young ruler question asked Jesus a similar question: "What good deed must I do to have eternal life?" (Matt 19:16). He too uses "must" and focuses on his personal responsibility. In response, Jesus directs him to the "only one who is good," who is God, implying that the young man could not do good deeds acceptable to God. Jesus then asked him about his keeping of the commandments, which is his responsibility before God. The rich man continues to talk from his delusion. In asking Jesus which commandments he must keep, he demonstrates that he has no understanding of the law in which to break one commandment is to break them all. After Jesus gives him examples of the commandments, the young man again answers from his delusion when he says that has always kept these commandments from the age they applied to him. Yet he perceives that he must still lack some quality to gain eternal life. Jesus now moves him to the reality of love. The young man lacks love, and so he neither knows the law nor knows God. Jesus says that if the young

---

1. To abandon one delusion would merely be to enter another.

man wants perfection – that is, to gain what he lacks – he must give his great wealth to the poor and follow Jesus. This is not a work of the law but an act of love. If the young man can gain love, he will have entered the perfection of the kingdom of heaven (the reign of Christ on earth). In following Christ he will have given up his own lordship and its power.

Entering the kingdom of heaven, and even the capacity to see it, requires the qualitative transformation of spiritual birth. This young man was left very sad. To gain that which he lacked he would have to follow Christ, which meant leaving his delusion, which was sustained by his wealth. Had he followed Jesus, recognizing him as the Messiah, his sin would have been atoned for and he would have gained eternal life.[2] But it seems he could not give up his wealth and power and remained in his lost state, lacking eternal life. The atonement was really what he lacked. Had he known the law he would have seen the reality that, in truth, he could not obey the law and so he must seek the Messiah. The question then would be "Who can save me?" Not "What must I do?"

In the radical change of world view from "What must I do?" (responsibility) to "Who can save me?" lies the solution to our impotence and the means of our freedom from the angst it induces. Our only task is to hand over our responsibility to the Lord Jesus, the Son of God. In handing over and following Jesus, we have access to great peace. Christ's perfect and completely adequate responsibility before God is imputed to us.

The great need is for a messiah, that is, a new representative of the human race who has the means to be responsible before God in our place. He must do for us what we ought to do, and this responsible action must be acceptable to God. This is what Jesus did, and so we who are guilty and condemned are no longer guilty and condemned. Because of the atonement, those who have truly received Christ as Lord and Saviour and so are in a saving relationship with him are justified, that is, they are accounted righteous. They are forgiven by God. Since they are justified and truly and absolutely forgiven, they have no guilt attaching to them and are forgiven three times – by the Father, the Son and the Holy Spirit, one God.

---

2. Here I am not making a statement about the doctrine of universal or limited atonement; I am merely stating that the benefit of the atonement did not appear to apply to the rich young ruler.

Freedom and Security

Fallen human beings are free to sin. That is the extent and nature of their freedom. It is the same freedom that Adam had, for he too was free to sin. This freedom should not be acted on but should be denied and given up. That is part of what Jesus meant when he said that his followers must deny themselves:

> If anyone would come after me, let him deny himself and take up his cross and follow me. For whoever would save his life will lose it, but whoever loses his life for my sake will find it. For what will it profit a man if he gains the whole world and forfeits his soul? Or what shall a man give in return for his soul? (Matt 16: 24–26)

Christians no longer have the freedom to sin. It is true that they can backslide, but they are not free to do so, as is evidenced by their unease (or dis-ease) when sinning and backsliding. When they act in sin, they act against their new nature and really against their converted will.

Not walking according to the flesh but according to the Spirit (Rom 8:4) and in newness of life is the new freedom. In Christ we are free to be in the Spirit, "For the law of the Spirit of life has set you free in Christ Jesus from the law of sin and death" (Rom 8:2). The old order is no longer binding; we are a new creation with a new freedom vastly greater than our first freedom. This is the freedom of the glory of God. The heart of our old freedom was our own glory. This was true even for Adam. But for us, it is the glory of Christ. We choose now in accordance with our renewed minds, which are set on the things of the Spirit.

To backslide is to fall back into our old captivity, for being free to sin is to be free to be imprisoned – which is a contradiction. In this captivity, we are free to lie and believe the lie and indeed chose the things of the lie. Real freedom is truth: "you will know the truth, and the truth will set you free" (John 8:32).

True freedom is experienced in the light of true being, and so leaping into the depths of the abyss or from the top of the highest mountain is no longer a possibility in our freedom. God is in the abyss and in the heights of the mountain, and so our freedom to leap is removed. Whether we leap or stay put, we are under the ultimate blessing of God: "For I am sure that neither death nor life, nor angels nor rulers, nor things present nor things to come, nor powers, nor height nor depth, nor anything else in all creation, will be able to separate us from the love of God in Christ Jesus our Lord" (Rom 8:38–39).

This is the declaration of our new, true freedom and "if the Son sets you free, you will be free indeed" (John 8:36).[3]

Our eternal and even temporal security must and does thus rest in God, and we must trust both the will and providence of God that unfolds before us as the history we are in. We leave the last word under this heading to Jesus.

> Therefore I tell you, do not be anxious about your life, what you will eat or what you will drink, nor about your body, what you will put on. Is not life more than food, and the body more than clothing? Look at the birds of the air: they neither sow nor reap nor gather into barns, and yet your heavenly Father feeds them. Are you not of more value than they? And which of you by being anxious can add a single hour to his span of life? And why are you anxious about clothing? Consider the lilies of the field, how they grow: they neither toil nor spin, yet I tell you, even Solomon in all his glory was not arrayed like one of these. But if God so clothes the grass of the field, which today is alive and tomorrow is thrown into the oven, will he not much more clothe you, O you of little faith? Therefore do not be anxious, saying, "What shall we eat?" or "What shall we drink?" or "What shall we wear?" For the Gentiles seek after all these things, and your heavenly Father knows that you need them all. But seek first the kingdom of God and his righteousness, and all these things will be added to you. Therefore do not be anxious about tomorrow, for tomorrow will be anxious for itself. Sufficient for the day is its own trouble. (Matt 6:25–34)

Aloneness and Adoption

Radical aloneness is a destructive force that penetrates deep into the soul. Many have to bear it continually, but not Christians, for we are no longer alone but have become adopted children of God and members of the body of Christ, the great assembly of the eternal *ecclesia*. We stand with this vast (dare I say infinite?) loving community before God's presence in heaven in life and love. Now and in the world to come we live in and have our being in the new community of God the Father, Son and Holy Spirit.

Because we are adopted into infinite and eternal being, we have an inalienable right to be. We are complete in God and in his multitudinous

---

3. The existentialists would have done well to read and assimilate the account of the new freedom in John 8 and Romans 8.

assembly. We are all princes and princesses of the eternal kingdom, sons and daughters of the King of the universe and of heaven. When we say "I," we also say "We" and God is all and in all. The penetrating pain of utter aloneness is healed by becoming partakers of the divine nature. We are joined or welded to the being of God.

The Blessing of Angst

Angst is an unwelcome visitor for some and a perpetual bedfellow for others. It is highly stressful, especially in its extreme form, so how can I say it is also a blessing?

Well, consider the parable of the rich fool once again (Luke 12:16–20). The man in this parable had such an abundant crop that his problem was where to store it. He solved his problem by building bigger barns and then put his feet up, thinking he was secure for many years and could "relax, eat, drink and be merry."

The problem for those who are like this man is that they confuse material wealth with security of being. They are relatively free of angst, but the grounds for this freedom are false. They have left God, the Lord of their life and soul, out of their calculations. "The fool says in his heart, 'there is no God'" (Ps 14:1). But God is not mocked (Gal 6:7). Those who deny him and live eating and drinking and being merry live the lie which relieves them from the problem of angst. They effectively bury their angst deeply in the false security of their worldly treasure, never to bother them again. But their day of reckoning is coming. They must return to the dust of non-being.

People like this appear to have abundant life but they have an inadequate knowledge of the true value of being and of real and eternal security in God. Their way of life is inauthentic, they have missed the mark and their hearts have become frozen.

For such people, angst can serve as a messenger of authentic being. If the foolish rich man had experienced angst calling him out of his indolence, he would have knelt in confession before the living God and might have saved his life for ever.

I would argue that angst is evidence of what is really real, and the really real is almighty God. Angst comes to remind us of true being and of what is really valuable. In this it is similar to bereavement. When someone close to a person dies, the reality of the death can cause the person to turn from the world to God, although, sadly, this effect often fades when the sense of ultimacy is overcome.

Kierkegaard talks about learning to be anxious in the right way: "Every human being must . . . learn to be anxious in order that he may not perish either by having never been in anxiety or by succumbing in anxiety. Whoever has learned to be anxious in the right way has learned the ultimate."[4]

Here the anxiety Kierkegaard is referring to is the inner pain of angst, the source of which is our own being. This angst arises from within. In a sense it is produced by us from the inside through reflection about being.

Kierkegaard goes on to say that only in this sense can we understand Christ's words in Gethsemane, "My soul is very sorrowful, even to death" (Matt 26:38). These words come from his inner being. He was about to be betrayed and go to the suffering of the cross. But the source of his profound angst was not fear of the cross but his pre-incarnational knowledge of the cost of salvation.

Kierkegaard is right when he claims that this type of angst is positive. Indeed, he says, the more profoundly someone experiences this type of angst, the greater they are. Such people face the ultimate truth and so come to a radical honesty about their own being.[5]

We cannot surely disagree with Kierkegaard when he says, "Anxiety is freedom's possibility, and only such anxiety is through faith absolutely educative, because it consumes all finite ends and discovers all their deceptiveness."[6] To face the ultimate, which is non-being, is to face God. And so the awful reflection of angst is a form of revelation, and the angst is educational in that the revelation of God's ultimate being becomes accessible to us.[7] Angst gives us, as it were, ears to hear. And what angst makes us hear has terrible proportions, for it attacks the veracity of our delusion about ourselves and leads us to see the truth.

Anyone who has experienced angst at this level knows that it is a fierce adversary: "no discerning judge understands how to interrogate and examine the accused as does anxiety, which never lets the accused escape."[8] Angst reorientates our vision back towards the infinite from whence it came from before the fall. However, it is grace and not angst that invites us back. Salvation may be described as angst meeting grace and handing over its role to it, as John the Baptist handed over his role to Christ. Yet even in the beautiful fragrance of grace received, angst remained as the thorn in Paul's flesh (2 Cor 12:7–10).

---

4. Kierkegaard, *Concept of Anxiety*, 155.

5. Calvin (*Institutes of the Christian Religion*, 1.1 and 1.2) implies something similar when he teaches that knowledge of God is knowledge of self.

6. Kierkegaard, *Concept of Anxiety*, 155.

7. This is the whole import of the book of Job.

8. Kierkegaard, *Concept of Anxiety*, 156.

Indeed Paul's elevation to infinite being necessitated the thorn as a messenger to facilitate his continuing in the world.

By thrusting us into the darkness, angst gives us a glimpse of the possibilities of life in the light. The awfulness and terror of angst give glimpses of the possibilities of infinite being. These possibilities are of the nature of hope. Hope reaches beyond despair into new and greater possibilities for life and happiness. "Whoever is educated by anxiety is educated by possibility, and only he who is educated by possibility is educated according to his infinitude."[9] When our view is towards the infinite, then all things become possible for us as God is infinite being and all things are possible to him. In the kingdom of heaven we are on a new and true journey into that which in the world was not possible. That which was not possible becomes possible for the creatures who are born anew. We go beyond that which was not possible in the world to a new concept of possibility itself. "Behold, the new has come" (2 Cor 5:17).

---

9. Kierkegaard, 156.

Part 2

The Suffering of Biblical Figures

In part 2 of this book we will focus on the role of suffering in the life of biblical characters. We will look at Job as the supreme example of undeserved suffering, at Jesus as the supreme example of suffering for others, and at Paul as the supreme example of suffering for God. Of course, these categorizations of suffering are not absolute, for Jesus endured undeserved suffering, as also did Paul, although on a different level. We conclude by looking at the suffering of the church, that is, the suffering of those who follow Christ and endure the suffering for God that we call persecution.

In this study we will be referring to passages of Scripture but will not be engaging in detailed exegesis. Our task is to see the broad sweep of the narrative and to see what role suffering plays in the life and mission of Job, Jesus, and Paul and the church. We will also seek to understand how their suffering relates to us, and how our suffering relates to theirs.

We will see that their suffering, and I believe, the suffering of all Christians, is in the will of God. It is part of the mysterious providence of God that his people undergo suffering. Clearly suffering is integral to *Heilsgeschichte* (the history of salvation), yet nowhere is it fully explained. This absolute origin is mystical, as we might expect, and may seem alien, but "since the supreme example of suffering lies at the heart of God's redemptive activity in Christ, it cannot be maintained that suffering is alien to the purpose of God."[1] In a real sense, faith is stepping out into this mystery.

---

1. Guthrie, *New Testament Theology*, 98.

8

The Suffering of Job

Job is the supreme example of undeserved suffering. Analysis of his suffering throws light on the ultimately positive nature of such suffering and the psychological, mental and emotional struggle that sufferers endure as they seek to grasp its meaning. Job's story reveals that the meaning of such suffering lies outside our present knowledge. What he received was a new revelation in and through a vastly more profound theology.

Job was an innocent and virtuous man. Yet he endured such great suffering that he wished he had never been born. His suffering began with great material loss when two different groups of raiders stole all his oxen and camels and massacred his servants. These losses coincided with a natural disaster in which his flock of sheep was struck by lightning, killing the sheep and their shepherds. In an agricultural society, these losses are the equivalent of sudden bankruptcy (Job 1:14–17).

As Job was being told about these disasters, another messenger arrived with news of an even deeper loss caused by something like a tornado that struck the house where his children were gathered, destroying the house and all within it (Job 1:18–19). Job was left to mourn his children and to adjust to life without posterity in a society that placed great value on having descendants.

All that Job has left were his health and his wife, and they too failed him. He broke out in "loathsome sores from the sole of his foot to the crown of his head" (Job 2:7–8) and his bereft wife counselled suicide, saying "curse God and die" (Job 2:9).

We are shocked at such loss, and even more shocked that God specifically allowed these disasters to come on Job and his family even though Job may have been one of the most virtuous men who ever lived. Although Job was a sinner like all who have inherited fallen human nature, God speaks of him as "a blameless and upright man, who fears God and turns away from evil?" (Job 2:3). In fact, God himself states that Job was afflicted for no reason, meaning no reason deriving from Job's life:

> And the LORD said to Satan,[1] "Have you considered my servant Job, . . . He still holds fast his integrity, although you incited me against him to destroy him without reason." (Job 2:3)

Here we are involved in the mystery of undeserved suffering that goes beyond human reason. What is at work here is the radically mysterious providence of God. The source of the suffering, and indeed the evil, that befell Job lies outside the world. The outside, the transcendent, is acting on a person in this world. When this happens, its effects can be devastating for that person. The foundations of their life may be so shaken that their understanding of life and the point of living is threatened. Their life context becomes negative as they enter the great mystery of repetitive futility and misery. We see this even in the dialogue between Job and his counsellors, which feels as repetitive and futile as the labours of Sisyphus. It goes nowhere. Round and round go the assertions of guilt and innocence. There is no release from the circle.

There are only two possibilities for breaking the cycle. One is for Job to commit suicide, as his wife urges him to do. But such an act is a denial of God's lordship. The other way out is for God to intervene to reveal the truth about why Job is suffering such apparent injustice. Job cries out for God to come and vindicate him by revealing the truth that will free him from his agony. In a sense, Job is like Sisyphus – only God can set him free from the curse that has been put on him and free him from his prison of suffering.

This same scenario holds true for all in Christ who are seriously afflicted by the apparent futility of undeserved suffering. They cry to the Creator to break in and release them from their pain. Effectively, they are asking him to set them free by transporting them outside the awful repetition.

Our suffering and bondage is not imposed on us by a pagan god, as was the case with Sisyphus, but is a result of our own sin and the sin of others. Yet God describes Job as blameless and upright. Unlike Adam, Job fears God and shuns evil. So why does Job suffer?

---

1. The word translated "Satan" literally means "the accuser." There is debate as to whether "the Satan" in Job is the same as the fallen angel Lucifer, who is also called "the devil." Surely the devil could have no place in the counsel of God in heaven? I would argue that the being identified as "the Satan" represents God's transcendence. Satan himself transcends the world, and is not yet cast down. (I am aware that the name Lucifer only appears once in the Bible, Isaiah 14:12 KJV.)

Truth and Ignorance

Before we can answer that question, we need to see another truth. Jesus told us that the truth sets us free (John 8:32). Freedom from limited sinful life comes by the transcendence coming into the world in the person of the Son of God. The way to freedom and abundant (or authentic) and eternal life now is to follow the Son, who is himself "the way, and the truth, and the life" (John 14:6). God the Son leads us out of our limited sinful repetition to life beyond. He de-limits us. This de-limitation requires our obedience to his commands and taking up our own cross, which is our suffering. This is suffering to be healed, and it is suffering to be free. Job's suffering, in the wonderful old covenant grace of God, was also to make him free, but the question is free from what?

When the transcendence of God visits the finite world of sinful human beings, the radical truth of the Logos of God can be clearly heard and distinguished by those who have ears to hear (Matt 13:13). They are called to leave behind their sinful delusion of self-sufficiency and self-glory and are led out to freedom through the process of sanctification and spiritual growth. In this light they see the truth about God and their own being, and this truth becomes their knowledge of God. This knowledge is the ground of their freedom. It is more valuable than silver and gold or the most precious stones. This wonderful knowledge is the "pearl of great value" (Matt 13:45–46).

I can now answer the question asked above. What is Job being set free from? He is being set free from ignorance. Elihu, Bildad, Zophar and Eliphaz, Job's counsellors, are arguing in terms of ignorance. Job knows that what they are saying cannot be true, but he himself is captured by the same profound ignorance of the nature of God and the nature of the law.

Ignorance of the nature of God

Job's error was not that he sinned as defined by the law or in terms of the Old Testament but that he was keeping God in a box. He insisted that God adhere to the formula of Old Testament righteousness or, more generally, to retribution theology. The basic tenet of retribution theology is cause and effect. In other words, it insists that sin causes suffering and so suffering is the direct result of sin. On this view, all suffering is deserved suffering.

Job and his counsellors, like all other Israelites, held with absolute certainty that God, the giver of the law, judged his people in terms of their keeping or breaking that law. Essentially, the Old Testament righteousness framework or righteousness formula is that you reap what you sow. That idea began with the covenant with Adam, which was that if you obey you will prosper but if you disobey you will die. Adam's disobedience reaped death, the ultimate disaster. It continued in Deuteronomy 27 and 28, where the people were warned that disobedience brings a long list of curses and disaster whereas obedience brings a list of wonderful blessings.

The belief is well summed up in these verses from Deuteronomy:

> And if you will indeed obey my commandments that I command you today, to love the LORD your God, and to serve him with all your heart and with all your soul, he will give the rain for your land in its season, the early rain and the later rain, that you may gather in your grain and your wine and your oil. And he will give grass in your fields for your livestock, and you shall eat and be full. Take care lest your heart be deceived, and you turn aside and serve other gods and worship them; then the anger of the LORD will be kindled against you, and he will shut up the heavens, so that there will be no rain, and the land will yield no fruit, and you will perish quickly off the good land that the LORD is giving you. (Deut 11:13–17)

By this equation, the disaster that came upon Job meant that he was unrighteous. He must have sinned, and sinned badly, to judge by the scale of his disaster. But Job knew, as does the reader, that he had not sinned. This is the great dichotomy and enigma of Job.

Retribution theology can be said to be an anthropological view of the universe in which human beings, rather than God, determine what lies ahead. God is acknowledged as having created the universe, but is then relegated to the position of judge and benefactor, punishing those who have sinned and rewarding those who have done good. God's essential nature then is that of an all-powerful judge, and his two key attributes are power and justice.

Jesus challenged this belief system when his disciples asked him, "Rabbi, who sinned, this man or his parents, that he was born blind?" He responded, "It was not that this man sinned, or his parents, but that the works of God might be displayed in him" (John 9:2–3). This answer and Jesus's restoration of the man's sight represent an early manifestation of grace over works of the law. They also show the providence and sovereignty of God. God is not bound by any particular expression of the law proclaimed as an early revelation to human beings. Nor is God bound by a limited world view.

A similar case concerns the cleanliness laws that specified which animals could be eaten (Lev 11). In the book of Acts, we read about the apostle Peter falling into a trance in which he saw heaven opened and something like a great sheet coming down. In the sheet were all kinds of animals, birds, and reptiles that the law would have proclaimed unclean and so not to be eaten. Peter heard a voice saying, "Kill and eat," but he refused, saying, "By no means, Lord; for I have never eaten anything that is common or unclean." He was rebuked: "What God has made clean, do not call common" (Acts 10:9–16). This is another New Testament revelation that God is not bound by the laws on cleanliness. Peter, however, was still operating under law and not under the revelation of grace that we may term the light of the kingdom of God.

The New Testament revelation of grace and Jesus's revelation that the true nature of God is love is seen to be overwhelmingly superior to the revelation of the law of Moses. There is no love in the letter of the law, and Job's counsellors, and possibly Job himself, were operating in terms of the letter of the law. They had an inadequate doctrine of God, which we will term ignorance. This ignorance was profound, and in the case of Job's counsellors it was in itself sinful and worthy of the wrath of God.

In the case of Job, it was not yet the time for the full revelation of the new covenant of grace, but it was the time for a greater revelation of God than that proclaimed in the theology of retribution. Through Job's great suffering he was prepared to receive a greater revelation of the true nature of God. Indeed, we can say that he was redeemed from captivity to his falsely held doctrine of retribution.

The first message of Job for suffering Christians, or indeed suffering people, is that, contrary to popular belief, suffering is not necessarily caused by personal sin.[2] The corollary to this is that good things do not necessarily follow from any virtue that we may have in ourselves. Self-righteousness is as filthy rags to God. The New Testament revelation is that the only righteousness acceptable to God is Christ's righteousness; imputed to us, but still his. In Christ, the doctrine of rewards for good acts and punishment for bad acts is a false doctrine.

Ignorance of the nature of God's law

Job's counsellors and Job himself were absolutely convinced that, in terms of obedience to the law, they were righteous. They thought that was all that mattered. They failed to recognize that the purpose of the law was to bring

---

2. Although there is still an element of reaping what we sow when it comes to deserved suffering.

blessing to other nations (Deut 4:6) and to show up sin. Paul describes it as a schoolmaster or guardian, teaching those under its instruction of their need for a messiah (Rom 7:7; Gal 3:24). The law leads human consciousness to the Messiah as eschatologically essential for the ultimate future of humankind, and certainly for Israel.

The law in itself does not save; it is a means to an end. But Job and his counsellors regarded the law as the end of the matter. As such, it became an idol for them, and even took the place of God. This is the evil for which Eliphaz, Zopher and Bildad were condemned. All of the players in the drama of Job were effectively in bondage to the idol of the law.

To worship the law is, ironically, to break the first commandment of the Decalogue. Yet by New Testament times, both the moral and ceremonial law were indeed worshipped, and the Pharisees had added hundreds of laws of their own making. The law had become a means whereby one group exercised power over another. Jesus responded with anger, referring to the Pharisees as hypocrites and whitewashed tombs (Matt 23:27). They had taught the people of Israel to worship the law but had left them ignorant of their responsibility to their neighbours. We see this demonstrated in the interaction between Jesus and a Jewish lawyer:

> A lawyer stood up to put him to the test, saying, "Teacher, what shall I do to inherit eternal life?" He said to him, "What is written in the Law? How do you read it?" And he answered, "You shall love the Lord your God with all your heart and with all your soul and with all your strength and with all your mind, and your neighbour as yourself." And he said to him, "You have answered correctly; do this, and you will live." But he, desiring to justify himself, said to Jesus, "And who is my neighbour?" (Luke 10:26–29)

The parable of the Good Samaritan followed in answer to this question. Interestingly, the command "you shall love your neighbour as yourself" comes from Leviticus 19:18, but there it is in the context of not taking vengeance against one's own people, implying that the neighbour is a fellow Jew. Jesus redefines the meaning of "neighbour," showing that a neighbour is a person who is in need of mercy. He extends the concept of neighbour beyond a particular group by showing love and mercy to all.

In Victor Hugo's profound book *Les Misérables*, Inspector Javert is a man who worships the law. He is totally without mercy and devoid of love, yet he appears to have the virtue of utter devotion to the law. When he finds himself in a situation where he recognizes that obedience to the law would be immoral, he is driven to suicide. He cannot live with a failed idol. That is the spirit of worship of the law. By contrast, Jesus shows that only love fulfils the law, and that the spirit of the law is compatible with love and mercy. The law calls for sacrifice, but God desires mercy.

Job's counsellors and Job himself should have seen that the virtue of the law is love and mercy. In this they failed. And so in the providence of God, Job's possessions, relations and self-worth were destroyed, but in so doing God also destroyed Job's profound ignorance of his true nature.

Reaching Out to the Transcendent

Job's pain seems to transcend what a human being can bear. He lost everything, and his acute mental and physical suffering pushed him beyond the desire to commit suicide into a desire for non-existence. There was no help from God, who remained silent for a long period. Job endured the ontological pain[3] of what seems to be a profound injustice. It is no surprise that he broke out into a great lament filled with "why" questions (Job 3). Yet in this lament we can see that he was beginning to move beyond a purely earth-bound perspective and reaching out to the transcendent.

The transcendent and lament

In many respects, Job's lament is in line with the genre of psalms of lament. Yet in the books of Psalms and Lamentations, and even in Jeremiah's laments, the writer is speaking to God or about God. But who is Job talking to?

> On a surface reading, Job's words here resemble those of a psalm of lament. Laments are prayers that are spoken to God when life is falling apart . . . Looking more closely at Job 3, we see that Job's words are far from this type of lament. First, Job does not even address his words to God. He is speaking to thin air in his exasperation.[4]

Let us look at Job 3 in more detail. We should note that Job is not asking to die. In Jewish thinking, to die would simply be to go to a place where his tortured existence would continue. Rather, Job asks "Why did I not die at birth?" (Job 3:1–12) or even before birth, "Why was I not as a hidden stillborn

---

3. Pain of his essential being.
4. Longman, *Job*, 106.

child?" (Job 3:16). His desire is not that he cease to be, but that he never was. How can he conceive of this "never was"? He must be reflecting on non-being, the total absence of any consciousness. Job may not realize it, but his unbearable pain is causing him to break out of his world view to an undefined and indeed indefinable (non)entity. Job has moved to the incomprehensible.

From his place of pain and utter meaninglessness, Job is reaching out to the transcendence in a theology of complaint, where his focus on non-being reaches beyond his theology of retribution. He does not curse God and die but continues to faithfully believe. "Though he slay me, I will hope in him" (Job 13:15).

Here we see a man fit for heaven. Job does not disobey as Adam did, even in his profound poverty. He is dressed in rags, and yet he is a citizen of heaven. Without revelation, through the quality of his lament, he manages to reach out to the transcendence in the fearful silence of God. In this capacity to reach beyond, Job is on the edge of a new order of meaning that will be inaugurated when God ultimately speaks.

Job has acquired the capacity to contemplate, through lament and complaint, a higher order and certainly a different order of meaning. His situation may be described as an epistemological crisis, that is, a crisis of knowledge, and specifically of knowledge of God. It is crisis that ends with Job moving "beyond the faith of his fathers to a new kind of faith, a faith in which Job turns in real hope to the God who speaks 'out of the whirlwind.'"[5]

Job's faith is shown to be equal to or greater than his crisis. It is a believing and a trusting beyond belief, similar to that of Abraham who also believed beyond belief (see Rom 4:18–25). In believing, trusting and surrendering the will, faith is not dependent on reason. While faith is supported by reason and is reasonable, there is much that is beyond reason in the unfathomable mystery of God. Faith requires us to believe in the incomprehensible, which seems impossible. But the creation of humankind in the image of God and the human capacity for innate knowledge of God renders the impossible possible.

Being-towards-death

Severe undeserved suffering is being-towards-death; living in the face of death and moving towards it. For all Job's desire never to have been born, it was actually death that lay before him. It stared him in the face, and offered his only possible hope of escape. Like a woman I knew who had terminal cancer,

---

5. Surin, *Theology and the Problem of Evil*, 26.

he would have said, "Let me now die." She had no hope of recovery or healing in this world, and so sought ultimate healing. What little life remained to her was going towards death.

Serious undeserved suffering is a life situation that faces death. Extreme depression, deep anxiety and catastrophic loss drive some to suicide. Job's lament and his words about non-being and non-existence suggest that he too is teetering on the brink. The mind can be overwhelmed with profound loss and what appears to be extreme injustice. Some react like the Jewish rabbi who, alighting from the train at Auschwitz Birkenau and seeing the piles of corpses, is said to have cried out, "There is no God." But Job neither turns to atheism nor commits suicide.

There are many today who ask how a sovereign, all-powerful, loving God can permit such suffering. A God of love could not permit it, and so the great suffering evident in the world militates against belief in God's existence. But this argument is rooted in ignorance of the true God. It is because a sovereign, powerful and loving God exists that there is such severe suffering in the world. This is a bitter pill to swallow, and Job has to do so.

Great suffering takes human beings down to the valley of the shadow of death (Ps 23:4). They have no option but to contemplate death. They are facing the ultimate human experience, and to face the ultimate is to face the truth. Satan's delusions fade, and his great lie, "You will not die," is exposed for what it is. To face death is to contemplate the truth of God's warning, "You shall surely die" (Gen 2:17). Facing and thinking about ultimate truth is facing and thinking about God.

All Christian theology is in some sense a contemplation of death, for we constantly remember the death of Christ through the regular celebration of Holy Communion. But Job was focusing on death before the incarnation and the resurrection, with his only context being the fear of God. Job feared God, but he was also held captive by the self-righteousness of his own theology. Yet as Job contemplates death, he faces truth, and he is prepared to receive the truth that will set him free when God finally speaks.

Gloom and the absence of meaning

Job "finds the mystery of evil to reside precisely in the inescapable tragic and sombre fact that the world is a 'land of gloom and chaos where light is as darkness.'"[6] Such a world is devoid of meaning. It is a place of depression and

---

6. Surin, *Theology and the Problem of Evil*, 66, quoting Job 10:22 (NRSV).

hopelessness where no purpose, whether noble or evil, can survive. Meaning cannot dawn and evil reigns victorious.

In this gloom, Job found neither mercy nor love but only the condemnation of his so-called friends whose hateful speeches and misunderstandings pinned him to the ground of his despair. It was as if he were already in Hades (*Sheol* in Hebrew), the place of the dead or the underworld, a place of tormented souls. Like the rich man in the parable (Luke 16:19–30), Job was enduring terrible anguish and torment.

But Job was not dead, and he had a purpose, which was to be justified and vindicated. But would this purpose raise him from his present anguish? Would meaning come if he gained the justice he sought? No, for Job conceived of meaning in terms of a just God who prospers those who do right. On these terms, if Job were vindicated, God would have to be condemned as unjust. What then would become of the meaning Job sought? There would be no way it could be redeemed.

So what is Job to do with the question of why God has brought this evil on him or why he allowed it to come? Job's only option is to redefine the concept of meaning. He needs to find a higher meaning, a meaning that cannot be found through reason but is a gift of God from beyond meaning as Job understands it.

Higher meaning has nothing to do with human achievements, greatness and glory, all of which are ultimately consigned to valuelessness and futility (Eccl 1:2; 12:8). Higher meaning has only to do with the glory of God. That is the key to the true meaning of human life. As the Westminster Shorter Catechism says, "Man's chief end is to glorify God." Through his profound suffering and repentance Job ultimately saw the glory of God (42:5). He received a higher meaning and a deeper knowledge of God.

Truth and the transcendent God

Revelation of God is revelation of truth. In contemplating death, those who are enduring severe suffering and undeserved suffering are facing the ultimate truth. It is this truth that makes them free (John 8:32). Receiving this truth into their being heals them from the effects of their captivity. Unbelievers who find themselves facing God may be set free from condemnation if they turn to him (although not all do so, and some do so only until the suffering ends). Believers who are enduring undeserved suffering ultimately experience a revelation of the truth of God that sets them free from their current theology. It is not that their current theology is necessarily bad or wrong, but it is not final. Believers should be continuing to grow in the knowledge of God, taking them always deeper into his being as Father, Son and Holy Spirit.

Truth is also a revelation of grace. Jesus revealed God's gracious nature. Grace is the essential hermeneutic (or principle of interpretation). Grace is the only way the force of the law can be fulfilled. Because retribution theology lacks grace, it lacks veracity and authenticity. When the law is the essential principle of any theology, it becomes that theology's limiting factor, for law is a limited revelation of an infinite God.[7] The principle of grace shows us that our knowledge of God can never be fixed; it must always be growing, and so our theology too must always be living and growing in depth. That is why one of the essential tenets of Reformation theology is *semper reformanda*, the principle of always reforming.

Because we are finite beings and our old nature is fallen, we long to arrive at the place where things are settled. In our uncertainty, we need certainty, and our quest for it can lead us to resist change. Thus we may hide from God in a body of doctrine that we regard as final. In some cases, this doctrine may even replace God for us.

But inadequate doctrine returns us to captivity, as happened to Job and his counsellors. Yet they were all set free through Job's suffering, in which he and they were confronted with truth. The delusion that sprang from their inferior revelation could almost be said to have become a lie that produced a great dilemma. They were confronted by the dichotomy between greater truth (grace) and lesser truth (the law).

Job had certainty in terms of old covenant law, and in terms of that certainty he knew all there was to know about the nature of God. The revelation he had was final. The covenant with God required perfect obedience to the law and such obedience would be rewarded with prosperity, conversely disobedience to the law would bring disaster, as it had for Adam. The problem was that God did not act in accordance with Job's certain knowledge of him.

In reality, the law only gives insights into the nature of God, who is infinite. Indeed the purpose of the law is to show the truth about fallen human nature. It showed up sin (Rom 7:7). We need to know the law in order to be able to distinguish good from evil, which is why the revelation of the law followed the radical change in human nature that came about first through Adam and Eve's disobedience and secondly through gaining knowledge of good and evil.

---

7. The law as an early revelation of God is good and authentic, but it cannot stand alone. Its vital function is to show up or even define sin, but it is clearly inferior to grace as a major principle of the knowledge of God and a living theology. The love within grace is the only means of fulfilment of the law.

Of course the law revealed God. But it did not sum up God. Yet Job believed that it did. He and the rest of the chosen people of God believed that people reaped what they had sown. Salvation was earned by doing the works of the law, and Job excelled in this respect. Undeserved suffering was thus an enigma. How could a righteous man like Job be struck with disaster?

Job sought meaning and indeed vindication in terms of his present knowledge of God. He found neither. It is reasonable that Job would seek the meaning of his suffering in terms of the knowledge of God that he presently held. All of his life he had acted in accordance with this knowledge, which for him and his counsellors was complete. It lacked nothing. Obedience in terms of this knowledge was the way of salvation.

Christians facing undeserved suffering face the same dilemma. We need to remember that meaning for life and being, unlike all other aspects of meaning, cannot be found within a finite system of knowledge and belief. God transcends all such systems and ultimate meaning is found in God alone. Job learned this truth when God at last spoke.

The Divine Silence and the Divine Voice

Those enduring undeserved suffering often feel that God is not present with them. Indeed they experience an absence of God, which they describe as his silence. This divine silence stands in stark contrast to the noisiness of suffering and the sufferer's great struggle for meaning. The divine silence gives a certain quality to the noise of suffering. Indeed it is the context of the pain.

Job's cry for validation of his innocence was noisy, as was the advice of his counsellors. His ringing cry for justice brought no response. In replying to Eliphaz he said, "Teach me, and I will be silent; make me understand how I have gone astray" (Job 6:24), but no teaching came. The noise of their debate continued, as did the divine silence. Job was on a journey of protest and demand for validation that was slowly moving towards his own profound silence. Such silence is surely pleasing to God, for God has told us to "be still [silent], and know that I am God" (Ps 46:10). God is saying "stop your noisy struggle and listen to me!"

But Job and his four friends were not listening to God. Rather they were intent on giving an authentic explanation from within their own theological and doctrinal position. They multiplied explanations within the same limited frame. They were like the Ptolemaic mathematicians who produced more and more complicated mathematical proofs to support their assertion that the planets and the sun circle a central stationary earth. But their whole system of thought had to be discarded when Nicholas Copernicus showed that it was actually the sun that was at the centre and that the earth moved around a stationary sun. Job's three friends are like those Ptolemaic mathematicians as they desperately seek sophisticated explanations for Job's situation from within their retribution theology.

The readers of Job, and Job himself, know that he has not sinned to the extent of deserving such disaster. There must therefore be another explanation, one which cannot lie within their theological boundaries. The meaning of Job's suffering transcends the present limitations of Eliphaz, Zopher, Bildad, Elihu and Job's knowledge of God. This transcendence is a whole new revelation that calls for life beyond the law and the perception of God as judge.

The divine silence as abandonment

In his suffering, Job felt abandoned by God. This was also the experience of the psalmist who wrote Psalm 22, the psalm of lament that Jesus quoted on the cross (Matt 27:46), lending weight to the belief that it contains a prophecy of his abandonment on the cross. Abandonment confronts us with the radical silence of God. No wonder the psalmist, and Job and Jesus all cry out, in a place of apparently hopeless personal disaster:

> My God, my God, why have you forsaken me?
> > Why are you so far from saving me, from the words of my groaning?
> > O my God, I cry by day, but you do not answer;
> > and by night, but I find no rest. (Ps 22:1–2)

There is, however, a vast qualitative difference between the cry of Job and the cry of Jesus. In the midst of wishing that he had never been born or had never existed, Job constantly cries out for justice. Job's adversary is God. However, in the prophetic prayer of Psalm 22, the psalmist speaks of the people who were his adversaries. In quoting this prayer, Jesus was not crying out to God for justice for himself. His prayer is framed in terms of his relationship with the Father and his relationship with his murderers, who were his own people. In other words, Jesus's cry had a social dimension, while Job's cry is about his own identity and standing. Job is consumed with himself and finding a solution to his own dichotomy of suffering despite being righteous.

Given that Job's lament is all about personal injustice, we could describe Job as radically selfish. His demand for justice could be taken as the demand of self-righteousness. Yet while saying this, we must admit that Job was a very godly man who cared for others. He declares:

> I delivered the poor who cried for help,
>   and the fatherless who had none to help him.
> The blessing of him who was about to perish came upon
>   me,
>   and I caused the widow's heart to sing for joy. . . .
> I was eyes to the blind
>   and feet to the lame.
> I was a father to the needy,
>   and I searched out the cause of him whom I did not know.
>   (Job 29:12–13, 15–16)

If we mistrust these claims because he is praising himself, we should also consider the biblical text's evaluation of Job as a man who "was blameless and upright, one who feared God and turned away from evil" (Job 1:1). This evaluation of Job is endorsed by God himself in 1:8.

Job's righteousness or blamelessness could not have been perfect. As Paul reminds us, "all have sinned and fall short of the glory of God" (Rom 3:23). Job acknowledges this when he says, "How can a man be in the right [i.e. righteous] before God?" (Job 9:2), and he speaks of "the iniquities of my youth" (Job 13:26; see also 14:17). But he was certainly one of the best men who ever lived.

Jesus, the only truly perfect man, made no such claim of righteousness; indeed he was baptized while sinless to fulfil all righteousness (Matt 3:13–17). He took the sin of the world upon himself and became sin (2 Cor 5:21). At the cross, we sense the absolute silence of God as the Son was abandoned and separated from the Father and the Spirit. He was judged and condemned on the cross in place of sinners in order to maintain the integrity and justice of God.[8] Jesus really died there, and his death and all of his passion are salvific for humankind. But this abandonment was for only a few days in the history of the world. The abandonment of Job, by contrast, has nothing to do with salvation; rather it is an extreme case of the abandonment experienced by those who must endure severe undeserved suffering in the purpose of God for their own spiritual advancement.

While Jesus was dying for others, Job wanted to die to escape his own pain and the ontological meaninglessness that beset him. What was happening was that Job was dying to self. God's silence was the space Job needed for this death,

---

8. We may call this forensic abandonment.

which would lead to a new identity in a deeper knowledge and therefore a new relationship with God.

God's providence

What is this silence about? The reader knows that God is in a kind of contest[9] with the angel called the Satan who was set the task of testing Job. Satan is used to inflict Job's suffering. This suffering was not arbitrary; it was in the providence of God. In the end Job would receive twice as much as he had enjoyed previously, including, most profoundly, a far greater revelation of God. God's silence can logically be seen as a necessary part of the process of moving Job from his limited being with limited knowledge to greater being with greater knowledge of God. Job's suffering was the process of setting him free from the constraints of his present knowledge.

Let us return to the story of the young man born blind (John 9). Jesus emphatically stated that this blindness was not because either the man or his parents were sinners, as the disciples believed given their retribution theology. The truth was that family's suffering and their experience of the silence of God over the years was in the providence of God to demonstrate God's glory. Unbeknownst to them, this young man had been assigned the task of becoming the person whose healing would symbolically reveal Jesus to be the light of the world. The man lived in darkness until Jesus healed his eyes and filled his life with light.

The ensuing conflict with the Pharisees because Jesus did this healing on a Sabbath encapsulates the sharp contrast between the letter of the law and grace. The Pharisees had developed hundreds of rules governing what was and was not allowed on the Sabbath. Jesus's failure to observe their rules (or laws) led them to condemn him as a sinner and to refuse to believe that a miracle had occurred.

> So for the second time they called the man who had been blind, and said to him, "Give glory to God. We know that this man is a sinner." He answered, "Whether he is a sinner, I do not know. One thing I know, that though I was blind, now I see." They said to him, "What did he do to you? How did he open your eyes?" He answered them, "I have told you already, and you would not listen. Why do you want to hear it again? Do you also want to become his disciples?" And they reviled him, saying, "You are his disciple,

---

9. Although superficially this may look like a contest, there is in fact no contest.

but we are disciples of Moses. We know that God has spoken to Moses, but as for this man, we do not know where he comes from." The man answered, . . . "If this man were not from God, he could do nothing." They answered him, "You were born in utter sin, and would you teach us?" And they cast him out. (John 9:24–34)

Like Job and his counsellors, the Pharisee held to a righteousness framework and proclaimed that they were the disciples of Moses, the lawgiver. Jesus's power to perform miracles and his apparently flagrant disregard for their laws greatly threatened them. Like Job's friends, they denounced the sufferer who had been born blind as a sinner. But far from being a sinner, the young man was the servant of providence.

It appears that providence is a harsh and cruel master. It brings suffering, sometimes of great proportions. But in God's plan, this suffering undergoes and is itself a metamorphosis. It is a caterpillar that turns into a butterfly; after the pain comes the glory of God. The man blind from birth receives sight in every way; spiritual as well as physical. Job receives double what he lost and a higher knowledge of God in a new, living theology. I would argue that Job becomes a prophet and a priest in his new life. Through his suffering of almost supernatural proportions, he is equipped to truly become the servant of God.

God's providence is also seen in the case of Lazarus. Mary told Jesus, "if you had been here, my brother would not have died" (John 11:21), but Jesus delayed his arrival in order that many would believe through Lazarus's resurrection. This providence was the will of God for the eternal salvation of sinners. The case of the young man born blind was about the re-establishment of the truth about God, who is light. Job's case was about coming to a higher knowledge of God in a living theology. The glory of Job is the transformation of dead knowledge to living knowledge of the true nature of the incomprehensible God.

God's voice

When God at last speaks to Job out of the whirlwind, he uses a string of questions – "Have you . . . ?," "Can you . . . ?," "Do you . . . ?"

> Have you commanded the morning since your days began,
>   and caused the dawn to know its place. . .?
>
> Can you bind the chains of the Pleiades,
>   or loose the cords of Orion?
>
> Do you know the ordinances of the heavens?

> Can you establish their rule on the earth? (Job 38:12, 31, 33)

And so on through chapters 38 and 39, until at the start of chapter 40 God thunders,

> Shall a faultfinder contend with the Almighty?
> He who argues with God, let him answer it. (Job 40:2)

Overwhelmed, Job can only respond:

> Behold, I am of small account; what shall I answer you?
> I lay my hand on my mouth.
> I have spoken once, and I will not answer;
> twice, but I will proceed no further. (Job 40:4–5)

The divine silence has ended and the silence of Job has begun. Job, who had been so certain of his theology, was shocked to recognize it as grossly inadequate and largely false. Acknowledging that he now had no grounds for his demand for justice, he fell silent. Through God's perpetual questioning, light at last shone into Job's situation. The drumbeat of questions led Job to the realization that the meaning of his trial lay outside his limited knowledge. God's questions and the hearing of God's voice marked the dawning of a new and higher revelation of God for Job.

God's method of questioning has some similarities with the method of the ancient Greek philosopher Socrates, who used a series of questions and answers as he sought to discern the truth of what was being discussed. His opponents were often reduced to silence. But Socrates, although far ahead of his pupils and adversaries, did not transcend them. God transcended Job, and hence Job had no base from which to answer him. But Job had heard God, and Job's silence was the evidence that this hearing had imparted a higher revelation. All of Job's suffering and his struggle for justice brought him to the point where he could receive this new revelation. Now he was ready to hear the mighty voice of God. He was prepared to reach beyond himself into the transcendence of God. That which was finite reached into the infinite and became a greater and richer being.

Karl Rahner states that human beings have a *potentia oboedientialis* for the word of God, that is, a potential to hear the word of God and receive a revelation that takes them beyond the present limitation of their knowledge and so increases their being. Rahner terms this "delimitation."[10] The limitation

---

10. Rahner, *Hearers of the Word*.

of Job's present knowledge and being were shattered when he heard the voice of God. He was taken from the law of God to the glory of God, and in this glory he found full and adequate meaning for his suffering. Like Elijah the Tishbite (1 Kgs 19:4), Job had come to the end of himself, and that was the beginning of a new journey into God as he confessed, "I know that you can do all things, and that no purpose of yours can be thwarted" (Job 42:2).

In response to God's question, "Who is this that hides counsel without knowledge?" (Job 42:3; quoting 38:2), Job confessed his foolishness, saying that he had spoken hastily about things he did not understand, and spoken of issues quite beyond his depth. Now that he had heard the voice of God from the whirlwind, however, he could see the kingdom of God and despised himself as he repented in dust and ashes (Job 42:5–6).

The Shame of Job's Counsellors

Job's friends and counsellors were also shamed by this revelation of the glory of God. They had argued too confidently, and often arrogantly, for their own righteousness. In the end they are seen to be disastrously wrong. Their apparent wisdom in terms of retribution theology is seen to be foolishness in the light of a greater revelation. The sages become shamed fools. They were, at best, noble princes in captivity, held captive by inadequate doctrine. They firmly held to the idea that they knew everything there was to know about God. They had pinned God down to an ethical structure of cause and effect. God was summed up as a judge of right and wrong and as a fountain of approval or condemnation. They failed to see beyond the condemnation to a God of mercy and grace. That was why the Lord addressed them saying, "My anger burns against you and against your two friends, for you have not spoken of me what is right, as my servant Job has" (Job 42:7).[11]

Job's counsellors had failed to recognize the truth about God proclaimed in Psalm 103:10–14:

> [The Lord] does not deal with us according to our sins,
>   nor repay us according to our iniquities.
> For as high as the heavens are above the earth,
>   so great is his steadfast love toward those who fear him;
> as far as the east is from the west,

---

11. Interestingly, the young man Elihu is not included in the condemnation. Perhaps because he spoke of his personal greatness and added nothing new to the debate, he was inconsequential to the main drama.

> so far does he remove our transgressions from us.
> As a father shows compassion to his children,
> so the LORD shows compassion to those who fear him.
> For he knows our frame;
> he remembers that we are dust.

But why were Job's counsellors condemned for having spoken wrongly of God, whereas the outspoken Job was not condemned, but is said to have spoken rightly? The answer may be as follows:

> Through God's constant questioning, Job came to realize the limits of his wisdom and knowledge. He tried to claim a knowledge of the workings of the universe that were vastly beyond him. . .
>
> Job had just been operating on hearsay about God. And what he had been hearing is that God rewards good people and punishes bad people. But the theology he had been taught (the "report" of God) was horribly deficient. God did not strictly operate the way Job thought. But now he has had a personal encounter with God and his understanding is vastly expanded.[12]

There can be little doubt that Job's suffering was a prelude to his greater knowledge. He was prepared to receive the higher knowledge through the dreadful process of his pain. What he did right was to honestly and rightly complain on the basis of his wrong theology. He was reaching in the right direction. In seeking to justify himself, Job ultimately justified God's use of suffering in his case.[13]

Job protested, but he did not turn away from God. His belief did not falter, and his faith was of a high order. Moreover, he did not only protest against what he perceived to be his unjust suffering; he also protested against the elaborate explanations of his plight offered by his counsellors. In this he was right and they were wrong. Job's spirit was alive; their spirits were dead. They displayed the arrogance and the ignorance of the Pharisees whom Jesus described as whitewashed tombs.

The approbation in God's reference to Job as "my servant" in Job 42:7 may also be related to Job's repentance.[14] There is a sharp contrast between Job's utter change of mind and heart and the poverty and foolishness of Eliphaz,

---

12. Longman, *Job*, 449.
13. And possibly in all cases of undeserved suffering.
14. Longman, *Job*, 459.

Bildad and Zopher. For Job there was no shame, but for the others there was considerable shame and the incurring of God's anger.

However, God still reveals himself to Eliphaz, to whom he speaks in anger. These men did not of themselves come to the place of repentance. God had to command them to bring animals for a sacrifice to Job. However, their obedience to this command and their apparently sincere and valuable burnt offering of seven bulls and seven rams suggest that they do repent, expressing their repentance in terms of the Old Testament sacrificial system. Job's prayer on their behalf propitiated God's wrath.

Job's repentance, however, sprang from deeper roots. He repented because of the greater insight he had been given through God's revelation of himself to him.

9

The Suffering of Jesus

In this chapter we reflect on the suffering of Christ, the GodMan, including both his inner suffering (as revealed in Psalm 22) and his physical suffering on the cross. Our reflection on the difference between Christ's suffering and all other suffering in the world is illuminated by an examination of the suffering servant prophecies in Isaiah. The chapter closes with a discussion of Jesus's suffering as grace.

The Son of God came into the world as Immanuel (God with us) to suffer and to save those who would believe in him and confess his Lordship. He entered the darkness of sin and evil in the world as our final representative, the last Adam. The actions of the first Adam led us into sin and death, but by becoming sin for us, Jesus, the last Adam, leads us out of sin and into eternal life. His suffering sets us free from the curses imposed on Adam and Eve.

Of course, Jesus did more than just suffer. He also taught the truth about God and performed many miracles of healing. But his suffering takes precedence when we speak of him, for it is the means of our salvation and eternal life. His suffering atones for our sin and frees us from the eternal prison of our finitude. Thus his suffering is to be venerated as the font of our new life, beautiful and free. He lived on earth in the ashes of suffering, but these ashes are infused with the wonderful grace of God who is love. It is his suffering that draws us to him. This truly is beauty from ashes (Isa 61:3).

Christ enters the darkness of death but rises victorious because the darkness cannot survive the light. Through the suffering of Christ, death died and the negation of human life and true potentiality was negated. We can say that he suffered for evil, not because he was evil but because his persecutors acted with evil intent. But he gloriously transformed that evil. Through his suffering, we are set free from evil and unrighteousness. And we are called to take up our crosses and follow him, sharing in his suffering. Such sharing makes our own suffering a privilege of infinite value. It does not save, but it does connect us to our Saviour. This attitude explains a story that is told about St Francis of Assisi (1181–1226), the founder of the Franciscan order and one of the most venerated religious figures in history:

> On a certain occasion when St Francis was suffering extraordinary physical pain, one of his religious brothers, meaning to sympathize with him, said in his simplicity, "My father, pray to God that he treats you a little more gently, for his hand seems very heavy upon you just now." Hearing this St Francis strongly resented the unhappy remark of his well-meaning brother, saying "My good brother, did I not know that what you just said was spoken in all simplicity without realizing the implication of your words, I should never see you again because of your rashness in passing judgement on the dispositions of divine providence." Whereupon, weak and wasted as he was by his illness, he got out of bed knelt down kissed the floor and prayed thus. "Lord, I thank thee for the sufferings you are sending me. Send me more, if it be thy good pleasure. My pleasure is that you afflict me and spare me not, for the fulfilment of thy holy will is the greatest consolation of my life.

The Nature of Christ's Suffering

Christ's death was not suffering that happened in spite of his status as the Son of God. It was part of an eternal plan of creation and re-creation as agreed on by all Persons of the Trinity. The eternal Logos, who was the creator of everything (John 1:1–3), foreknew the suffering that would come to him in his incarnate history. But when he emptied himself (Phil 2:7) he laid down this knowledge to make possible the functioning union of his humanity and his deity.[1] Born as a human being, he did not know all things, yet as he grew in wisdom and was granted supernatural knowledge, he came to know who he was and what his ministry would entail. Thus from an early age he must have known something of the quality of the suffering that lay ahead and what it was intended to achieve. Such knowledge would mean that his entire existence was

---

1. Theologians speak of Christ's self-emptying as *kenosis*, and hold that it refers to his emptying himself of God's omniscience and omnipresence, which are incompatible with true humanity, but not of his fundamental divinity. He remains consubstantial with the Father.

shaped by suffering, for suffering was his raison d'être. That was why Isaiah described him as "a man of sorrows and acquainted with grief" (Isa 53:3). Yet despite his suffering, both present and in prospect, he possessed a great peace that he gave to his disciples: "Peace I leave with you: my peace I give to you" (John 14:27). In Jesus, peace and suffering were compatible; they could exist together in a wonderful harmony. I want to term this harmony "the love of God" or "the love God loves with." In Jesus, God's love identifies with sinners and with human infirmity and grief.

Jesus's peace was the peace of the infinite depth of his knowledge of God. On the basis of this knowledge, he revealed a God whose essence is grace – not grace as understood by men and women but something far greater than they can ever conceive. Similarly, his suffering was not the same as ordinary human suffering, no matter how great, but embraced the infinite pain of all being. It extended beyond all being to embrace the pain of the eternal Trinity in his pre-existence as the eternal Logos. He came to suffer in the world. His joy was set before him; it was not yet. He revealed the great suffering of the love of God for human beings, who despite the fall were still the pinnacle of God's creation.

Jesus suffering was not the result of some cause-and-effect relationship in this world; rather, it was the great means of re-creation, which we call redemption. His suffering came from outside this world, from heaven itself, and was rooted in his nature. His suffering through incarnation was the outworking of a prior agreement within the Trinity whereby the Son would enter human history as man, to satisfy the absolute, infinite and eternal integrity of God concerning the salvation of at least a part of his human creation. *Heilsgeschichte* would enter human history to reveal and inaugurate the kingdom of heaven in the world.

As with all things relating to God, we can seek to understand Jesus's suffering and passion only by an analogy that gives us a glimpse of the transcendence.[2] So what we can say is that the Father required the Son to suffer and die in the body he assumed in Bethlehem in the womb of Mary.

But how does this suffering relate to the types of suffering we know? It fits into all the categories. It was deserved suffering in that he identified with sinners and suffered the penalty for sin, and it was undeserved suffering in that he himself never sinned. It was suffering for others, suffering for God and

---

2. This is true of all knowledge of God. We know God by analogy with creation, trusting that the creative work of God is logically continuous with heaven.

ontological (inner) suffering, all coming together in the much greater mystery of suffering that he entered and wholeheartedly took upon himself.

But I would also like to propose a new category of suffering appropriate to the passion of Christ: the suffering of eternal love (John 3:16). This suffering is the ground of our eternal life. Christ's suffering and death satisfies the justice of God and so propitiates the Father's righteous wrath. It expiates the guilt of the human beings who collectively constitute the bride of Christ. It reveals the grace of God to humanity.

Christ's Inner Suffering

Scripture leaves us no doubt about Christ's inner suffering. We see it vividly in Matthew's account of the events in Gethsemane (Matt 26:36–56), and above all in the cry of anguish, "My soul is very sorrowful, even to death" (Matt 26:38). Luke tells us that his suffering was so profound that "his sweat became like great drops of blood falling down to the ground" (Luke 22:44). This was the first blood to be spilt: the next time blood would spill onto the ground would be at his scourging, and then on the cross on the hill of Golgotha (Calvary).

The sixteenth-century English statesman Sir Thomas More wrote poignantly about Gethsemane:

> The blessed and tender heart of our most holy saviour was cumbered and panged with manifold and hideous griefs, since doubtless well wist [knew] he that the false traitor and his mortal enemies drew near unto him, and were now in manner already come upon him; and over this that he should be despitefully bounden, and have heinous crimes surmised against him, be blasphemed, scourged, crowned with thorns, nailed, crucified, and finally suffer very long and cruel torments.[3]

More wrote these words when he was a prisoner awaiting execution in the Tower of London, and so he would have empathized profoundly with Jesus's experience in Gethsemane. He also spoke of Christ having to pass over the brook Kidron on the way from Jerusalem to the Mount of Olives (John 18:1) and comments that the name of the brook carries overtones of "sorrow or heaviness." After describing the depths of Jesus anguish in graphic terms, he comes to the issue of Christ's deity:

---

3. More, *Sadness of Christ*, 6.

Some man may haply here marvel how this could be, that our saviour Christ, being very God equal with his almighty Father, could be heavy, sad, and sorrowful. Indeed, he could not have been so, if as he was God, so had he been only God, and not man also. But now seeing he was as verily [truly] man as he was verily [truly] God, I think it no more to be marvelled that inasmuch as he was man he had these affections and conditions in him, such I mean as be without offence to God, as of common course are in mankind, than that inasmuch as he was God he wrought so wonderful miracles. For if we do marvel that Christ should have in him fear, weariness, and sorrow, namely seeing he was God, then why should we not as well marvel that he was hungry, athirst, and slept, since albeit he had these properties, yet was he nevertheless God for all that?[4]

We have little difficulty understanding that as a human being Jesus was hungry, thirsty and tired and needed to satisfy these basic physical needs that are an inextricable part of our human nature. Things are less clear when it comes to spiritual facets of human life. It seems that there may be a merging of the Holy Spirit and human spirit in the unity of God and man. We see a similar merging when Jesus performed miracles with the power of the Holy Spirit. Here it is far less easy to distinguish what belongs to his human nature and what to his divine nature, for they are consubstantial. Even in regard to the bodily need for food, we could say that Jesus redefined nourishment when he instituted Holy Communion. Nourishment is now to be thought of in spiritual terms as we eat and drink what was everyday food in Christ's day while remembering his sacrificial death for us, symbolized in the physical realm by bread and wine. This merging of body and spirit was also seen when God provided manna from heaven, which is a metaphor Christ used when he referred to himself as "the living bread that came down from heaven" (John 6:51). In all that he does, the unity of the person of the GodMan is fully and always engaged.

The infinite proportion of Christ's sorrow could not be borne by a human being for no human can go beyond his finitude. But sin against God is sin against an eternal, infinite being, as Anselm argues when speaking of the necessity of the incarnation. A human being has sinned, and so a human

---

4. More, *Sadness of Christ*, 7. Note that More's comment is in line with Thomas Aquinas's teaching on the impassibility of God. Aquinas, quoting Athanasius, states: "The passion is to be attributed to the supposition of the divine nature not because of the divine nature, which is impassible, but by means of the human nature which is passible" (*Summa Theologica*, part 3, question 46, article 12, reply to objection 3).

being must pay the debt of sin owed to God, but as humans we do not have the ability to pay such an infinite debt. We have to rely on the GodMan.[5] By the unity of God and a human being, God can be satisfied and humanity redeemed.

Responsibility for the salvation of mankind was and is an infinitely great responsibility. It was met perfectly by the Messiah (the Christ) a man who was and is God, but is still fully a man. He was the representative new man who obeyed whereas Adam, the first representative, disobeyed. In Gethsemane, Christ rose up from his great anguish to accept his awful responsibility in the words "not my will, but yours, be done" (Luke 22:42). Christ took our sin upon himself, and in so doing he also took our sorrow. Ultimately tears will be wiped from our eyes and we will be eternally glad.

Psalm 22: An Inside View of Christ's Suffering

We have already discussed Psalm 22 with respect to the suffering of Job. Now it is time to consider what Christ's quotation from that psalm in Mark 15:34 tells us about his own suffering on the cross. Although I would advise you to read the whole psalm, let me focus here on only a few verses.

> My God, my God, why have you forsaken me?
> > Why are you so far from saving me, from the words of my
> > > groaning?
> O my God, I cry by day, but you do not answer,
> > and by night, but I find no rest.
>
> . . .
>
> But I am a worm and not a man,
> > scorned by mankind and despised by the people.
> All who see me mock me;
> > they make mouths at me; they wag their heads;
> "He trusts in the LORD; let him deliver him;
> > let him rescue him, for he delights in him!"
>
> . . .
>
> Many bulls encompass me;
> > strong bulls of Bashan surround me;
> they open wide their mouths at me,
> > like a ravening and roaring lion.

---

5. Anselm of Canterbury, *Cur Deus Homo* (Why God Became a Man) in *St. Anselm Basic Writings* (Chicago: Open Court Publishing, 1962).

> I am poured out like water,
>> and all my bones are out of joint;
> my heart is like wax;
>> it is melted within my breast;
> my strength is dried up like a potsherd,
>> and my tongue sticks to my jaws;
>> you lay me in the dust of death.
> For dogs encompass me;
>> a company of evildoers encircles me;
> they have pierced my hands and feet –
> I can count all my bones –
> they stare and gloat over me;
> they divide my garments among them,
>> and for my clothing they cast lots. (Ps 22:1–2, 6–8, 12–18)

While this psalm has the superscription "a psalm of David," no known incident in David's life matches the details of this psalm, which seems to refer to an execution. Traditionally, the church has seen it as a prophetic description of the death of Christ, and so as giving us insight into Jesus's own experience on the cross.

The Lord Jesus gives credence to this interpretation by using the opening words, "My God, my God, why have you forsaken me?" in his great cry of abandonment in Mark 15:34. But it is striking that in this psalm this sense of abandonment is balanced by a profound confidence and unity with God, expressed in words of unshakeable unity in the second half of the psalm (from verse 22 on).

The psalmist who wrote this psalm may have been experiencing God's withdrawal from him and divine silence, which is a known human experience and elicits a unique genre of prayer. But if this psalm were merely about David's experience, we would expect it to include some confession of sin, but there are no words of confession. This too suggests that it applies to Jesus.

It seems that Jesus was experiencing something very different from an ordinary person praying this prayer. Theologically, it appears that his temporary abandonment by God was necessary for the reconciliation and acceptance of sinners with God. As he took up the load of human sin, Jesus the Son felt abandoned by the other members of the Trinity – the Father and the Holy Spirit. He prays to the Father without ceasing, but is met with silence. This seeming abandonment does not detract from Jesus's continuing unity with God. But his is the only voice we hear speaking. It is met with a terrible silence, in itself a profound absence; yet this divine silence facilitates the sacrifice for the salvation of fallen human beings.

The mocking and scourging and other attacks on Jesus's dignity appear to have taken away his self-worth, as they were designed to do, so that he says with the psalmist, "I am a worm and not a man." He speaks of the torrent of mockery, which is actually profound blasphemy. He feels as if he is being gored by cruel bulls and mauled by savage lions. All his strength is gone: "I am poured out like water." Not only his blood pouring out from his wounds, but his life is ebbing away. His limbs are wrenched to the point of dislocation, and his heart muscles can no longer sustain him but are becoming as flabby as melted wax. He has a ravening thirst, so that his tongue sticks to the roof of his mouth. Indeed, he can say, "you lay me in the dust of death." The curse in Genesis that human beings would return to dust was becoming real in the experience of the Son of Man. But, as we know, although Jesus did die on the cross, his body would not return to the dust.

The psalm's final amazing prophecy of pierced hands and feet and the division and casting of lots for garments, which were normal practices at a Roman crucifixion, cement for us the belief that this psalm truly reveals the inner pain of Jesus from the cross.

In verse 20 David cries to be delivered from the sword. Jesus too cries out for deliverance, but from the cross. His prayer is both unanswered and answered: he is not delivered from his immediate suffering, but he is delivered from death by his resurrection. We hear the note of confidence in the words from verse 22 on, where Jesus focuses not on his pain but on his task as the one who will bring salvation. We see his total commitment and trust in the unity of the Father and Son as he shifts from a focus on his pain to his great task of "bringing many sons to glory" (Heb 12:10), tying these passages firmly together. It is thus worth noting the full context in Hebrews, "For it was fitting that he for whom and by whom all things exist, in bringing many sons to glory should make the founder of their salvation perfect through suffering" (2:10). The suffering of Jesus would not be relieved until the appointed time.

What Was Different about Christ's Physical Suffering?

In the final week of his life, Jesus endured great physical pain, sparked by the hatred of the Jewish religious leaders and inflicted by cruel Roman soldiers. We find it hard to read about or even imagine what he endured. Yet we need to ask the question, in what way was his suffering any different from that of the two thieves who were crucified with him? In terms of physical suffering, their ordeal was very similar to that of Jesus. They too were nailed to crosses by their hands and feet. They experienced the pain of hanging from the nails. So let us begin this section by considering the shared elements in the suffering of all who were crucified, for to the Romans this was a common method of execution.

The whole process of crucifixion from beginning to end was designed to shame and humiliate the victim. The soldiers who were to carry out the execution made no secret of their contempt for those who were about to suffer this terrible death. In the case of Jesus, they ridiculed him as a crazy fool who claimed to be a king. So they dressed him in fake robes, and made him wear a crown made of thorns and hold a reed for a sceptre. Then they paid him mock homage, and then spat on him and beat him (Matt 27:28–30). In the same vein, they prepared a placard to hang over his head on the cross, declaring him to be "the King of the Jews." The crosses of the other criminals would also have had placards listing their crimes, but Jesus was the focus of the soldier's mockery because of the uniqueness of his claims.

Crucifixion was usually preceded by scourging. Jesus was certainly scourged (Mark 15:15), and so it is likely were the two thieves. Again, Jesus probably received more severe abuse from the soldiers because of the attention his case had attracted.

Scourging was a barbaric beating with

> a short whip . . . with several single or braided leather thongs. Iron balls or hooks made of bones or shells were placed at various intervals along the thongs and at their ends. The person was stripped of his clothing and whipped along the back, buttocks and legs. The scourging ripped the skin and tore into the underlying muscles, leaving the flesh in bloody ribbons. The victim verged on circulatory shock and the blood loss would help determine how long he would survive on the cross.[6]

In the messianic prophecy of Isaiah 53:5 we read that we are healed by Jesus's wounds, or as some translations have it, "by his stripes." Surely this refers to the bloody stripes of this relentless, inhumane flogging. As Christ endures this almost unbearable pain, he stands in our place, taking the full brunt of suffering for us and for our healing.

After the flogging, the condemned men had to carry the crossbar on which they would be hung to the place of crucifixion, where the poles on which the crossbars would be fixed stood waiting. It has been estimated that the crossbar

---

6. Fr William Saunders, "The Passion of Jesus Christ."

would weigh between 34 and 57 kilograms, a heavy weight on one whose muscles have already been torn by the scourging. The journey to Golgotha along what has become known as the Via Dolorosa was not long, no more than half a kilometre, but Jesus had been so severely whipped that he did not have strength to carry the burden that far. Simon of Cyrene was compelled to carry the load for him.

Roman crucifixions were not done in back rooms. They were done at public places like crossroads, theatres, and on high ground so that the fate of the victims would serve as a warning to others. Golgotha was such a place. When the three condemned men arrived there, they were further humiliated by being stripped naked, exposed to mocking public gaze while the soldiers cast lots for their clothing.

Before being nailed to the cross, each man would have been offered a bitter drink of wine mixed with myrrh to dull their pain. The two thieves probably drank it, but Jesus refused. He did not seek to escape any element of his suffering.

Then the men's arms would have been stretched out over the crossbar and large iron spikes would have been driven through their wrists into the wood.[7] The crossbar was then hoisted up to the pole that was already in place, and the victim's feet were nailed to the vertical post.

Those who had been crucified did not just hang limply on the cross. Their physical position made breathing extremely difficult or even impossible. So in order to take a breath, they would have to raise their bodies each time putting a load on their nailed feet. The pain in their feet would cause them to collapse down again, returning the load and the pain to their wrists. With each breath, the cycle would be repeated. Meanwhile, the rough wood of the cross would tear at their wounded backs, while the strain would keep their wounds from closing. It was a slow and excruciatingly painful death that Jesus and the two thieves endured. We can judge how severely Jesus had been scourged by the fact that he died after only six hours on the cross (John 19:33). The two thieves took longer to die, as is evident from John's account which tells us that the soldiers broke the legs of the two men. This would soon result in asphyxiation because they could no longer lift their bodies in order to breathe (John 19:32).

Was Jesus's suffering any different from the suffering of those two men, or of the thousands of others crucified by Roman soldiers over the years? Physically, no. He suffered the same dreadful death as thousands of slaves,

---

7. According to Fr Saunders in "The Passion of Jesus Christ," the nails were usually iron spikes around 18 cm long with a shaft end of around 1 cm.

criminals and rebels – for they were the only ones crucified. Roman citizens could be executed, but they were granted a swift beheading. It was in fact one sign of the "foolishness" of the Christian gospel that it encouraged worship of someone who had died such a humiliating death.[8]

But there was something about Christ's death which made a hardened Roman soldier, who had no doubt witnessed many other executions, say "Truly this man was the Son of God!" (Mark 15:39). The difference was that Jesus was indeed the royal Son of God. He was profoundly and eternally innocent. He was and is the King of kings and the Lord of lords, not simply the King of the Jews as the placard over his head mockingly proclaimed. Both the Roman soldier and one of the two thieves crucified with Jesus had the truth of who he really was revealed to them. Just as the Holy Spirit revealed Jesus's identity to Peter (Matt 16:13–17) so the Holy Spirit must have revealed Christ's deity to the soldier and the thief. If so, then the Holy Spirit was manifestly present in some way at the crucifixion event, although perceived only by the blessed two. Illuminated by the Spirit, they perceived that God was on the cross in the person of the Son. It is this reality that Christians born again by the Spirit discern, and it is this reality which shocks them.

Many seeking souls are converted when they see the cross on which the Lord hung. This is a truth that Jesus spoke of before his death when he said, "as Moses lifted up the serpent in the wilderness, so must the Son of Man be lifted up, that whoever believes in him may have eternal life" (John 3:13–14). He also said, "I, when I am lifted up from the earth, will draw all people to myself" (John 12:32). He was seeing his crucifixion as foreshadowed in the story told in Numbers 21:

> And the people spoke against God and against Moses, "Why have you brought us up out of Egypt to die in the wilderness? For there is no food and no water, and we loathe this worthless food." Then the LORD sent fiery serpents among the people, and they bit the people, so that many people of Israel died. And the people came to Moses and said, "We have sinned, for we have spoken against the LORD and against you. Pray to the LORD, that he take away

---

8. Commenting on Paul's reference to the foolishness of preaching a crucified saviour (1 Cor 18:23) Martin Hengel comments, "Justin puts us on the right track when he describes the offence caused by the Christian message to the ancient world as madness, and sees the basis for this objection in Christian belief in the divine status of the crucified Jesus and his significance for salvation: "They say that our *madness* consists in the fact that we put a *crucified man* in second place after the unchangeable and eternal God, the Creator of the world." (*Crucifixion in the Ancient World*, 1). The quotation from Justin is from his *Apology 1*, 13.4.

the serpents from us." So Moses prayed for the people. And the LORD said to Moses, "Make a fiery serpent, and set it on a pole, and everyone who is bitten, when he sees it, shall live." So Moses made a bronze serpent and set it on a pole; and if a serpent bit anyone, he would look at the bronze serpent and live. (Num 21:5–9)

The people of Israel repented, but it was looking at the bronze snake on a staff that healed them. They looked in full belief that if they did so, they would be saved. Belief is involved in the looking that saves. At the start, the crucified thieves, the Roman soldier and those who mocked at Christ did not believe, but two of those who were there were marvellously converted and saw the cross in a new light. Enlightened by the Holy Spirit, they beheld the royalty of the one who hung there, and his radical innocence.

In the cross, we have an extreme example of the spiritual acting through the physical. The spiritual was salvation history (*Heilsgeschichte*) and the physical was world history in the form of the historical figure of Jesus, who lived and taught and performed miracles and was crucified.[9] Spiritual history and salvation history came together at the cross, and Karl Barth sees them as continuing together in the forty-day period in which the resurrected Christ was in this world.[10] During this period, Christ appeared as a man but in the mode of God.

Jesus suffered in human history. His suffering was witnessed by many, most of whom perceived it only as physical suffering. Those who saw him again after his resurrection would have had a very different perception of who he was and what his physical suffering meant. The witnesses of the resurrected Christ had the necessary presence of God before them.

Isaiah 53: A Prophecy of Christ's Suffering

Christians believe that the Servant Songs of Isaiah 52 and 53 are a revelation of the suffering of the Messiah, the Son of God. Let us read some of these verses before looking at them in more detail.

> He was despised and rejected by men,
> a man of sorrows and acquainted with grief;
> and as one from whom men hide their faces
> he was despised, and we esteemed him not.

---

9. I am not referring here to the so-called historical Jesus of Albert Schweitzer but to the Jesus of history as opposed to Bultmann's Christ of faith.

10. Barth, *Church Dogmatics* 3.2, 450.

> Surely he has borne our griefs
> and carried our sorrows;
> yet we esteemed him stricken,
> smitten by God, and afflicted.
> But he was pierced for our transgressions;
> he was crushed for our iniquities;
> upon him was the chastisement that brought us peace,
> and with his wounds we are healed.
> All we like sheep have gone astray;
> we have turned – every one – to his own way;
> and the Lord has laid on him
> the iniquity of us all.
>
> . . .
>
> Therefore I will divide him a portion with the many,
> and he shall divide the spoil with the strong,
> because he poured out his soul to death
> and was numbered with the transgressors;
> yet he bore the sin of many,
> and makes intercession for the transgressors. (Isa 53:3–6, 12)

What stands out in this passage is the vicarious nature of the servant's suffering. He suffered and died for us, for our sin, in our place. If our iniquity was laid upon him by God's decree, if we are healed by his wounds, and if he was pierced for our transgressions, then this servant, whom Christians take to be the Messiah, is the substitute for humankind. He is sacrificed by God. He is the scapegoat for us. It is through this amazing sacrifice that the path of salvation leads.

The cause of the Messiah's passion is clearly stated in this prophecy; it was "for our iniquities" that he poured out his soul to death. God provided atonement for us through the sacrifice of the Christ, his only begotten Son. Christ was "numbered with the transgressors" – he was seen by God as being one of us, he represented us in his passion.

Our griefs and sorrows, our own suffering, is taken up by Christ. Our suffering becomes his suffering. Our fallenness, in all of its evil, becomes his. He becomes a curse for us (Gal 13:13). The answer to the question, "Why did Christ have to die?" lies here in the heart of Isaiah's prophecy. The human suffering of those who would believe in him is borne by him. He suffers with us, as he suffered for us. All of our suffering from beginning to end became his suffering and is his suffering. This is the root of his great sorrow. When and as Christians suffer, they ought to be aware of this truth. From eternity[11] Christ is suffering with them. He shares in our suffering and has borne it and is bearing it with us, healing our souls through the anguish of his soul.

This prophecy also makes it clear that despite this wonderful grace, humankind as a whole despised and rejected the Messiah. He was rejected first by his own people, the Jews, and then by all who hear of him but will not believe. The truth is that we hide from God; we do not want him to see our sin. We cast aside his offer of saving grace. Before their conversion, those who are now Christian were among this great crowd who reject him.

Grace as Jesus's Suffering

True love involves suffering. Christ is the eternal Logos, the Second Person of the Trinity, the Son whose ever-begottenness means that he is ever being sent forth by the Father. He is ever coming forth. In the economic Trinity, the Father is the creator, the Son the redeemer or re-creator, and the Spirit is the applier of re-creation to all of creation (see Rom 8:19–23). Re-creation is accomplished by the dynamic of the Son becoming incarnate in world history, sent by the Father, followed by the Spirit. The nature of the Father's creation is grace, and the nature of the Son's re-creation is grace. Grace follows the Son in the Person of the Spirit.

The sending of the Son is proclaimed in John 3:16. The Son is sent into the world through the love of God as its redeemer, so that those who truly believe in him will gain eternal life. Those who do not believe are already condemned and so, terrifyingly, will perish.

The sobering truth of Scripture is that the Son is sent to suffer, and so we can say that grace suffers. Saving grace, as grace always is, is the suffering of Jesus. This is the divine providence to which St Francis of Assisi so ardently submitted.

The begottenness of the Son can now be seen as meaning "sent to suffer." Clearly the character of the suffering of the Messiah transcends any form of human suffering. Its meaning is beyond our present limitations. Such higher suffering is experienced only by Jesus. Lower suffering, the suffering we endure as men and women, will pass away:

---

11. For his suffering for us is eternally applied. The eternal Son of God being omniscient would have known substantially, before he made the earth, the precise reality and nature of what he was foreordained to suffer both on the cross and before the cross. That is what I mean by "from eternity."

Behold, the dwelling of God is with man. He will dwell with them, and they will be his people, and God himself will be with them as their God. He will wipe away every tear from their eyes, and death shall be no more, neither shall there be mourning, nor crying, nor pain anymore, for the former things have passed away. (Rev 21:1–3)

In the new heavens and the new earth, God's presence will be immediate and all human tears, mourning, pain and suffering will cease. None of these have any place in the new order of creation, which is the order of heaven.

This new order is the omnipresent grace of God in which we will live and move and have our being. There the Son is perceived as the Lamb of God who sits on the throne of grace. When resurrected men and women behold this throne, they will understand the great value of their suffering in the world and be greatly glad of it. Jesus's suffering will be seen as the sacrifice that evokes eternal worship and utter adoration and love. There will be no need for the freedom of the old creation. Human beings will at last be absolutely fulfilled in Christ, higher than the angels and living in surrender and obedience that cannot be corrupted. The possibility of sin will no longer exist and so theirs will be a higher freedom of selves in the perfect community of the eternal kingdom of God.

It is the unity of the Person of the GodMan who suffers. He does so in order to bring about the perfect peace of the new heavens and the new earth. Revelation 21 is about this triumph of grace. But because God is immutable, such a triumph involves no change in his nature. Amazing grace, which is beyond our imagination in being efficaciously extended to the saved humanity, was not a new thing; it is eternal in all of its fullness.

What then does it mean to speak of Jesus as the one who "for the joy that was set before him endured the cross, despising the shame, and is seated at the right hand of the throne of God" (Heb 12:2)? Did he experience change? Or have we mischaracterized suffering? Should we be referring to it as "the means of joy"? The suffering of Jesus the GodMan does not undergo a spiritual metamorphosis to become joy. This divine joy is joy before the foundation of the earth and indeed the universe. The GodMan is the sin-bearer, but at the end of six hours on the cross he states, "It is finished" (John 19:28–30). The abandonment is complete and the joy is set before him. Nothing can now impede our community of complete love with Christ at its centre as the blessed Lord of life. God through creation and re-creation has created love in creatures who were not programmed to love but who come to love at the cross and believe, and so freely become love. Redeemed men and women are partakers of the divine nature (2 Pet 1:4) and there is no possibility of disobedience. True love of God with all of our heart, soul and mind, and in the same love, the love of each other, is our new nature. We became love, but God eternally is love.

10

The Suffering of God

Contemplation of Jesus's suffering as the GodMan leads to the question of whether it is possible for God to suffer. Thus this chapter deals with the impassibility/passibility debate. Discussion of God's immutability and immanence leads to the paradox of the logical necessity of impassibility and the biblical evidence of passibility, which reveals the grace of God and the glory of this grace. The chapter closes with a discussion of the ascended body of Christ as the passible body, the body which endured suffering.

In the previous chapter, we simply accepted Jesus's status as the GodMan. But we need to think more about what this means, and a key problem it presents. If Jesus was God, how could he suffer? This question is rooted in classical theology, which demands that God be impassible, meaning that he cannot experience pain or pleasure from the actions of another being. The purpose of this definition is to distinguish God from the many pagan gods who were consumed by emotions like rage and jealousy and were susceptible to flattery. The God of the Bible is nothing like this. But how then is it possible for Jesus, who is God, to suffer?

This problem has been recognized for a long time. Some have attempted to solve it by using the Christological doctrine of the two distinct natures of Christ, one human and one divine, saying that it was only his human nature that suffered. One of the strongest proponents of this teaching was a man called Nestorius, who insisted that Mary was not the *Theotokos* (God-bearer) but rather the *Christotokos* (Christ-bearer) because it was only the human Christ whom she bore in her womb. This type of teaching establishes such a radical division between the two natures of Christ that they are almost two distinct and separate persons, with only an artificial unity. At the Council of

Ephesus in AD 431, this teaching was condemned, and today it is known as the Nestorian heresy.

Twenty years later, in AD 451, the Council of Chalcedon debated the issue of the divine and human nature of Christ and issued the following statement, which has been widely accepted by the church.

> We, then, following the holy Fathers, all with one consent, teach people to confess one and the same Son, our Lord Jesus Christ, the same *perfect in Godhead and also perfect in manhood; truly God and truly man*, of a reasonable [rational] soul and body; *consubstantial [co-essential] with the Father according to the Godhead, and consubstantial with us according to the Manhood;* in all things like unto us, without sin; begotten before all ages of the Father according to the Godhead, and in these latter days, for us and for our salvation, *born of the Virgin Mary, the Mother of God, according to the Manhood; one and the same Christ, Son, Lord, only begotten, to be acknowledged in two natures, inconfusedly, unchangeably, indivisibly, inseparably; the distinction of natures being by no means taken away by the union, but rather the property of each nature being preserved, and concurring in one Person and one Subsistence, not parted or divided into two persons, but one and the same Son, and only begotten God, the Word, the Lord Jesus Christ;* as the prophets from the beginning [have declared] concerning Him, and the Lord Jesus Christ Himself has taught us, and the Creed of the holy Fathers has handed down to us.

This almost universally accepted statement affirms that the two natures of Christ concur in the "one Person and one subsistence." Christ's two natures do not belong to two persons. They are united in a way that means neither nature is in any way reduced or removed by the union. Somehow in the mystery of God two entirely different natures are unified into one person. The GodMan is a perfect unity of the Son of God and the Son of Man.

But, we may ask, how can the human and the divine be united in one person without the infinite personhood of God completely overwhelming the finite human person? Our answer to this is a partial doctrine of *kenosis*. In taking a human body, Christ emptied himself of the divine knowledge, that is, the omniscience of God, as well as God's omnipresence, so that he learned as a human being learns. But unlike other human beings, Jesus is sinless and absolutely virtuous.

When we reflect on the mystery of the unity of God and man, we need to remember that men and women too are created in the image of God, and that thus we all embody some synthesis of the divine and the human in our human nature, albeit on a very different quality and scale to Christ. We are created in the image of God, Christ "is" the image of God.

One of the fundamental differences between the divine and the human is our physicality and mutability. God is incorporeal, immutable and impassible. But how do we understand these characteristics in relation to the incarnation?

Impassibility and Immutability

Impassibility and immutability are very distinct attributes of God, yet they are held together in what we may term a necessary relationship. The traditional doctrine of impassibility holds that God does not suffer. No external body can act on him. He is totally self-sufficient and self-determined. He exists above and beyond human emotion. He cannot be touched by us. This belief is seen as a logical consequence of belief in God's immutability. We know from experience that emotions change us, and thus if God has emotions analogous to human emotions, he would be changeable as his emotions changed from, say, joy to grief.

But God does not change, and so it follows that he must not have emotions. He so transcends human life that he is absolutely beyond being touched by human emotions. This means that there is no analogy between human pain and suffering and God's experience. It suggests that it is absurd to think of God as suffering – and even more so to assert that he can die on the cross.

To sum up, according to classical theism, God is immutable, he does not have feelings or emotions, he cannot suffer and he cannot die. You can see that this presents a problem for Christology, which asserts that Jesus is God and that he suffered terribly and died on the cross.

If God is immutable, it also follows that none of the three persons of the Trinity can change. God the Father, God the Son and the Holy Spirit are all immutable. How then can the Second Person of the Trinity, the eternal Logos, become incarnate in a human body? How can he change to indwell human being as a true man while retaining his Godhead? As asserted at the Council of Chalcedon, Christ is both very God and very man. He is really God and really human, two natures unmixed, in one person. It would seem to human logic that in the incarnation the eternally begotten Son of God must have changed his state of being.

Some would respond by saying that human logic has no place when talking about the transcendence of God and the doctrine of impassibility, but if so, we must conclude that we cannot talk about God at all! Ruling human logic out of court leaves no place at all for theology. So we are left with the basic theological dilemma, how can we talk about a transcendent God? The answer would be that it is possible to do so if we use the principle of analogy, which we will discuss more later in the chapter. First, let us look at two further examples of the problems we have to wrestle in regard to these issues.

The problem of inconsistency

Thomas Aquinas, a great proponent of the immutability of God, shows inconsistency when he denies emotions and feelings or suffering to God yet upholds God's passion and love. The Westminster Confession similarly states that God does not have passions but is at the same time "most loving, gracious, merciful, and long-suffering":

> There is but one only, living, and true God, who is infinite in being and perfection, a most pure spirit, invisible, without body, parts, or passions; immutable, immense, eternal, incomprehensible, almighty, most wise, most holy, most free, most absolute; working all things according to the counsel of his own immutable and most righteous will, for his own glory; most loving, gracious, merciful, long-suffering, abundant in goodness and truth, forgiving iniquity, transgression, and sin; the rewarder of them that diligently seek Him; and withal, most just, and terrible in his judgments, hating all sin, and who will by no means clear the guilty.

How can God be loving and merciful if he is beyond being in touch with us? If God is long-suffering, does that not mean that he suffers? Even if we agree that God's mercy transcends our mercy and that God's long-suffering is not the same as our long suffering, must there not be some connection to our understanding of these concepts? Surely there must be some analogy, even if not identified in these spheres?[1] God transcends the world. Surely his transcendence is homogenous. Is he more transcendent in some things and less so in others?

---

1. Philosophers talk of the analogy of proportionality and the analogy of being.

The problem of the biblical evidence

The Bible strongly asserts that God does not change (Mal 3:6; Jas 1:17). Yet God is also often spoken of as being compassionate and empathizing with his people: "The LORD will have compassion on Jacob and will again choose Israel, and will set them in their own land" (Isa 14:1). We are told that he is angry at sin: "There is no soundness in my flesh because of your indignation" (Ps 38:3). Jesus, the Son of God, was pained at the rejection of his love and grace: "When he drew near and saw the city, he wept over it" (Luke 19:41). He showed us the Father in that he revealed the Father's nature to us (John 14:8–10). He empathizes with us in our weaknesses (Heb 4:15). If to see Jesus is to see the Father, then we must assume that the Father has the same emotions as Jesus does when it comes to his people. In other words, the Bible presents the Father as not impassible but passible. It shows that God suffers with and for us. So what is it about God that does not change?

God's Nature

God cannot change in his essential nature. If this statement is true, it means that the incarnation did not change God's essential nature. Nor can any of God's relationships with the beings created in his image. Somehow, the incarnation of the eternal Logos now residing in a human body in heaven did not necessitate any change in God. We can understand this more clearly if we meditate on his omniscience and his immanence and transcendence.

Omniscience

While we must be very careful to avoid any hint of anthropomorphism when speaking about God, we must believe that he knows our pain and the disastrous effects of the fall and his curses upon us. Indeed, God knew our pain and the extent of our sin through our fallenness before he created the world. The whole of human history and *Heilsgeschichte* is known to God before its beginning. God is eternally aware of the incarnation, and all things come together in God's providence. The reality of the suffering of the eternally begotten Logos and of human suffering were already in God's conscious awareness before their actual occurrence in history. Leftow argues:

> It's standard theism to hold that God has full foreknowledge of what is to befall us: he sees our pain before we feel it, not just while we feel it, and so grieves it beforehand if he ever grieves it at all.

There would be no difference in the quality of God's grief before and while the pain occurs. For were there anything about it he did not know beforehand, the foreknowledge would not be full, and full knowledge beforehand should elicit the same reaction as full knowledge during.[2]

God's compassion and grief would thus be part of his essential unchanging nature before events happen, and so before our perceived relation with him.

Obviously thinking in this way involves thinking about the nature of providence. We can define providence as the coming to pass in world history of that which existed beforehand in God's consciousness, or what we think of as his foreknowledge. The nearest analogy to this would be human memory, although that looks back, rather than forward. Our knowledge is stored in our memory. It exists there as real, as does what we retain of our personal history. Our grief over past events and realities may no longer have real cause in the actuality of the world, but it remains real in our consciousness. Indeed our consciousness of our history, including our gained knowledge, is the ground of and so defines our present real life moments.[3]

Using this analogy, we can argue that the events of world history evoke the same grief that God knew in his foreknowledge without involving any change in God's essential being. All things that actually happen in time do so in terms of God's providential decree. Even if an event were to involve a change in God's grief, such change would be of a different, infinitely higher order than perceived change in the world.[4] Again Leftow's words are helpful:

> It's standard theism to hold that God is cognitively perfect. If he is so and exists in time, he has a past to recall and so has perfect memory. If God perfectly remembers your pain, it is as fresh for him years later as it was while it occurred, and if he perfectly loves you, perhaps he never gets over it. So we can make sense of unchanging grief; if God does grieve, we might well expect it from a God with full foreknowledge, cognitive perfection and a perfect

---

2. Leftow, "Immutability."

3. Our actual present grief, for example, passes with profound immediacy into our past and so into our memory. Thereafter the feeling of grief involves recalling the cause of that grief. Grief is thus an iterative process involving memories and actuality in the present passing moment.

4. It can be seen that we are using human logic to reach beyond human logic. However, I believe, as does theology, that there is a necessary principle of continuity between both planes. We may compare this with the couplet of God's transcendence and God's immanence.

affective nature. If he is timeless, an immutable but passible God would just timelessly suffer for us.[5]

Transcendence and immanence

In the above discussion we are making a quantum leap with respect to the possible suffering of God. We are saying that suffering is an aspect or element of the essential nature of God. We are also claiming that a possible analogy exists between our suffering and God's suffering, offering a valid way to retain the doctrine of immutability. If we are right, then the way is clear to further analogy between our suffering and God's suffering, and also between our personhood and love and God's personhood and love.

But what does it actually mean to say that God is love? This appears to be the most essential question. We want to affirm with biblical support that God is love; we also want to affirm that one of the persons of the Trinity came into the world to suffer and die for us in order that our sin would no longer condemn us if we believed in him (John 3:16). The incarnation of the eternal Logos is not only evidence of the immanence of God in the world (continued in the person of the Holy Spirit so that we are not left as orphans – John 14:18), it is evidence of suffering as essential to the salvation wrought by God himself, before the foundation of the earth.

The immanence of God in the person of the Son is a fully present immanence, while at the same time it is a presence of the transcendence. Christ on earth is simultaneously with us and transcends us. We may quote here Karl Rahner's famous maxim: "the 'economic' Trinity is the 'immanent' Trinity and the 'immanent' Trinity is the 'economic' Trinity."[6] This is true because Christ is simultaneously a member of both.[7]

On the ascension of the Son, the Spirit continues a different mode of personal immanence. In other words, God was immanent in Christ in his time on earth, and he is immanent in the Holy Spirit at this time. However, the standard doctrine of God's immanence holds that God was always transcendent

---

5. Leftow, "Immutability."

6. The "immanent Trinity" refers to the relationships within the Trinity in God's transcendent aseity. The economic Trinity, as the economy of salvation, relates to the roles of the Persons towards us: the Father as creator, the Son as the re-creator or redeemer, and the Spirit as the applier of redemption. These are the relationships of the Trinity active in creation and *heilsgeschichte* within the world.

7. Rahner, *The Trinity*, 23.

to and immanent in his time-space creation. He has been immanent in the material world since its creation.

The manifestation of this immanence, I would propose, is the inner logic and idea of the things that were made. These material things can be seen as symbols pointing to heavenly spiritual realities.[8] This is the basis of what is called general revelation.[9] For example, the infinite sky with its myriad stars, the great seas and the high mountains reveal something of God's vast power and majesty. The intricacy and mystery of the human eye, light and vision, reveal that God sees and is in the light and is the giver of this light. The amazing intricacy and complexity of this world should also lead us to ask about the power and genius of its designer. He has provided trees that provide us with shade, food, building materials, furniture, and fuel. His sun provides light and heat and life to vegetation, water is the life-giving fluid that quenches our thirst and refreshes and sustains not only us but all plant and animal life.

The immanence of God in creation or nature is a wonderful mystery that human science seeks to know and categorize. The mystery I believe is the manifestation of the transcendence or the infinitude in and through and peeking out from the apparent limitation of the finitude. This mystery is talked about in children's tales as fairies, goblins, wizards, talking animals and the like. In theology it is the realm of the mystics and mysticism.

God's Activity

The arguments for impassibility seem to present a God who is static and does not in any way act upon or within the creation. But the revelation of God in the Bible is of an active personal being both in creation and recreation. Throughout the Old Testament we see God (the Father) in action, and in the New Testament both the Son and the Spirit are continually active.

The Spirit is the applier of redemption won through the active atonement of Christ. This is his place in the economic Trinity. Regeneration is by and

---

8. Plato's theory of forms or ideas may be helpful in thinking about this. To Plato this present world is only a shadow of the form (or idea) of the real and essential world, which transcends this immediate world. The real world is the perfect world of which the things of this world are copies. So we have two worlds: this world, which is imperfect and temporal, and the transcendent world, which is perfect and eternal. In this immediate world we have, for example, the copy or shadow of a horse, but the essence of horse, or horseness, the true form or idea, exists in the transcendent world.

9. General revelation is the revelation of God through his works of creation, just as the pots made by a potter are a revelation of the nature of the potter. This form of revelation is both impersonal and shadowy (see Rom 1:20; Ps 19:1–4).

through him and no other. He is the giver of the gift of faith and the agent in rebirth. And now the way to follow Christ is to walk in the Spirit. The Spirit is the transcendent God and the transcendence of God in power and wisdom and always in the world. The Spirit is not static energy but a person in relationship with and eternally proceeding from the Father and the Son.[10] This is the great joy of those who can see and have entered the kingdom of God on earth. Such a dynamic is the defining essence of God's action. God will "neither slumber nor sleep" (Ps 121:4).

We see the activity of God in the Old Testament in relation to Abraham, who lays hold of him through an amazing faith. We see God's promise and the fulfilment of that promise when Abraham and Sarah have a son in their old age. We see Isaac, the son of the promise, being used to test Abraham's faith when the father is called to sacrifice his son. We see God in relation to Moses in the exodus and the giving of the Decalogue, written on stone by "the finger of God" (Exod 31:18; Deut 9:10). We see God at work in relation to Joshua in the conquering of hostile nations and the entry into the promised land, and to King David in the slaying of Goliath and the administration of Israel, and to Solomon in the building of the temple. And to Elijah, Isaiah, Jeremiah and other major and minor prophets. We have two possibilities here: either the Old Testament Scriptures are inauthentic or God was extremely active with the players, including in his choice of Israel as his special people.

When it comes to immutability in the Old Testament, God seems to change his mind on a number of occasions. He does so when in his righteous judgement he sends the flood and preserves only Noah and his family. And then God "repents" and covenants not to do such a thing again, using the rainbow to symbolize this promise. In Exodus 32:14 we are told that the Lord changed his mind about what he would do to the people (see also Jer 26:19; Amos 7:3, 6). Yet in 1 Samuel 15:29 we are told that God will not (cannot) change his mind (see also Isa 31:2).

I have merely listed these texts, and no doubt careful exegesis would show that God does not change and that the doctrine of immutability is not under threat. I am happy to accept such arguments, for the doctrine of immutability is overwhelmingly right and necessary. However, what has been shown here is that passibility does not cancel out immutability. There is abundant evidence that God does feel emotions in the Old Testament and in the New Testament.

---

10. In holding to the *filioque* position, no offence is intended to those who hold to procession from the Father only.

Appearance and reality

In the sixteenth-century there was much debate about Joshua's commanding the sun to stand still (Josh 10:12–14). What sparked this debate was Nicolaus Copernicus's challenge to the belief that the earth was the centre of the universe with the sun and the planets revolving round it. Instead, Copernicus argued, the sun was at the centre and the earth travelled round it. This theory worked mathematically and in terms of what was observed, whereas the older Ptolemaic theory did not. But church leaders insisted that the heliocentric cosmology could not be true because it would mean that Joshua 10 would be wrong, and so the Bible would contain error and its authority would be lost.

Here there was a conflict between absolute truth (the earth literally stood still) and relative truth (the earth merely appeared to stand still from Joshua's perspective). To resolve the conflict between science and the Bible, it had to be universally accepted that the sun only appeared to stand still. Can we use this same approach in reverse when it comes to theology and the Bible as regards God's immutability and claim that God only appears to change, whereas the essential and absolute truth is that he does not? That is what I would argue.

There is also, of course, evidence of God's changelessness in the Scriptures. This doctrine of immutability is vital for human security and for stability of belief and faith. God is our rock of justice and perfection and is righteous without any trace of evil. If God can change in his essential nature, human beings are lost. The symbolism of the rock of perfect righteousness and faithfulness is the symbol of immutability and absolute ontological security for us. Indeed, no other eternal and infinite security is available.

Listen to the words of the Song of Moses:

> For I will proclaim the name of the Lord;
> ascribe greatness to our God!
>
> The Rock, his work is perfect,
> for all his ways are justice.
> A God of faithfulness and without iniquity,
> just and right is he. (Deut 32:3–4)

God does not change in his essence. Our task is to understand how God can appear to change existentially in his actions to and with us but not change in his essential being.

It is the nature of change itself that we need to consider when we talk of immutability and indeed impassibility. We are talking about non-essential change, change that is outside of God's essential nature. The change involved in the incarnation was an enactment of God's essential nature of grace. I contend that if God did not act in salvific providence through the suffering and atoning death of the Son, then he would have denied, and so effected change, in his essential nature. The incarnation was an act of God as our Rock. God's love was seen in its full glory in the passion of Christ. This is unfailing immutable love. His act of incarnation and sacrifice was forged outside of time, and so we may say in eternity.[11] It was an act that was predestined and so involved no change. Similarly, the passible wonder of grace was predestined in eternity. This higher order of possibility we may term impassibility.

The Paradox and Its Possible Resolution

The position we have now reached is the same paradox that Thomas Weinandy identifies when he writes that "the impassible suffers."[12] We could equally well speak of the passible impassible, or the empathetic apathy. These, like all paradoxes, are contradictions in terms, suggesting that this supposition must be invalid. However, we are also dealing with the transcendence of God, which is utterly beyond our understanding, and so paradox may have a new authenticity in this milieu.

Throughout the biblical text God is seen to empathize with his people so much that he sent his Son, the eternal Logos, to suffer and die by crucifixion. Christ's passion was foreordained and in a real sense it defined suffering for human beings, and most certainly for Christians. His suffering up to and through death is heralded by John 3:16 as the supreme evidence of God's love for his people. The message is very clear: God empathizes with humans in their fallen plight and pays the cost of their sin through sacrificing himself in the person of his eternally begotten Son.

The incarnation was a coming of the transcendence into finite human being to save finite human being from its lostness. In this we see great and profound compassion. We are able to derive from this act, as we seek to know and understand it, that the transcendence is a compassionate loving person. We can know this person through the analogy of our own feelings of compassion and love.

Christ revealed God as a compassionate loving person. Further, this loving compassion of God draws us to love him and others whom we term our

---

11. We cannot talk about eternity as we do not have an adequate analogy. We must use simply a *via negativa*: eternity is not time. Eternity involves some different, infinitely higher, order of being.

12. Weinandy, *Does God Suffer?*, 213.

neighbours. From this viewpoint it would appear to be almost blasphemous to claim that God does not have feelings for or care about his people. Impassibility seems to deny the gospel of Jesus the Christ.

The limits of revelation

But at this stage we also need to ask another question: Do we know anything at all about God's aseity (i.e. of his being in itself)? What do we really know about the immanent or ontological Trinity, about God in himself in heaven in his Trinitarian relationships? The answer must be that we know nothing about it. This knowledge would be too high for us. The aseity of God is the milieu of God's impassibility. It is not revealed to us. Such revelation would be completely and utterly beyond us, belonging to the realm of God alone.

The key principle of revelation is that it is about the self-disclosure of God's being towards us, about our relationship with God. Further than that we cannot go, just as we cannot know what lies beyond the thousands of millions of stars in the night sky. We can think about what lies beyond the stars, but we cannot know it. All we can do is contemplate the stars with wonder. Similarly, there are boundaries imposed on us by our finitude. Impassibility is one such boundary. God in Christ came into our finitude to reveal the true nature of God. If we have seen him we have seen the Father (John 14:3–7).

The boundaries to which we are subject means that we can see only the existence of God, his omnipotence and his majesty, but nothing else (Ps 19:1; Rom 1:20). When we try to move beyond those boundaries, we enter the realm of metaphysics and have no revelation but only human reason. We begin perhaps from the biblical revelation, but more immediately from the general revelation of God in nature, influenced by philosophy. Note that none of these things are bad. Indeed, they are good.

We all begin from our idea of God, for we all have an idea of God as the most perfect being (if he were not so, he would not be God). From this root, we seek to work out God's attributes and define his nature. The Bible gives us the boundaries. It teaches that God is creative, God is love, and God is unchanging – the same yesterday, today and tomorrow. My question is, do we seek to apply a right hermeneutic and proper rules of exegesis to these great concepts, seeking to understand their meaning in terms of the *sitz im leiben* into which they are spoken? Or do we take them as boundary statements, which we cannot plumb except by human reason?

The way that we must proceed, of course, is by analogy. However, when we cannot find an applicable analogy, we have to revert to philosophy. While it is not wrong to do this, we must remember that philosophy lacks the authenticity of revelation.

Let us take two of God's primary attributes, as summarized in clear biblical statements "God is love" and "God is spirit" (1 John 4:8; John 4:24). We do have analogies for these two concepts. Our love for each other is analogous to God's love, and there is a possible analogy between our spirit or our concept of spirit and God as spirit. We can begin to build on these analogies, always bearing in mind that we are dealing with the boundaries of transcendence and so our analogies struggle for adequacy.

Let us consider the development of the concept that God is spirit. We understand it to mean that God is incorporeal, doesn't have a body and so does not have "parts." We find it hard to say much more about this. We cannot develop the analogy because we do not really know what spirit is.

We can go a little further, however, in bringing spirit and person together. Jesus revealed God as person, and so we can pose that God as spirit has something to do with God's person. We might say that God is a personal spirit. "Person" to us implies care, and so love. So we can go on to say that God is a personal spirit of love. The nature of this love is grace. The love of God acts in and through grace. And so grace is the motive and essence of God's good creation.

Impassibility and grace

In this discussion of God's attributes we have not been able to explore all the boundaries, although we have produced a valuable skeleton of concepts that we claim define the nature of God. However, I think that there is more that can be said about the nature of grace. We know what grace is because we have many cases of undeserved mercy in the world. We are deeply touched when we witness grace in a human person. It disarms us and moves us to tears. Grace is glorious; it is true glory. The superlative example of grace is Jesus raised up on the cross in our place. Yet even in this profound knowledge, which connects us to the heart of God, we cannot know the grace of God as it exists in himself as an attribute of his wonderful being. We are created in his image, however, and grace images God to us and through us to others.

It seems difficult, however, to move from grace to God's attribute of impassibility. These appear to be dialectic qualities – we would say "impassibility versus grace" rather than "impassibility and grace." But let us step further in seeking to understand God better.

Logically, God does not feel emotions as we feel emotions. His foreknowledge and omniscience mean that he already has all knowledge of our feelings, knowledge that he cannot possibly share with us. God perfectly and eternally knows all things, and so he is always conscious and aware of all things. If this is true, then he is vastly beyond, deeper and higher than empathy. The mere idea of an infinite being empathizing with a finite being seems absurd.

Similarly, how could an infinite being, absolutely self-sufficient and at eternal peace, suffer as we understand it? He knows the cause and effect of all suffering eternally. We have moments of grief and suffering, but there are no moments involved with an eternal being who lives outside of time from all eternity to all eternity. The case for impassibility seems both undeniable and conclusive. It seems to be essential to God's being.

How then can God's nature be grace? In human terms, grace is understood as flowing from the heart of true love but it is very rare, dispensed only by those whom we regard as saints and heroes. Fallen human beings rarely show grace; they live by laws of their own making and the laws of the land, which they both make and break. So true grace has something of the nature of transcendence.

But the grace of God far transcends fallen human nature and finite human being. The grace of God is the creative action of God communicated explicitly through the incarnation and the cross. Before the historical point of the cross, this grace was revealed in a shadowy, more implicit, way through the being of creation. It was both creation's motive for existing and its spiritual power.

God's incommunicable and communicable attributes

As we wrestle with the paradox of the impassible passible, it seems that the solution may lie in the sphere of communicability. God's love and grace appear to be communicable attributes; impassibility is not. The paradox is resolved by recognizing that we are dealing with two completely different categories.

Immutability and impassibility are incommunicable attributes of God. They are intellectual boundaries that cannot be passed. They are indeed beyond the possibility of human knowledge. This means that they are unknowable in any way. They are of the category of God's absolute being.

However, "while the incommunicable attributes emphasize the absolute being of God, the communicable attributes stress the apparent fact that He enters into various relations with his creatures."[13] God's attributes of love and

---

13. Berkhof, *Systematic Theology*, 60–61. I would not use the term "fact" here; perhaps "reality" would be more accurate.

being spirit are in the category of communicable attributes. We can understand something of them. Immutability and impassibility, however, are perceived as merely the names of transcendent realities. Love and spirit relate to us as they are close to our own principles for an authentic and abundant life. Incommunicable attributes must relate to communicable attributes in the reality of God, but the exact nature of that relation appears to us as unknowable mystery.

Indeed, *mystery* is the only way in which we can relate the transcendence of God to us. The objects of the mystery are unknowable and can only be described allusively in folklore within the weave of human cultures. We talk about the mystery through narrative (story), and the narratives themselves can and are often used by human reason to fill out meaning.

Impassibility is of the category of mystery. We can tell stories about impassibility or discuss it in terms of its relation to other of God's incommunicable attributes. We can think of it as pertaining to the absolute being of God and we can make certain statements with respect to the nature of absolute perfect being, as we have been doing. Confusingly, we can define the elements of absolute perfect being as we project our idea of it, but we can in no way know it. We can only really skate around the boundary. We remain in the clouds of mystery in any discussion about this attribute.

Relationship of Absolute Being with Created Finite Beings

The absolute immutable being of God is seen in biblical revelation to have relations with the beings of his creation, and most especially with human beings created in his image. That which is incommunicable and completely incomprehensible communicates love and spirit through grace. He who is utterly transcendent with an infinite gulf between himself and us bridges the gulf and reaches into the finitude; supremely through the incarnation. This reaching is both phenomenological and through the Logos. We seek to receive the phenomenological in terms of description[14] and the Logos in terms of human reason (involving metaphysics). While we cannot know absolute being in its infinitude, we can be aware of it as a fly can be aware of a human being, or an ant at the foot of an elephant can be aware of the elephant. This awareness

---

14. In terms of Edmund Husserl's phenomenological descriptive method. We might say that the universal Logos appears in the world as an historical phenomenon whom we can describe but not know essentially. We are aware of the appearance and can act only in terms of this awareness. We cannot know his transcendence which remains a mystery. The philosophical and theological method of merely describing the phenomenon leads to mysticism.

of infinite being is, according to Rudolf Otto, the *mysterium tremendum* which is *fascinans*, the terrible and fascinating mystery.[15]

According to biblical revelation, God suffers in Jesus, the GodMan who died on the cross. The cost of grace is the suffering of Christ to the point of death and beyond.[16] This is the meaning of the Lord's Supper or Holy Communion. Grace was supremely revealed through the sacrifice of the only begotten Son of the absolute being of God.

The act of grace is the relational act of the infinite to the finite. Infinite being creates finite being through a loving act and redeems finite being in and through grace. Human beings are the supreme finite beings created in the image of the infinite being and so are capable of a special epistemic relationship with him. This we may term "seeing the kingdom of heaven," which is the capacity to know God.

Original sin was the devastating act of human freedom, stepping into the evil life of rebellion and rejection of God through which our special, and indeed filial, relationship with him was destroyed. The image of God in human beings was, if not entirely lost, completely corrupted and so its capacities were rendered inoperable. The gift of faith, producing regeneration, removes the corrupting virus and restores the capacity for relationship with the transcendent God.

Non-Christian philosophers' understanding of absolute being derives from the world view of fallen human beings. They do not have the perspective of faith and so they apply reason, which does not take account of the possibilities of relationship with absolute being. Thus scholastic philosophers from the twelfth to the eighteenth century attempted to construct a natural theology, that is, a theology based only on general revelation in nature. They sought to determine the attributes of God apart from any element of faith or the special revelation of the Bible. According to Berkhof, they propounded three ways in which God's attributes could be determined. These were causality, negation and eminence:

> By *the way of causality* we rise from the effects which we see in the world round about us to the idea of a first Cause, from the contemplation of creation, to the idea of an almighty Creator, and from the observation of the moral government of the world, to the idea of a powerful and wise Ruler. *By way of negation* we remove

---

15. Otto, *Idea of the Holy*.
16. I am arguing here that the cost of the penalty for human sin as an offence against God is an infinite cost that Christ is able to bear.

from our idea of God all the imperfections seen in His creatures, as inconsistent with the idea of a Perfect Being, and ascribe to Him the opposite perfection. In reliance on that principle we speak of God as independent, infinite, incorporeal, immense, immortal, and incomprehensible. And finally, *by way of eminence* we ascribe to God *in the most eminent manner* the relative perfections which we discover in man, according to the principle that what exists in an effect, pre-exists in its cause, and even in the most absolute sense in God as the most perfect Being.[17]

This method of determining God's attributes focuses on the impersonal principles of God as absolute first cause (*primum mobile*) and as the absolute, most perfect being. It is a *remoto Christo*[18] method (setting Christ aside temporarily) that by its very nature does not and cannot take account of the nature of the relationship between the infinite absolute God and finite created human beings.

The list of attributes in the quotation from Berkhof above all pertain to God as absolute. We could include in the list all the attributes that are termed incommunicable, including immutability. In ontological terms, change implies either more or less of something. But concepts like "more" or "less" cannot be applied to the most perfect being. The most perfect being cannot become more perfect or he would not be most perfect and so not God. This same problem with "more" applies to all of God's perfections. Nor can God be "less" perfect in any respect, as then too he would not be God. This is the central principle of the doctrine of immutability.[19]

We have already, I hope, given adequate grounds to disassociate immutability from impassibility. However, I would also argue that impassibility communicates possibility through the special relationship of God and those created in his image. I am saying that in creating us in his image, God passes something of his absolute and infinite being to us. This is the basis of innate knowledge. In the regeneration of our relationship with God, we gain immortality of a higher order, we gain comprehension of a higher order and achieve absolute ontological and existential security. Effectively, salvation is the absolute and infinite or wholly other reaching through the boundaries into

---

17. Berkhof, *Systematic Theology*, 54–55.

18. As used by Anselm in *Cur Deus Homo* in an attempt to do theology by setting Christ aside (remote Christo) using only reason.

19. This doctrine echoes the views of Plato, Socrates and the pre-Socratic philosophers on change and changelessness.

the fallen world of the finitude,[20] taking hold of and converting an immense part of humanity, and taking us out of the world to the place of absolutes and infinite perfections.

The infinite and absolute abundant life of heaven in terms of the immediate presence of God to the unfallen finite world is seen through the accessibility of God to humankind through his immediate presence with Adam and Eve before the fall. In this immediacy we see a radical change in a relationship but no change in God's essential nature. While, this filial relationship, which did not require mediation, was destroyed and replaced by death, it does reveal the possibility of a relationship between the absolute and the finitude. This relationship of the impassable with the passible implies that the one, while retaining fully ontological integrity, can pass wholly into the other and be passible. And so the absolute and perfect God who cannot suffer passes through the relationship of his son the GodMan into suffering in the world. As far as we are concerned he suffers in terms of the possibility of the communicable attributes of love and spirit.

The Human Body Ascended

Our lives as human beings are most properly and happily summed up as a relationship with God in Jesus, the eternal Logos and the Son of God, consubstantial with the Father and the Spirit, who now has corporeal life in the Trinitarian order of heaven. Jesus was resurrected; his body was raised from death. He ascended in the resurrected body to rejoin the council of heaven, a movement symbolized by the statement that he is "seated at the right hand of . . . God" (Luke 22:69). Being at the right hand of the Father implies that he possesses the power of God: "From now on you will see the Son of Man seated at the right hand of Power" (Matt 26:64; Mark 14:62). The raised and ascended Christ is omnipotent; he has all power and he is for us. His very corporeality is the eternal witness to this truth. He is our heavenly representative, our advocate in the Trinity. He is our absolute security and so our negation of suffering.

In the return of the GodMan to the Trinitarian order of being, the passible person returns to the impassable Trinity. This is itself a great mystery. In this return, even although Jesus's body is a glorified body, it is still a physical entity. The Westminster Confession of Faith 8.4 reads:

> On the third day he arose from the dead, with the same body in which he suffered, with which also he ascended into heaven, and

---

20. Ultimately through incarnation, but also before this through the prophets.

there sits at the right hand of his Father, making intercession, and shall return, to judge men and angels, at the end of the world.

Effectively then physicality is given entry to the aseity of God who is spirit, with no change taking place in his essential nature. This body, we believe, will bear the scars of the wounds of the cross, as shown to Thomas (John 20:27).

It is hard for us to grasp the immutability of God in relation to this return to the aseity. In terms of human logic, there has definitely been a change. The Trinity in its aseity was spirit, and with the return of the Son it is now spirit and an added physicality in Jesus's human body. The authenticity of the attribute of immutability is seriously challenged.

The Westminster Confession, with scriptural proofs, states that Christ ascended into heaven in the same body in which he suffered. In view of the arguments for impassibility, there is an element of irony here. God in his aseity cannot suffer; yet if the confession is right, the Son returned to the aseity in the body in which he suffered. Thomas Aquinas, while rigorously on the side of the immutability and inaccessibility of God, appears to hold a similar view:

> But Christ's body after the Resurrection was truly made up of elements, and had tangible qualities such as the nature of a human body requires, and therefore it could naturally be handled; and if it had nothing beyond the nature of a human body, it would likewise be corruptible. But it had something else which made it incorruptible, and this was not the nature of a heavenly body, as some maintain, and into which we shall make fuller inquiry later . . . but it was glory flowing from a beatified soul: because, as Augustine says (*Ep. ad Dioscor.* cxviii): "God made the soul of such powerful nature, that from its fullest beatitude the fulness of health overflows into the body, that is, the vigour of incorruption." And therefore Gregory says (*Hom. in Evang.* xxvi): "Christ's body is shown to be of the same nature, but of different glory, after the Resurrection."[21]

This body ascended and amazingly, in some great mysterious way, was compatible with the perichoresis of the Trinity. The body that received the stripes, the nails and the spear is now a heavenly body. It is this body in which Christ will return to the world in the second coming at the eschaton. To take physicality into the Godhead without change to the essential nature of the Trinity is a profound communication of the special relationship of God and

---

21. Thomas Aquinas, *Summa Theologica*, Part 3, Q54, Article 2 (reply to Objection 2).

saved, and therefore eternal, humankind. In this relationship it is human beings and not God who undergo a radical change, becoming partakers of the divine nature.

> His divine power has granted to us all things that pertain to life and godliness, through the knowledge of him who called us to his own glory and excellence, by which he has granted to us his precious and very great promises, so that through them you may become partakers of the divine nature, having escaped from the corruption that is in the world because of sinful desire. (2 Pet 1:3–4)

In Christ the GodMan, human beings can share in the divine nature, which is incorruptible. The human body of Christ was already glorified in the incarnation. As Augustine describes it in the quotation above, the soul overflowed into the body of Christ, giving it the fullness of health, which is the vigour of incorruption. This human body and soul were received into the Godhead when Christ assumed it. The glorified relationship between God and human beings is forged in the person of the GodMan who has immediate access into the Trinitarian unity in heaven.

Because this was decreed and foreordained by God as the great revelation of his nature of grace to humankind, absolutely no change took place with respect to God's essential nature. The blessed union with a creature created in his image flows from and is commensurate with his essential nature. In the incarnation, then, the human body and soul is already given access to the Trinity. The human nature assumed by Christ himself becomes a partaker of the divine nature, and so do all who are in Christ. This amazing miracle is evident in the ascension, in which no new element was added.

Summing up, we can say that the Person of the GodMan suffered while in the perfection of the incorruptible human body and soul in his relationship with corrupted human bodies and souls, and so God is perceived as suffering. But this suffering is of the nature of grace, which is God's essential nature.

We have termed God's grace towards human beings the suffering of God. Grace is the cost of love, and this cost is God's responsibility towards his promises, which he keeps eternally and to infinite proportions. This responsibility to his promises is the primordial fact of God being true to himself. It is because of this truth that the story of the salvation of sinners has the nature and character that it has.

I am saying that Christ's suffering was the grace of God that is God's essential nature. And so the grace of God communicated as the suffering of Christ is the greatest glory of God beheld by regenerated human beings who are in the world but not of it.

11

The Suffering of the Apostle Paul

Paul's letters are written from the foundation of his personal suffering, which was part of his path to apostleship. He shared so passionately in the suffering of Christ that readers of his letters are drawn to perceive that in some sense suffering is intrinsic to Paul's view of salvation. Thus he told the Corinthian church, "I decided to know nothing among you except Jesus Christ and him crucified" (1 Cor 2:2). Meditation on Paul's focus on the death and resurrection of Christ reveals a dialectic in which death is followed by resurrection, suffering by healing, and humiliation by the glory of God. Weakness, not power, is Paul's modus operandi. All of his suffering comes together as a pathos that is the persuasive power of his ministry to the Gentiles.

We often fail to pay sufficient heed to the great suffering of the apostle Paul, preferring to focus on his exhortations to rejoice rather than on what he suffered. But as Karl Plank reminds us, "Paul draws on the language of affliction, in virtually all of his letters, to interpret human life and the gospel he understands to empower that life."[1] He, more than any other, appears to have understood his life and ministry in Christ in terms of suffering. I would argue that, after Christ, he is the greatest sufferer in the New Testament, so much so that he could even be called the second suffering servant.

Paul's suffering is what we might call apostolic suffering or representative suffering. An apostle (*shaliach* in Hebrew or *apostolos* in Greek) was originally

---

1. Plank, *Paul and the Irony of Affliction*, 3.

someone who was sent on a mission by his master as his master's representative. The mission of Christ's apostles was to communicate the gospel of Christ. To do this among the Gentiles, Paul had to first communicate the suffering of Christ.

Paul's suffering would validate and authenticate his own apostleship, and in this authentic authority reveal the gospel of Christ to the Gentiles and to those who would follow, who would read his letters. In this authority Paul planted churches to whom he wrote letters inspired by the Holy Spirit.

Like the suffering of his master, the ultimate Suffering Servant, Paul's suffering was absolutely necessary for his ministry and so derived from the will and plan of God. This much is plain from God's words to Ananias, whom he sent to heal Paul's blindness after the vision on the road to Damascus: "I will show him [Paul] how much he must suffer for the sake of my name" (Acts 9:16). There is nothing arbitrary about Paul's suffering – it was clearly foreordained in the great plan of God. Through witnessing Paul's suffering and his triumph over it, sinners would come to belief. They would be confronted by Paul's great resolve and integrity, which was unmovable in Christ.

The Mystery of Suffering

There is little mystery about the law to which the young Saul (later Paul) was so utterly committed: law is strictly defined and demands obedience even if it is not understood. By contrast, the passion of Christ cannot be defined, nor is it comprehensible. Yet the cross constitutes the most profound revelation of grace the world has encountered. When we are confronted by grace we are confronted by the infinite mystery of God.

To share in the suffering of Christ is to be thrown face-to-face with the mystery of God. For Paul, the revelation of this mystery began with his encounter with the Son of God on the Damascus road in which he experienced the fear of God. I suspect that Paul knew very little of this fear before his conversion; he was in awe of the religious power of the Pharisees and so feared men more than God. On the Damascus road, he learned the awful fear occasioned by the in-breaking of the transcendent.

The fear of God involves an entirely different psychology to worldly fear, and Paul's natural reaction to the new light was blindness. To be blind and led by the hand is to return to a kind of childhood; it is going back to begin again as it were. The blindness and helplessness, along with the great anguish of the fear of God that came to Paul through this miracle, marked the beginning of Paul's new faith in Christ.

Before his encounter with Christ, Paul was single-minded and acted with purpose, using his great gifts of zeal and resourcefulness. But when Christ appeared to him, all was thrown into confusion. In abject submission, he asked, "Who are you, Lord?" and "What shall I do, Lord?" (Acts 22:8, 10). He had been cast out of definition and into awful mystery that would involve suffering.

The mystery of suffering derives from the mystery of God himself. God reveals himself to us but remains incomprehensible. His ways are past finding out, even when revealed to us. We see something of this in Paul's hesitancy when describing his vision of the third heaven, which he may possibly have received during his trance in the temple in Jerusalem sometime after his encounter with Jesus on the Damascus road (Acts 22:17–21). In this trance, the Lord appeared to him and commanded him to leave Jerusalem for his own safety. Speaking of this vision or some other vision, Paul says:

> I know a man in Christ who fourteen years ago was caught up to the third heaven – whether in the body or out of the body I do not know, God knows. And I know that this man was caught up into paradise – whether in the body or out of the body I do not know, God knows – and he heard things that cannot be told, which man may not utter. (2 Cor 12:1–5)

Paul's uncertainty as to whether he was physically transported to heaven or received a revelation as a disembodied spirit underlines the profound and evocative quality of mystery. So does the statement that the things Paul heard would not be beneficial or perhaps even bearable for the churches to hear. Indeed the revelation was so powerful that it had to be balanced by suffering (2 Cor 12:7).

The point I am making here is that receiving a revelation of the mystery of God produces suffering on earth. This was true for Paul, and it is true for us. Any revelation of God received into our fallen being imposes responsibility and demands a response. Part of this response must be the awe that constitutes the fear of God, which is the beginning of wisdom (Prov 9:10). It is a revelation that shakes the roots of our human identity.

The Intensity of Paul's Suffering

In chapter 4 we noted that Paul endured all types of suffering. In the present chapter we consider more his inner (or ontological) suffering. Such suffering was inevitable, for a revelation received through a living theology produces ontological growth (growth of being and as a person), and ontological growth results in intensity of being, which results in suffering. Authentic being in Christ is intense being. This intensity may be measured by the capacity to respond to God. To use a somewhat crude analogy, a battery is capable of a response directly proportional to its charge. The greater the capacity of a battery, the more it can be charged; and the greater the charge stored in the battery, the greater the task it is able to support. Analogously, the greater the capacity of a believer to receive the being of God, the more highly charged he or she must be. So great being is highly intense being. And because intense being absorbs suffering, great being, in the fallenness of the world, is necessarily suffering being.

The words appropriate to intense being can take the form of confession, as they did with Paul and Augustine. For both, their confession was basic to their identity, one as an apostle and the other as a bishop and theologian. But there is also a great difference between them. In Augustine's *Confessions*, which is a theological reflection of great power, Augustine confesses his personal immorality. But while the apostle Paul confesses that he sins, he confesses more that he suffers. The sin is integrated in the suffering and shows itself through great angst. Paul is a called and appointed human being who is chosen by God to suffer and through suffering reach the Gentiles, but he is also inspired to write letters that would later be included in Holy Scripture.

We see aspects of confession throughout the Pauline corpus. He confesses sin, he boasts of personal weakness, he confesses his former persecution of the church. He agonizes over his apparent incapacity to overcome his personal sin, even crying out, "Wretched man that I am! Who will deliver me from this body of death?" (Rom 7:24).

What is significant in this confession is that it appears to consolidate his authority as an apostle. Strikingly, he confesses not as a criminal but as an apostle of Christ. Paul is strong. He has apostolic authority and is prepared to wield it. But his authority is empowered by his suffering and apparent weakness. Yet at no time is he seen to lose control. He has great being, which does not take authority but has authority. This authority is given to him proportional to his having his being in Christ. It does not come from Paul's great learning and scholarship under Gamaliel, nor from his natural gifts of leadership or worldly status. No doubt Paul had genius, but his authority did not derive from it; it was given to him by God through revelation.

In understanding Paul's identity as an apostle, it is helpful to consider the distinction Søren Kierkegaard makes between a human genius and an apostle. According to Kierkegaard, Paul's human genius had nothing to do with his apostleship. He was called by a revelation to be an apostle. A genius relates to the finitude; an apostle relates to the transcendence. A genius is born; an apostle is appointed. Paul was called by God and sent by him on a mission:

> An apostle has no other evidence than his own statement, and at most his willingness to suffer everything joyfully for the sake of that statement. His speech in this regard will be brief: "I am called by God; do with me now what you will; flog me, persecute me, but my last words will be my first; I am called by God and I make you eternally responsible for what you do to me."[2]

Paul states his authority with meekness and submission, but yet it has the force of the transcendence of God. The quality of this authority is seen through his suffering and joyful willingness to suffer, which validates the veracity of his apostleship and his apostolic authority. His suffering is laid before his opponents and those who read his letters, demanding a response. Both are eternally responsible for what they do with Paul. This we may term the power of Paul's confession.

Paul's suffering, his utter dedication and his inspired teaching reveal his character. He is seen to be a man of the highest integrity and a trusted role model for the churches. This contrasts greatly with his life before conversion. The hand of fellowship extended to him by the apostles at the Jerusalem Council became the universal hand of the body of Christ.

Paul's Understanding of Suffering; Meaning and Purpose

There is an element of irony in the fact that the list of Paul's sufferings in 2 Corinthians 11:23–29 forms part of Paul's defence of his apostleship. In fact, his suffering is the major element in the authentication of his ministry as an apostle. The two major factors militating against such authenticity were his persecution of the church and the fact that he missed the Christ event. He was not one of the chosen Twelve, indeed he was an outsider. He encountered the risen Christ, in what was, perhaps, the final resurrection appearance, but he did not walk with Jesus on earth. He did not see Jesus's miracles, listen to him teaching, or witness the crucifixion (or if he did, there is no mention of this in Scripture). In short, Paul had no experience of the incarnate Suffering Servant, the Lamb of God who would take away the sin of the world, and he would not in any way have associated Jesus of Nazareth with the coming Messiah.

---

2. Kierkegaard, "Difference between Genius and an Apostle," 105.

But as we learn from Paul's letters, and have stated above, his suffering validated his ministry. He is readily perceived to be a suffering servant of the Son of God. We can see this more clearly if we examine three couplets that define his understanding of his role: death and resurrection, suffering and healing, and humiliation and the glory of God.

Death and Resurrection

For Paul, Jesus's statement that his disciples must deny themselves, take up their cross and follow him (Matt 16:24) literally meant following Christ to the cross. He did indeed follow Jesus to a violent death, probably by beheading.[3] But the reality and intensity of Paul's sharing in the passion went far beyond this. For him, following Christ involved sharing in Christ's suffering, which meant dying to self and living in him. The way of the cross meant death to the ego and the flesh (the old nature) and new life in the Spirit. As Paul said to the Galatian church, "I have been crucified with Christ. It is no longer I who live, but Christ who lives in me" (Gal 2:20).

Roman Catholics tend to interpret Paul's suffering (and that of other believers) as having salvific force.[4] In other words, Christ gave himself up for us in the salvific act of his passion and death, and Paul perceives himself as doing something similar in his participation in the passion and death of Christ. Christ lives in him when he is "crucified with Christ" and so through his suffering grace accrues to others. Thus, for Roman Catholics the crucified Christ is the model for Christian life:

> the crucified Christ provides the meaning of life and the meaning of death, even the meaning of life to come! The suffering of Christ does not prevent our suffering on earth, but it does allow us to suffer with dignity and meaning.[5]

While there is truth in this, there are also problems with it. One is that Catholics refer to Paul as Saint Paul, which assigns him, and other saints a higher quality of being than ordinary mortals. As a "saint," he is perceived as being almost in a state of sinless perfection, hence his sufferings qualify as salvific as do those of other Roman Catholic saints.

---

3. There is little doubt that Paul was martyred. But that he was beheaded is speculative. He would not have been crucified as there was a prohibition on the crucifixion of Roman citizens.

4. John Paul II, *Salvifici Doloris* [Apostolic letter on the Christian Meaning of Human Suffering], 1984.

5. Marshall, *Catholic Perspective on Paul*, 208.

But clearly that is not how Paul sees himself. He acknowledges that he continues to be a sinner. His focus on the cross was not simply because he sought to save others but because he knew that he needed to confess his own sin and take it to the cross, as all must do. He knew that the cross was the answer to his anguished cry "Who will deliver me from this body of death?" (Rom 7:24).

Given Paul's intensity of being in the Lord, he would have been constantly aware of sin. Confession would have been vital to his ministerial energy. Augustine's *Confessions* constitute a genre through which Augustine did theology, but for Paul confession was existential in that he lived his confession of sin and his suffering.

So what did Paul mean when he said, "I decided to know nothing among you except Jesus Christ and him crucified"? Was he speaking of what he would teach, or in terms of what he knew about the Corinthian church? Was Christ crucified among the Corinthian church community? Given that Paul goes on to speak of the spiritual status of the community, it seems that the spiritual meaning is central to his thinking. His goal was to focus the attention of the Corinthian church on this central reality. The cross is the fountain of their salvation, and he would rather they drank from that fountain than listened to lofty words, no matter how wise.

The point I am making is that Paul did not stand at the cross alone; he stood there as part of the community of believers in the churches he founded. Both Paul's letters and the Lord's Supper encourage us to remain at the cross as our first true home on earth. The Christian "Way" is undoubtedly the way of the cross, which is the way of the suffering of Christ.[6] In taking up our own cross and following Christ, we take our own suffering to the cross of Christ and then share in his suffering.

A further problem I have with the Catholic formulation is that if we take the crucifixion of Jesus, and our own crucifixion, as our sole focus for eternity, we are confronted by a blessed meaninglessness and a false view of grace. The great suffering of the crucifixion is only meaningful for the church in view of the hope of resurrection, which bestows infinite meaning on the cross. We see this link clearly in Philippians 3:10–11, where Paul follows his great catalogue of suffering with the statement that the purpose for which he has endured is "that I may know him and the power of his resurrection, and may share his sufferings, becoming like him in his death, that by any means possible I may attain the resurrection from the dead."

---

6. The Christian faith was originally known as "the Way" (e.g. Acts 9:2).

The crucifixion and the resurrection are inviolably linked. The ultimate purpose of Paul's suffering with Christ is to attain "the resurrection from the dead." In grace, the meaning of the crucifixion is resurrection, both of Christ and of all the believers who constitute the body of Christ. Romans 6:5 has similar force: "For if we have been united with him in a death like his, we shall certainly be united with him in a resurrection like his."

Paul's greatest teaching on the resurrection is found in 1 Corinthians 15. There he has this to say:

> If Christ has not been raised, then our preaching is in vain, and your faith is in vain. We are even found to be misrepresenting God, because we testified about God that he raised Christ, whom he did not raise if it is true that the dead are not raised. For if the dead are not raised, not even Christ has not been raised. And if Christ has not been raised, your faith is futile and you are still in your sins. Then those also who have fallen asleep in Christ have perished. If in Christ we have hope in this life only, we are of all people most to be pitied. (1 Cor 15:14–19)

In Paul's mind, there is a perfect balance of crucifixion and resurrection. The salient point for believers is that we need to be crucified with Christ (not necessarily implying shedding physical blood) in order to be resurrected with him. This is "the way" which Paul teaches. It is the path that followers of the Way must walk. To put this differently, the root cause of our suffering is finally healed in resurrection to eternal life in a new order of being.

That having been said, however,

> the glib Protestant adage, "But we worship the resurrected Christ, not the crucified Christ" finds no traction in the writings of Paul. One cannot divide Christ. There is not a "resurrected Jesus" and a "crucified Jesus." There is one Lord Jesus Christ and His resurrection possesses meaning for us only in so far as we appreciate His crucifixion. Moreover, Saint Paul indicates that if we wish to attain the resurrected glory of Christ we must first enter into the sufferings of His death.[7]

---

7. Marshall, *Catholic Perspective on Paul*, 208.

Suffering and healing

If the ultimate balance lies in the couplet of death and resurrection, the penultimate balance for Paul involves the couplet of suffering and healing, which he speaks of in the opening passage of 2 Corinthians:

> Blessed be the God and Father of our Lord Jesus Christ, the Father of mercies and God of all comfort, who comforts us in all our affliction, so that we may be able to comfort those who are in any affliction, with the comfort with which we ourselves are comforted by God. For as we share abundantly in Christ's sufferings, so through Christ we share abundantly in comfort too. If we are afflicted, it is for your comfort and salvation; and if we are comforted, it is for your comfort, which you experience when you patiently endure the same sufferings that we suffer. Our hope for you is unshaken, for we know that as you share in our sufferings, you will also share in our comfort. (2 Cor 1:3–7)

As the Christians in Corinth shared in the suffering of Christ, they shared also in his comfort. And this leads to a clear statement of a purpose for suffering: God comforts us in our suffering so that we may be equipped to comfort others. This implies that suffering should not be thought of in isolation but should always be seen in relation to the comfort that comes with and through healing.

The Greek term translated "comfort" in the above passage is *paraclesis*. Its root meaning is "calling to one's side" for either exhortation or consolation. More fully, it means calling someone to one's aid. Sharing in the suffering of Christ means that we are called to Christ's side, and in so doing we become ministers of this aid. This aid is the source of comfort, but sustained enduring comfort comes only from substantial healing. We see overwhelmingly that Jesus's ministry is predominately one of healing, both physical and spiritual. Through suffering we are called to share in Christ's ministry of healing. Suffering thus brings healing.

As death is to resurrection, suffering is to healing. They are two sides of the same coin. There can be no healing apart from some degree of suffering. We have here a profound (although not comprehensive) answer to the question, why do we suffer? We suffer to be healed and to bring healing to others. In healing, and only through healing, we receive sustainable comfort.

When God heals us spiritually, our whole being is healed for eternity. Being healed is being Christian, as it brings healing to others. The church suffers to gain the capacity to be a healing body for its members and for others who are drawn to its doors. And so the Corinthian church suffered to share in the suffering and the healing ministry of Christ. That is why Paul assured them, "our hope for you is unshaken, for we know that as you share in our sufferings, you will also share in our comfort" (2 Cor 1:7). He is sharing in Christ's suffering, and so then are the members of the church. The principal positive element is that this suffering will be followed by the fruit of the suffering, which is healing and real comfort.

Because of Paul's suffering for others, he was empowered to bring healing to others, so continuing the ministry of Christ. His suffering for the healing of the Gentile church in itself provided evidence of the truth and validity of his gospel. Yet though suffering is central to Paul's ministry and his apostolic identity, it does not sum up the entirety of his ministry. We must consider both Paul's power of suffering for others and his power to heal and restore life.

As with Jesus's healings, Paul's healings restored both physical and spiritual life. We see this illustrated in the case of Eutychus, who fell from a third-storey window and was declared to be dead. Paul brought him back to life (Acts 20:7–12). This miracle is said to have comforted the believers in Troas, and no doubt others who had gathered to listen to Paul's teaching. We see here the supernatural connection of suffering and healing, and that even death can be healed by Paul.

Both Eutychus and Lazarus suffered and were restored to life in this world, but this is not always the case. Suffering does not always lead to the restoration of temporal life, but it always leads to spiritual and eternal life for the believer. Physical healing is a symbol of spiritual healing, and one often follows the other.[8]

Supernatural healing reveals God. The miracle of the restoration of life to Eutychus revealed a new dimension of Paul. It showed him to be an authentic apostle endowed with apostolic power. He who had suffered like Jesus had healing power like Jesus, including the power to restore life. Paul lived in suffering, he shared in the suffering of Christ, and he lived in his healing of others that followed as a product of his own pain.

In Paul's ministry we see victory over suffering, and God was revealed to those who saw this victory. Perhaps the most mysterious and indeed shocking element of that victory is that the means of the victory was not power and glory but weakness and shame.

---

8. As in the case of the healing of the man born blind (John 9).

Humiliation and the glory of God

Paul was known for his ethical and moral integrity. He was a man of truth and great fortitude, completely loyal to his task of preaching the gospel of Christ to the Gentiles and the Jews. He was in every way a giant of faith, meek when he was with his flock, though fiery when writing letters (2 Cor 10:10). Yet what comes through from the pages of his letters is not great strength but great weakness.

In the present day Middle East, appearance is everything, and honour comes through the appearance of power. The same dynamic was at work in Paul's time, most prominently through Rome. The Romans used naked power to conquer and dominate the known world. The Jewish religious authorities enjoyed wielding the power they derived from being the keepers of the law. Both groups misappropriated power that they believed to be the power of God (or the gods). But the power of God is the force and energy of being. It was what Adam and Eve wanted when they sought God's knowledge. They believed that it would give them the freedom of self-determination. The great delusion is that power is the means of glory for the one who holds it.

In modern secular thought, power is often associated with the fitness that determines which species survive and evolve and which do not. The philosopher Friedrich Nietzsche[9] wrote of the superman (*Oberman*) and the master race who would have power over the servant race. Influenced by such thinking, Adolf Hitler defined pure Aryans (Germans) as the master race and consigned the Jews and other groups to the inferior servant race.

By contrast, the Son of God came into the world with powerless parents in the weakness and vulnerability of human childhood. Immediately after his birth, Mary and Joseph had to flee to Egypt to avoid the assault of the powerful king who sought to murder the baby. From the time of his entry into the world in a human body, the Son of God was persecuted. He is the Suffering Servant of Isaiah 53, the Lamb of God who came to suffer and die as a ransom for sinners (Mark 10:45). There seemed to be no power in his sacrificial death on the cross; it gave every appearance of weakness. Indeed Christ's life from birth to the cross displays great meekness, for he laid down his divine power and made no attempt to wield it against his enemies.

Saul of Tarsus, however, wielded his power as a Jewish leader and rabbi, but this power was removed when he came to conversion on the Damascus road. What followed was a pattern of humiliation and weakness. Yet Paul

---

9. Nietzsche, *Will to Power*.

rejoiced in this weakness "for he understood that weakness was the means by which the powerful word of the cross took effect in people's lives."[10] Paul had heard God say, "My grace is sufficient for you, for my power is made perfect in weakness," and he responded, "Therefore I will boast all the more gladly of my weaknesses, so that the power of Christ may rest upon me" (2 Cor 12:9).

In the weakness of Christ is hidden the infinite, eternal and absolute power of God being brought to bear for the salvation of sinful humanity. For those who have eyes to see, the power and glory of the grace of God is seen in the human weakness of Jesus. What we might term the weakness of the cross is, I propose, the essential element that draws human beings and changes their hearts. Indeed the weakness of the cross is the pathos[11] that breaks human hearts. It is the amazing revelation of the grace of God that causes sinful human beings to repent.

Paul's weakness, his pathos, is in amazing contrast with his triumph in the power of the risen Christ and is almost miraculous in its effect on those who witness it. He was continually humiliated and shamed, and continually triumphant. The essential triumph was that Gentiles were persuaded to accept and follow the Jewish Messiah. They knew nothing of this Messiah. Few Gentiles had encountered Jesus himself during his earthly ministry. Thus while the pathos of Jesus and the cross touched a multitude of Jews, it would not have affected the Gentiles. Moreover Paul's new teaching about the death and resurrection of a man who was God would have been strange to Gentile minds steeped in the teaching of Socrates and Plato.[12] Yet Paul, talking from the praxis of profound suffering, becomes the means God used to reach and convict Gentile hearts and minds and to establish churches filled with Gentiles.

It was the pathos of Paul as the intrinsic and real extension of the pathos of Jesus that enabled him to accomplish all this. This was the triumph of Paul's pathos as an authentic extension of the pathos of Christ. We might say that Paul was a type of Christ to the Gentiles, while Paul's great focus was the cross of Jesus.

Paul's weakness finds its zenith in his humiliation and shame. He communicates this humiliation in his letters, and sees it as sharing in Christ's humiliation. In this humiliation is the essence of the persuasive force to believe. The humiliation is the cost of bringing others to salvation.

---

10. Schreiner, *Paul – Apostle of God's Glory*, 99.

11. I take pathos to mean a poignancy that evokes sadness and even a sense of tragedy. The cross has great pathos, as also does the suffering of Paul. This pathos draws human hearts.

12. We see evidence of this in Paul's interaction with the philosophers in Athens (Acts 17:22–31).

Here I want to introduce the concept of the humiliation of God, that is, God taking on himself the full shame experienced in the human arena. It was human shame that Paul wore as a mark of his ministry. But as in the case of Christ, through this shame and this humiliation came glory. This is the glory of the grace of God.

Raising the Cross

We have now identified three essential couplets, death and resurrection, suffering and healing, and humiliation and the glory of God. Resurrection, healing and glory are all supernatural. Death, suffering and humiliation are the means of the valid re-entry of the transcendence of God into human finitude. Resurrection is the ultimate work of the Son, healing is the work of the Holy Spirit, and glory is the triumph of the Trinity.

We are, I believe at the heart of Paul's amazing vision as perhaps the most outstanding apostle. Just as the forgiveness of God for his children must be extended through the forgiveness those children show to others (Matt 18:23–35), so the death, suffering and humiliation of the Son of God must be extended through Paul and other true and zealous believers to other people. We must all then, take up our cross, and indeed raise up our cross, as Paul did. He raised up his own cross in the hidden power of the cross of Calvary. Moses raised up a snake on a pole, and all who looked at it who had been bitten by snakes were saved. To look is to believe. Jesus said, "And I, when lifted up from the earth, will draw all people to me" (John 12:32). Paul was not raised up on a cross to draw all men to him as Jesus had been, but he was taken down into humiliation and degradation. He was imprisoned, beaten and mocked as the leader of the new faith to the Gentiles. This was the cross that Paul endured. The church today must similarly be raised on its own cross – evidenced through great suffering – in order that unbelievers today will look and believe.

If we can say that suffering is death working in us as in Paul, and that this quality of suffering leads to both our own healing and the entry into healing and abundant, or authentic, life of others, then we have gained a new perspective on the positive nature of suffering.

We may also posit that those who are not or have not suffered undeservedly for others are not equipped as ministers of the gospel to work for the extension of the kingdom of God. It is through suffering and weakness that God acts in grace to save the world. It certainly cannot be done in puny human strength and power. Neither can it be done through human wisdom and knowledge, which in the end will be seen to be foolishness before God.[13]

Completing the suffering of Christ

On the basis of all that has been said so far, we can argue that Paul's suffering was a corollary to the suffering of Christ.[14] When Paul states "Now I rejoice in what was suffered for you and I fill up in my flesh what is still lacking in regard to Christ's afflictions, for the sake of his body, which is the church" (Col 1:24 NIV), he is stating that he fills up that which is missing or incomplete in Christ's suffering by his own suffering. So Christ's suffering is extended and completed in Paul's suffering.

We understand, however, that Christ's suffering is and must be complete with respect to the salvation of sinners from every nation. Such is the import of Jesus's cry from the cross, "It is finished" (John 19:30). This being the case, Paul's suffering, while a corollary to that of Jesus, must be of a different quality. There is no saving power in the suffering of Paul, and he suffers as a sinful human being. Paul was not a lamb without blemish; he could not atone for himself, nor could he atone for the Gentiles. He expresses his profound gratitude for the fact that Jesus the Messiah died even for him "the least of the apostles" (1 Cor 15:9).

But what Paul's suffering does have in common with the suffering of Christ is that it is revelatory. It is the communicative power of the cross, not the saving power of the cross, which is lacking in the case of the Gentiles. In other words, through Paul's own suffering the passion of Christ is effectively and powerfully communicated to the Gentiles. In Paul's suffering the suffering of Christ is revealed, and so Paul's suffering, and its pathos, is the medium of revelation of the cross to the Gentiles. This was the ministry of Paul. When we remember that in the world today there are thousands of Hebrew Christians but billions of Gentile Christians, we gain a perspective on the great purpose of Paul's struggle to communicate salvation for all nations of the world.

Paul's mission is to bring in "the fullness of the Gentiles" (Rom 11:25); to achieve this he must effectively communicate the cross to the Gentiles. The Gentiles knew what a cross was, and that it was used to execute criminals, but they had no concept of a messiah, even as a political or military figure. They

---

13. This is not to say that theology is futile. It is as a result of theology that I can make this statement. Theology must seek the truth and the authentic meaning of the revelation of God, even though it will be seen as foolishness compared to the majesty and infinite wisdom of God.

14. Schreiner, *Paul – Apostle of God's Glory*, 95.

would have lacked even the most basic understanding of the Jewish sacrificial system and the concept of atonement. Yet Jesus was the Jewish Messiah, and his life, ministry and death could only be understood in terms of the tenets of the Jewish religion and the Old Testament. Jesus himself used the Old Testament Scriptures to help his disciples understand the true nature of the passion and great purpose of the cross. The Gentiles' lack of knowledge of this essential background is the only lack in the cross of Christ.

> Paul is surely not saying that the Lord Christ lacks anything as the messianic agent of God's salvation; nor does he mean that the redemptive results of his death need to be supplemented by Paul . . . .The images of a suffering Christ in Paul's writings are usually employed to illustrate and interpret his own suffering as a missionary. Here suffering is exemplary of servanthood, but not expiatory of sin. In this way Christ's suffering is logically parallel to his own; like Christ, Paul is God's "suffering servant."[15]

This extension of the motif of the suffering servant to Paul fits within the extension of Jesus's mission to Paul. Jesus's mission is the content and inspiration of Paul's own missionary task, and Jesus's suffering is seen in Paul's own life as a sufferer. Indeed Paul is authentically sharing in the mission, task and suffering of Christ, and so of God himself.[16]

Paul, in turn, reveals that this task done in this way is the responsibility and the essential life of the church in his own day and in our day. This is the way in which the "fullness of the Gentiles" will come in (Rom 11:1–24). When this happens and the Israelites return to God, the Lord will return (Rom 11:25–26).

The words "I fill up in my flesh" stress Paul's personal sacrifice: "I fill up (*antanaplēroo*) in my flesh – is to complete his mission: to present to you the word of God in its fullness (*plērosai*)."[17]

> The means by which Paul "fulfils" the word of God by bringing the gospel to the Gentiles is suffering. The "filling up" of Christ's afflictions is the pathway by which the gospel is "fulfilled in the lives of the Gentiles."[18]

The message that was hidden from the Gentiles in the Christ event is now revealed to them through Paul, a suffering servant.

---

15. Wall, *Colossians and Philemon*, 87.
16. The suffering of God is dealt with in chapter 10.
17. Wall, *Colossians and Philemon*, 88.
18. Schreiner, *Paul – Apostle of God's Glory*, 101–102.

The suffering of Christ on the cross was effectively a revelation of the grace of God to the Jews. Gentiles who were exposed to that revelation believed (e.g. the thief on the cross and the Roman soldier). Paul's suffering was effectively a revelation of the grace of God to the Gentiles, but this revelation did not focus on Paul but on Christ. In Paul's suffering the mystery of the cross is revealed to those outside of Israel.

Reflective Summary

The life of Paul reveals something essential about the nature of suffering: suffering and victory over suffering reveals God. Throughout the miracles of Jesus we see victory over human suffering as the blind see, the lame walk, the dead are raised. The power of revelation in these cases is undeniable. Jesus himself delayed coming quickly to his friend Lazarus in order that he would die and be raised, resulting in many converts (John 11:38–44). In Paul's suffering and his overcoming of his suffering there is a sense of miracle. And one of the key features of miracles is that they reveal God.

The passion of Jesus is seen to continue in the suffering of Paul. Jesus's prayer in Gethsemane, "if it be possible, let this cup pass from me" (Matt 26:39) is reflected in Paul's, "Wretched man that I am! Who will deliver me from this body of death?" (Rom 7:24). Implicit in the second part of the verse is Paul's total resolve to do the will of Christ.

Paul had the great privilege of "sharing in the suffering of Christ" and so do all Christians who suffer. This suffering was the necessary experience that equipped Paul to continue, with great efficacy, the healing ministry of Christ among the Gentiles and, of course, the Jews. In this dynamic we see that suffering is a vital element in healing, and healing, not suffering, is the result.

In Paul's utter focus on the death and resurrection of Christ, we are at the core dialectic of salvation. Jesus dies and is the first fruit of resurrection. His resurrection secures the resurrection of all who believe and are in him. Christians must die twice: they must die to self, to their own fallen egos, and they must undergo a physical death. But through the atonement of Christ this death has no sting. It is a going down not to the pit but to the gateway of eternal life.

The true nature of the death of Christians is resurrection to eternal life. Similarly the true nature of the suffering of true believers is healing. Our proper focus then is not on death and suffering but resurrection and healing.

From the writings of Paul we have the revelation of suffering as entirely positive, meaningful and even joyful. Suffering does not defeat us; rather, it produces a right and humble attitude through which the sanctifying work of the Holy Spirit takes effect. Suffering kills the old man or woman and prepares the way for the new.

Paul's suffering is most essentially the channel of Christ's suffering to the Gentile churches. They must follow his example of suffering, and so the churches themselves must suffer as the body of Christ. The example extends to Christian families and individual Christians. Suffering in the body of Christ is never entirely individual, but the cross that each must take up and bear is individual. In this, each must bear the weight of their own burden, but in bearing this weight we also help bear the weight of the cross of Christ. Paul is our example of helping to bear the cross of Christ. And as we too bear the cross of Christ, we too play our part in the healing ministry of Christ.

12

The Suffering of the Church: Persecution

In this chapter we consider the form of suffering for God known as persecution and its bedfellow risk, or living in perpetual risk. At its most extreme, persecution can result in martyrdom, as was the case for Stephen and others in the early church. Underlying persecution are lies, that is, false accusations. We restate the presupposition that mission is the serious expression of association with Christ, which can be perceived as a form of religious and social revolution that produces, or results in, persecution. Persecution then is a necessary part of divine providence and so cannot prevent God's ultimate triumph.

On 12 February 2015, twenty-one Coptic Christians were beheaded by the terrorist group known as ISIL. The terrorists posted a video of the killings, showing the men singing and praying to Christ as they went to their deaths. At a memorial service for these men in a Coptic church in Amman, Jordan, the patriarch preached that the blood of these beloved brothers was an extension of the blood of Christ.

These men are only a few of the vast number of Christians who have died for their faith since the earliest days of the church and who continue to die to this day. "Statistics show that since the church's inception nearly 70 million Christians have been killed for their faith with 65% of these martyrs dying in the twentieth century alone. Including victims of persecution who do not die for their faith, but rather live daily with threats, ridicule, torture, and/or imprisonment would further inflate the numbers."[1] It is thus vitally important that we reflect on the nature of persecution and how we as Christians are to understand it and withstand it.

Defining Persecution

The English word "persecution" comes from the Latin *per sequor*, which means to hunt down, pursue or follow. The Greek noun with the same meaning is *diogmos*, which has the meanings of putting to flight, driving away, and pursuing. In the Old Testament the Hebrew word that is used is *radaph*, the meanings of which include oppression, harassment and affliction. Throughout the Bible there are examples of physical, social, mental, and spiritual persecution.

For our purposes, persecution can be defined as systematic oppression that seeks the destruction of an individual or group by another individual or group through inflicting suffering, harassment, isolation, imprisonment, fear, pain or exclusion. Sometimes a group may be targeted because of its ethnicity, as when the Nazis persecuted the Jews in Europe, Hutus attacked Tutsis in Rwanda, and Whites oppressed Blacks in apartheid South Africa. Such persecution sees the other group as different, and such difference is perceived as threatening in a fallen world. Sometimes a group may be targeted for religious reasons. This differs from ethnic persecution in that the difference is perceived to be more pervasive as it affects the whole of life. Religious persecution often involves a campaign to exterminate, drive away, or subjugate people because of their religious beliefs. Such persecution is not only directed at Christians of course; it is also part of the experience of adherents of other religions like Judaism and Islam.

The Nature of Persecution

Persecution or suffering for God is the type of suffering Christ referred to in the Sermon on the Mount: "Blessed are those who are persecuted for righteousness' sake, for theirs is the kingdom of heaven. Blessed are you when others revile you and persecute you and utter all kinds of evil against you falsely on my

---

1. Tiesze, "Striving Towards a Theology of Persecution." Originally presented as "Mission in Contexts of Violence: Forging Theologies of Persecution and Martyrdom" at the Northeast Regional Conference of the Evangelical Missiological Society, April 8, 2006. Statistics derived from David B. Barrett and Todd M. Johnson, *World Christian Trends: AD 30 – AD 2200* (Pasadena: William Carey Library, 2001), 227, 229.

account. Rejoice and be glad, for your reward is great in heaven for so they persecuted the prophets who were before you" (Matt 5:10–11).

All Christians will experience undeserved suffering and suffering for others (see chapter 4), but the question is whether we will all experience suffering for God, or more specifically for Christ. Paul certainly assumed so, telling Timothy,

> You, however, have followed my teaching, my conduct, my aim in life, my faith, my patience, my love, my steadfastness, my persecutions and sufferings that happened to me at Antioch, at Iconium, and at Lystra – which persecutions I endured; yet from them all the Lord rescued me. Indeed, all who desire to live a godly life in Christ Jesus will be persecuted. (2 Tim 3:10–12)

All Christians who strive to deny themselves, follow Christ and confess him will experience some degree of persecution, no matter where they live in the world. The exceptions are those who hide their light under a basket and those who are backslidden. But the rest, both those with deep faith and those of weak faith, may well face some level of persecution. When contemplating this reality, it is important to remember Charles Spurgeon's words:

> Between the very lowest degree of faith and a state of unbelief there is a great gulf. An immeasurable abyss yawns between the man who has even the smallest faith in Christ and the man who has none. One is a living man, though feeble, the other is "dead in trespasses and sins"; the one is a justified man, the other is "condemned already, because he has not believed in the name of the only-begotten Son of God." The weakest believer is on the road to heaven; the other, having no faith, is going the downward road, and he will find his portion at last among the unbelievers . . . Although we speak like this of believers as all of one company, yet there is a great distance between weak faith and strong faith. Thank God it is a distance upon the one safe road – the King's highway. No gulf divides little faith from great faith.[2]

Persecution may not come to those who have little faith, because they might not be able to bear it, but those who have strong faith will know the suffering of the pain of persecution to some extent. Great faith must confess the truth of the gospel of Jesus Christ or it would not be great faith. Yet persecution

---
2. Spurgeon's Sermons in the Metropolitan Tabernacle Pulpit, Sermon 2173 available at https://www.thekingdomcollective.com/spurgeon/sermon/2173/.

of Christians comes in many shapes and sizes. It is not all violent and not all apparently life-threatening or of the same intensity.

Persecution and living for Christ

In Western societies that claim to focus on human rights, persecution is understood in political, ethnic or perhaps economic terms. There is little evidence of explicit religious persecution of Christians. Thus Christians in the West are often "unable to see the subtle, mild, and infrequent persecution that does occur in their societies. Consequently, what is perceived to be non-existent is not appropriately addressed or it is left to those portions of the church who may experience persecution more."[3] However, rising secularism and government legislation aimed at protecting and empowering minority groups may have the effect of opening the door to state persecution of committed Christians who oppose certain lifestyles. What we may also see is social persecution, that is, discrimination against an individual or group, effectively driving them away or with the intent of driving them away and making them outcasts.

In other parts of the world, however, the physical persecution of Christians continues on a large scale. Recently, there has been well-documented persecution of Christians in the Middle East and Asia by Islamic fundamentalist governments and groups such as ISIL. Christians in Northern Nigerian are under attack by Boko Haram. Similar fundamentalist groups exist in other African countries. Persecution is also widespread in much of Asia.

For Christians, persecution may be understood as "suffering for righteousness,"[4] which it is, since Christ is our righteousness and we are suffering for him. But we could also look at it from the perspective of Paul, who taught that the reality of our suffering in Christ is that it is sharing in Christ's suffering, as we saw in the previous chapter. However, I would argue that whereas undeserved suffering and suffering for others are sharing *in* the suffering of Christ, persecution is of a different order in that it is suffering *for* Christ, just as the Old Testament prophets suffered for God.

Of course, the categories of suffering are not watertight compartments; they overlap and each type of suffering may be involved in some of the others. But when we share *in* the suffering of Christ, we also share in his healing ministry, both for ourselves and for others (2 Cor 1:3–4), whereas when we

---

3. Tieszen, "Striving Towards a Theology of Persecution," 3–4.
4. Penner, *In the Shadow of the Cross*.

suffer *for* Christ through persecution, the outcome is not necessarily healing on earth, although there is a great heavenly reward. To be persecuted and prevail is to store up riches in heaven, as the letters to the churches in the book of Revelation make clear. Temporary oppression on earth leads to an eternal reward.

Jesus predicted that his disciples would suffer persecution (John 16:1–4), and this prediction began to be fulfilled soon after his death. In Acts 3, we read of Peter and John's healing of a man who had been lame from birth. This healing took place at the temple gate and was specifically done "in the name of Jesus Christ" (Acts 3:6). The general amazement at what had happened led to a crowd forming, and Peter seized the opportunity to preach about Jesus, accusing the people he was preaching to of murdering Christ, the Author of Life, and urging them to repent. The apostles insisted that it was not they who had healed the lame man; the healing was by faith in Christ's name.

The two apostles were then arrested, and dragged into court. Once again, Christ's name became the focus as they were asked "By what power or by what name did you do this?" (Acts 4:7). The court before which they appeared may well have been the same one that condemned Jesus and sent him to Pilate for execution. Despite knowing this, Peter "filled with the Holy Spirit" fearlessly answered,

> Rulers of the people and elders . . . let it be known to all of you and to all the people of Israel that by the name of Jesus Christ of Nazareth, whom you crucified, whom God raised from the dead – by him this man [the lame beggar] is standing before you well. This Jesus is the stone that was rejected by you, the builders, which has become the cornerstone. And there is salvation in no one else, for there is no other name under heaven given among men by which we must be saved. (Acts 4:10–12)

The rulers were afraid to take action against popular figures like Peter and John – many people had seen the healing and heard Peter preach, and some 5000 people had believed in Jesus (Acts 4:40). So they merely ordered them "not to speak or teach at all in the name of Jesus" (Acts 4:15–18).

Association with Jesus is still association with the name of Jesus, and this is the root of persecution. Evil powers hate and fear those who speak the truth in the name of Jesus. They know that this truth shows up their own corruption and threatens their power. That is why they seek to silence those who proclaim him as Lord.

Peter and John refused to be silenced, despite repeated attempts to do so (Acts 4:19–20; 5:17–18, 40), and the young church continued to grow rapidly, attracting "even a great many of the priests" (Acts 6:7). God intervened to protect the apostles when they were attacked, using both miraculous means (Acts 6:19–20) and the human wisdom of some of their enemies (Acts 6:34–39). But as the number of believers grew, so did the ferocity of their opponents. The same dynamic is at work today.

Persecution and dying for Christ

It is clear from the New Testament that God does not always intervene to protect his people. Sometimes those who are persecuted have to flee (Acts 8:1) and sometimes those who are persecuted lose their lives for Christ. Those who endure this most extreme form of persecution are known as martyrs and are honoured for their very special end of life on earth and entry to heaven. Martyrdom is the supreme sacrifice and a testimony to real and true faith to those who witness or hear of the martyrs' death. That truth is present in the very word "martyr," which comes from the Greek *martys*, which means "witness." A profound witness to the truth that Christ is the Son of God is the holy purpose of martyrdom in the will and economy of God. The act of suffering up to and including death for Christ is the ultimate sacrifice for God. It was the noble end of all the apostles, except the traitor Judas who committed suicide and the faithful John, who is said to have died of old age. Let us look at some of the accounts of martyrdom in the New Testament and the early church.

Stephen, the first Christian martyr, is described as "a man full of faith and of the Holy Spirit" (Acts 6:5). He served as one of the seven deacons appointed by the apostles to serve the rapidly growing church in Jerusalem and he "was doing great wonders and signs among the people" (Acts 6:8) when he was arrested on a trumped up charge of blasphemy. In court, Stephen gave a powerful address in which he outlined the history of the people of Israel from the time God first appeared to Abraham, through the events of the Exodus, to the building of Solomon's temple, and the ministry of the prophets that followed. Then he accused his hearers of following in the footsteps of their ancestors who had resisted and persecuted those prophets who foretold the coming of the Messiah, "the Righteous One" (Acts 7:1–53).

His words enraged the court, but Stephen did not keep silent. Instead he told them about the vision he was seeing: "Behold, I see the heavens opened, and the Son of Man standing at the right hand of God" (Acts 7:55–56). He was seized, dragged out of the city and stoned to death. But as the stones rained down, Stephen cried out, "Lord Jesus, receive my spirit" and then uttered his last words, "Lord, do not hold this sin against them" (Acts 7:59–60).

Stephen's courageous speech uncompromisingly proclaimed Jesus and showed up the hypocrisy of the Jewish leaders. Both his teaching and his life showed them to be liars who created an environment of lies that they peddled as the true religion of the people of God. Yet what also stands out about Stephen is that he was superlatively Christ-like. His dying words are strikingly similar to Jesus's words on the cross, and reveal his love even for his persecutors.

Stephen's vision of Christ standing at the right hand of the Father spoke to him and speaks to us of the triumph of God and the absolute integrity and justice of God's providence. The truth is real and eternal, whereas the lies concocted against us are paper castles and plastic walls. False religions, ideologies and political systems may appear to prosper, but they are built on lies and hypocrisy. They are an appearance with no substance, and will crumble before the truth of Christ.

James the brother of John was the first of the apostles to die a martyr's death. He had been one of the inner circle of the disciples (James, John and Peter), yet God allowed him to die by the sword at the orders of King Herod Agrippa at a time when persecution was ravaging the church (Acts 12:1–2).

James the brother of Jesus, also known as James the Just, was the author of the letter of James in the New Testament. He became the leader of the church in Jerusalem (see Acts 12:17; 15:13; 21:18) and has been described as the first bishop of Jerusalem. Eusebius's account of his martyrdom in AD 62 presents him as a man of great virtue and faith who was deeply respected even by non-Christians. His persecutors were the same people who had persecuted Jesus, Paul and Stephen. They publicly confronted James, demanding that he cease preaching and renounce his faith in Christ. When James refused, he was thrown from the roof of the temple, and when this fall did not kill him he was stoned and finally beaten to death with a club.[5]

In these accounts of martyrdom we see familiar themes such as attempts to prevent believers from speaking in the name of Christ and the martyr's refusal to remain silent. We see also that those who were persecuted were admired by believers and had a good reputation with non-believers, all of

---

5. Eusebius, *Ecclesiastical History* 2.23. "The Martyrdom of James, who was called the brother of the Lord."

which contributed to their being singled out for attack. But we also see that their steadfastness was an enduring witness to the authenticity of Christ – both in the record of their words and on the tombstone that Eusebius says was erected over James the Just. Their witness showed up the lies and deceit of their persecutors. In time, the church came to accord special authority to words of those who were imprisoned awaiting martyrdom as they were believed to speak truth from God. Paying the ultimate cost came to be seen as the ultimate honour. It was an honour that Paul too shared, although we do not know the precise details of his death.

Martyrdom arises from a murderous hatred of Christ and his people by dark forces of opposition. Those who live in regions of extreme persecution know that the forces arrayed against them are very real and very deadly. Yet Christians there live courageously and are prepared to die for their faith if called on to do so. Some may condemn such deaths as pointless, yet as Jim Elliot said, "He is no fool who gives what he cannot keep to gain that which he cannot lose."[6] Such acts of faith proclaim that the one in whom the martyrs have faith is alive and true and is worth dying for.

Persecution as God's Plan

When the apostle Paul revisited churches he had established in Lystra, Iconium and Pisidian Antioch, he spent his time "strengthening the souls of the disciples, encouraging them to continue in the faith, and saying that through many tribulations we must enter the kingdom of God" (Acts 14:22). He was not intimidated by the prospect of suffering because he understood that it is rooted in divine providence. It is part of following in Christ's footsteps and will lead to believers sharing his eventual triumph.

Persecution as divine providence

Persecution is rejection; its goal is destruction of human identity even to the point of death. It is thus the antithesis of the gospel of acceptance and eternal life. It is a repetition of the tension between God's creation and the forces of destruction that have been at work since the fall. As such, it has a place in God's plan for the world.

---

6. Jim Elliot was a missionary killed in Ecuador. The quotation comes from his diary entry for 28 October 1949. See Elizabeth Elliot, *Shadow of the Almighty* (New York: Harper Collins, 2009), 15.

> Persecution is not viewed as an accident by Luke. It is not simply an obstacle to be overcome or the unanticipated or surprising negative response to the gospel. Persecution is firmly located within divine providence.
>
> The persecution of the disciples in Acts fulfils the prophecies of Jesus made in the Gospel. Jesus as a prophet of God reveals the will of God for his disciples. Included in that will is their suffering persecution because of their association with him. . . . The persecution of the apostles and Peter in Acts 4:1–31 and 5:17–42 fulfils these prophecies in a particularly poignant manner. The inability of the Sanhedrin to contradict the testimony of Peter and John is in fulfilment of Jesus's prophecy that the opponents of the disciples would not be able to resist them (Luke 21:15 and Acts 4:14). Stephen is martyred just as Jesus had predicted . . .
>
> Since these revelations are from the mouth of God the narrator assures the reader, in the words of Paul, "I have faith in God that it will be exactly as I have been told."[7]

Nothing that happened to the apostles, or will happen to us, falls outside the providence of God.

Persecution as continuity with Christ

There is continuity between the persecution of the prophets, the persecution of Jesus, the persecution of the apostles, and the persecution of the church. Regardless of whether this persecution comes from worldly authorities or religious leaders, we are part of this pattern, and can say that to be persecuted for Christ is to be joined with Christ in his conflict and passion. After having been beaten, the apostles rejoiced "that they were counted worthy to suffer dishonour for the name" (Acts 5:41). They recognized that suffering is nothing to be ashamed of, but is significant in that it connects us firmly to the *missio dei*, that is, the way God works in the world. Through persecution, we become part of *Heilsgeschichte*, part of the body of Christ that lives to tell the truth about God to the world.

The value of suffering for God is inestimable. It is an infinite value and is therefore the greatest of riches. I believe that the truth about God and his creation, proclaimed and taught, will produce persecution, and truth and persecution are the essence of infinite worth in the finite world. When you

---

7. Cunningham, *Through Many Tribulations*, 287.

are persecuted for the truth about God who is love, you are a disciple of Christ, you are a partaker of the divine nature, and you have a living and fruitful faith. While you are in prison you are free.[8]

Persecution and the triumph of God

Human beings may throw all kinds of obstacles in his servants' path, but nothing can stop God's purposes from being fulfilled, as Gamaliel warned the Sanhedrin (Acts 5:39). This truth was vividly demonstrated in the three prison rescues recorded in the book of Acts (Acts 5:19; 12:6–7; 16:25–34). They are evidence that "the word of God cannot be imprisoned."[9] God allows his servants who preach the gospel to be persecuted to the point of imprisonment, but then he steps in to rescue them, leading to the salvation of sinners. Persecution becomes an occasion for the triumph of God. Persecution captures souls, but God sets them free. The truth cannot remain in prison; it will come out.

I believe that this quality of being set free through and from persecution – moving from radical rejection to utter acceptance – is the reward of persecution. Being persecuted for Christ is suffering for God, and the freedom of release is a wonderful eternal reward.

The Character (Ethos) of Persecution

Lies and false accusations

Persecution relies heavily on false accusations and lies about the persecuted. We see this on the mundane level where persecutors sometimes resort to character assassination. But it is also true on the spiritual level, where persecution can be seen as an attempt to turn the truth about God and his people into a lie. It is a manifestation of what Paul was referring to when he spoke of the "ungodliness and unrighteousness of men, who by their unrighteousness suppress the truth" and consequently exchange "the truth about God for a lie" (Rom 1:18, 25). The ultimate goal of persecution is to suppress the light and maintain the confusion of darkness so that wicked religious and even national leaders can maintain their status and power. Its roots are satanic, for in its hatred of God and the truth it reflects the nature of the one whom Jesus described as "a murderer from the beginning, and . . . the father of lies" (John 8:44).

---

8. Compare Matt 5:10 and 11, 2 Pet 1:4.
9. Cunningham, *Through Many Tribulations*, 261.

Look at the first lie: "You will not surely die," the serpent said to the woman. "For God knows that when you eat of it your eyes will be opened, and you will be like God, knowing good and evil" (Gen 3:4–5). This lie spawned hamartia and an alternative world view that seeks to put God to flight and see him effectively murdered in human hearts. Thus we now live in a fallen world, an inauthentic world based on lies about God built upon the primary lie. The maintenance of this lie requires the careful covering or hiding of the truth through sowing confusion, false teaching and doctrine. The face of the truth cannot be allowed to be seen.

Alexandre Dumas's book *The Man in the Iron Mask* tells the story of two princes who were twins. Confusion over who would be king posed a threat to the monarchy, and so one of the twins was imprisoned and fitted with an iron mask so that no one would recognize him. Similarly, the truth about the evil world is well hidden under a mask. Those sent by God to proclaim the truth, namely the prophets and the incarnate Son of God himself, were murdered to maintain the lie. Little has changed in the era of the church, which is called to proclaim the truth of the kingdom of God and which has also had to endure persecution and martyrdom. Those in power and authority in the dark world of lies still rage against God and his Son (Ps 2:1–3). The world is in a perpetual state of war with God and with itself, and the first victim of war is the truth.

Persecution today still operates through a complex system of lies that are used to accuse believers, both in the Middle East and Asia and in the West.

Mission and division

The presence and power of the Holy Spirit in true missionaries of the gospel produced thousands of converts in the early days of the church. As the number of Christians grew, so did the ranks of their persecutors. But the believers continued in their missionary task of proclaiming the truth about God that is the gospel of Jesus Christ, and will continue to do so until Christ returns.

The events in the book of Acts show that there can be no mission without persecution. We also see that mission is revolutionary in the sense that it insists that "there is salvation in no one else, for there is no other name under heaven given among men by which we must be saved" (Acts 4:12). This implies that all other ways of seeking salvation are flawed and empty, like fig trees that bear no fruit. Christians uphold that which is authentic and true against that which is inauthentic and untrue.

Authentic mission is thus a form of revolution. It uses the language of revolution in that it points to the corruption in human societies, and thus also to the corruption of human authorities and powers. It understands that the world is in rebellion against God and loves lies, and it seeks to change this by the revolutionary approach of proclaiming the truth and seeking to draw others to Christ.

This revolution is non-violent and works by persuasion empowered by the Holy Spirit. But it does produce division among the people and persecution by those who have set themselves against Christ. This was foretold by Christ:

> Do not think that I have come to bring peace on earth; I have not come to bring peace, but a sword. For I have come to set a man against his father, and a daughter against her mother, and a daughter-in-law against her mother-in-law; and a person's enemies will be those of his own household. Whoever loves father or mother more than me is not worthy of me, and whoever loves son or daughter more than me is not worthy of me. (Matt 10:34–37)

In various parts of the world, family members have reported others in the family who believe in and follow Christ to hostile authorities, fulfilling Jesus's prophecy, "Brother will deliver brother over to death, and the father his child, and children will rise against parents and have them put to death" (Matt 10:21). This is not what Christ desires, but is an inevitable result of proclaiming the truth to a hostile world.

Mission and persecution are thus the poles of a dialectic. Persecution is the antithesis of mission. We have all heard the saying that "the blood of the martyrs is the seed of the church." Insofar as this is true, it is because authentic mission always takes place in a context of persecution. This is because mission divides people into new believers who join the mission dynamic and are themselves the fruit of it, and those who will not believe in Christ and who become the persecutors.[10] There is often no neutral zone; only a harsh dialectical reality.

The persecution of those who are good and true followers of Christ is itself the witness of true mission. The lifeblood of the church must remain the truth that is proclaimed and lived, but this truth is evidenced by persecution and guaranteed by the Holy Spirit. Those who have suppressed the truth and exchanged it for a lie must persecute those who proclaim the truth and teach it in the power of the Spirit and the name of Jesus Christ.

Mission calls people to leave the place of powerlessness and through faith in the truth of Jesus Christ, the Son of God, enter authentic or abundant life.

---

10. I am referring here mostly to mission in Eastern countries rather than in the West, although some forms of minor persecution do occur in pluralistic countries.

Abundant life proclaims Christ; it is compelled to do so. And the mission to proclaim this vital new life evokes persecution.

Persecution as Risk

The maintenance of a full commitment to Christ in a context that strongly opposes Christianity and hates Christians is done at considerable risk. It invites personal threats, even to one's life. Those who live in such circumstances know what it is to live with a deep fear of what form of persecution is coming next. This fear is the root of the pain of risk. But let us now look risk in the face and reflect on it in detail.

Risk as inner suffering (angst)

We have already understood, I hope, that suffering is a necessary part of Christian life and of our moral and ontological growth (growth of our being). The same applies to the suffering that comes with risk. Such suffering is also normal for Christian life. To risk for God is to suffer for God. In this it is noble.

The fear and suffering involved when the risk is substantial moves into the realm of angst. As you will remember, angst is prompted by our awareness of the threat of non-being. It can involve an acute sense of loss. Those who are enduring risk for God can experience the fire of profound ontological and existential insecurity that increases as the risk increases. The greater the risk, the greater the angst. To follow Christ and be openly associated with him is to accept this pain.

The balancing factor, indeed the counterweight, to this is faith and trust in God. Faith is the healing and calming balm of the pain of risk. Indeed it is the counterbalance of risk. The joy of total submission to Christ renders risk powerless. Jesus the Son of God is our eternal and absolute security. Therefore, risk for Jesus's sake is not risk as the world understands it. This is life against the currents of the world. Risk in God through stepping out in faith and remaining in faith is eternal life. Yet for those living in substantial risk, this faith is continually being tested.

To be alive in Christ, Christians must take risks. All Christians should to some extent be out on a limb. It is a blessed, rich and fruitful state of being. Our weakness as human beings means that from time to time our faith wanes and the sharp pain of risk returns. The reality is that when we are out on a limb with no visible safety net, our life, identity and security are on the line. All of our eggs are in one basket. That is why those who go out to proclaim Christ are, in the world's terms at least, fools for Christ.

Risk as vulnerability

In general terms risk is vulnerability. To take risks and live with risk is to enter the emotional and spiritual state of vulnerability, in which we are dependent on something outside of ourselves. Of course, all human beings are vulnerable. We are dependent on medical doctors for our lives. We are dependent on those who supply our food, from farmers to shopkeepers. We are dependent on governments and banks and oil producers and aircraft pilots. We have become dependent on machines and almost universally on computers. In the post-modern twenty-first century world, advanced technology has produced a new dependency on scientists and technicians, who have become the high priests of modern life.

All vulnerability must involve a type of faith, whether it be faith in a surgeon or faith in a pilot and the integrity of an aircraft. But faith in God for all things in one's life involves a different and higher order of vulnerability.

Saving faith involves believing in, utterly trusting in and surrendering our wills to God the Father, God the Son and God the Holy Spirit. It involves our minds, our wills and our desires. This is not faith in the finitude or in anything finite but in the infinite and transcendent Person. Through saving faith, we let go of security in finite beings and lay hold of the infinite, eternal Person who is beyond our horizons, utterly transcending us, yet radically available to us in saving love. What I am saying here is that our vulnerability in Christ is our capacity to let go of our limited finite being and, in holy fear, grasp infinite being as our true home and fountain of eternal life.

In Europe and America, the eighteenth century is known as the era of the Enlightenment. It was a time when philosophers like Immanuel Kant attacked the viability and integrity of Christian theology. In response, Friedrich Schleiermacher sought to reconstruct Christian theology in a form more acceptable to those who demanded that reason and not faith was the only ground of knowledge and truth. Accordingly he sought to move the ground of theology from faith to feelings.[11] Most centrally he defined religious faith as a sense of utter dependence. I am not generally in agreement with Schleiermacher, but I do find his concept of a sense of utter dependence is

---

11. Schleiermacher, *The Christian Faith*; Gerrish, *A Prince of the Church: Schleiermacher and the Beginnings of Modern Theology*; and most especially F. W. Schleiermacher, *On Religion*.

enlightening. I believe that we get closest to God when we sense our utter dependence on him. When we come to the place of almost total abandonment of the self and total giving over of ourselves to God, we are totally and utterly vulnerable. We confess this vulnerability and our total inability and weakness to God and we trust him totally with our lives. In this vulnerable state of confession and utter dependency, God becomes immediately present to us.

This powerful feeling of utter dependence comes when believers feel small. It comes at the end of our journey of risk and vulnerability as it is the end of ourselves. The prophet Elijah risked his life when he confronted the priests of Baal on Mount Carmel and when he learned of Jezebel's threats, his awareness of his extreme vulnerability overwhelmed him. He had nowhere to go but God (1 Kgs 19:1–4). Accepting risk for God involves dependency; we have no control over the outcome.

Risk as faith in action

Risk involves stepping out in faith into vulnerability. Those who hold back from stepping out of their security base – their precious home, the place of their identity support and comfort – have somewhat of a dormant faith. Faith in action requires risk, which is always to some extent a risk of our lives.

The classic example of stepping out is, of course, Abraham who left everything – his home his security his comfort – to live in a tent. "By faith Abraham obeyed when he was called to go out to a place which he was to receive as an inheritance. And he went out, not knowing where he was going. By faith he went to live in the land of promise, as in a foreign land, living in tents with Isaac and Jacob" (Heb 11:8–9).

Abraham's faith was greatly tested in that God called him to offer the life of his son Isaac as a sacrifice. Abraham knew that Isaac was the son of the promise, and so he believed that Isaac would be raised again from the dead (Heb 11:17–20). Abraham's willingness to sacrifice his son entailed a great risk, which was why it was seen as evidence of great faith in action. Ultimately, Isaac's life was not required, but the test of Abraham's faith was.

Jesus calls Christians to show their faith in action when he tells us to take up our cross and follow him (Mark 8:34). He is calling us to leave home, to leave our worldly connections and to take a great risk in following him totally. We can thus summarize what risk in God is. It is trusting in Jesus upon whom we are utterly dependant. Risk is surrender to God in whom we believe absolutely. Risk is believing God's promises.

Hebrews 11:1 defines faith as "the conviction of things not seen." We can say that faith has to do with certainty, while risk has to do with uncertainty in this world. But in the kingdom of heaven, risk can be taken with total certainty because it is faith in action.

Risk as folly

In the world's view, risk has to do with potential loss. The higher the risk, the greater the potential for loss. Risk is always understood in negative terms as insecurity. In the world of finance, risk involves financial loss, and risky ventures are equivalent to gambling. But relationships can also be a gamble, and even marriage can be a gamble, for it too involves risk. So does leaving an old job for a new job. Risk in the world always involves some element of gambling.

Risk-as-gambling has the potential for success (gain) and therefore joy, or for failure (loss) and therefore regret and sometimes despair. Some enjoy taking calculated risks. Rock climbers and skydivers enjoy the sense of exhilaration that comes from overcoming potential danger. The greater the danger, the greater the risk, the greater the exhilaration. Those who bet on horses may enjoy a brief moment of exhilaration, but mostly they experience regret and a degree of despair. They try to add to their lives by placing their money, and so their economic substance, at risk. Through gambling, without work and without skill, they seek to increase their substance and therefore their being. In a kind of fatalistic faith, they set their hope on Lady Luck smiling on them.

But gambling is an empty faith and a false and foolish hope, and the end result is that gamblers become smaller persons, and not bigger as they desire. They suffer loss and decrease and not gain and increase. I would call their kind of risk the risk-of-idols. It is faith in something that does not exist. They place all their hopes in a false god whose temples are betting shops and casinos. This forlorn faith is the blind faith of the world in that which is empty and fruitless; again a fig tree that has no fruit.

Risk in the world requires uncertainty, and uncertainty is not boring. It is frightening, and so risk in the world requires fear as a necessary component. It also produces angst. For the majority of people, uncertainty is dangerous and frightening and so to be avoided at all costs. This avoidance we may call risk aversion. Risk aversion sees risk only in negative terms, producing negative results that one will only escape if one is extremely lucky.

Risk is a radical form of insecurity, and so taking risks adds to the feeling of insecurity and vulnerability. It is to stare loss in the face. It is to tempt providence, and so on. Taking risks is sometimes necessary, but it is considered a bad thing, to be avoided if at all possible. Indeed it is considered foolishness, worthy of mocking.

Yet if we consider the psychological phenomenon of "framing," it appears that even in the world's terms great risks are taken in the face of foolishness. Framing is the term for the boundaries on human rationality. The human mind gets overloaded, so to speak, and so what we might term adequate rationality is not applied. Human rationality in dealing with risk fails because the risk is merely framed out, as happens, for example, in the case of drinking and driving. Drunk drivers totally ignore the high risk of a serious accident.

Cultural, political and even emotional biases frame out balanced rationality, and therefore entry into great risk can occur by holding fast to the bias. Greed or jealousy can frame out risk factors, as can a crowd mentality. The result may be extreme folly.

Insurance companies insure persons and objects at premiums dependent on their probability calculations. The higher the probability of an accident or failure, the higher the cost of the policy. Probability is a way of seeking to make some form of concrete statement about uncertainty. Calculations of very high risk make a person or object uninsurable.

The world's concept of risk then is almost entirely negative; risk is something to be avoided and even feared. The pain of risk would cause extreme evasive action. The sensible world cannot live with risk. Risks taken by those who do not understand the risk they are in or who are driven to risk-taking by some kind of inner compulsion are deemed to be recipes for disaster.

Risk as putting one's life on the line

Godly risk is not a risk with money or possessions, although these things may be involved. Rather, it is total risking of one's life and being. It may be termed a Kierkegaardian "leap of faith," but it is not a leap into the darkness of an abyss, it is a leap into the light of Christ. And so it is a leap of certain hope, risking our lives to gain God. It is most definitely a risk in the fear of God beyond the world, and so is a risk taken in wisdom, for the fear of God is the beginning of wisdom. The life of the Christian could be described as total risk by living with intentionality to work for the kingdom of God on earth.

The Bible contains many verses that speak of a literal risk to life. For example, in the Old Testament, Gideon's son reminded the people of Shechem that "my father fought for you and risked his life and delivered you from the hand of Midian" (Judg 9:17). Here and in many other locations, the risk is undertaken for the sake of others. The New Testament also speaks of Barnabas and Paul being commended by the apostles as "men who have risked their lives for the name of our Lord Jesus Christ" (Acts 15:26). Later Paul praises his co-workers Prisca and Aquila for having "risked their necks for my life" (Rom 16:4). In another letter, he says that Epaphroditus "nearly died for the work of Christ, risking his life to complete what was lacking in your service to me" (Phil 2:30) and commends him to the care of the church in Philippi. Clearly these verses speak of the ultimate risk, the risk of death. The early missionaries willingly risked not only their property and their occupations but also their lives to gain and proclaim the kingdom of God.

Risk as sacrifice

In 2 Samuel 23:13–17 we have an account of an incident that happened one harvest season when David had set up his base in the cave of Adullam. Given the time of year, the weather was hot, and it seems that water was scarce in the vicinity of David's stronghold. David told his men how much he longed for a drink of the cool water from the well in his boyhood home of Bethlehem. Unfortunately Bethlehem was about ten kilometres away, and there was a Philistine garrison encamped near it. David was probably only expressing a wish, not expecting anyone to take his words as a command. But three of his soldiers "broke through the camp of the Philistines and drew water out of the well of Bethlehem that was by the gate and carried and brought it to David" (2 Sam 23:16).

David would not drink the water. Instead, he offered it to God, saying, "Far be it from me, O Lord, that I should do this. Shall I drink the blood of the men who went at the risk of their lives?" (2 Sam 23:17). David was so deeply moved by his men's love that he perceived the water to be of such value that it was almost sacred. It would have felt like blasphemy to drink it. Indeed, he perceived it as being like sacrificial blood, and so he poured it out as a libation to God. The water had been obtained at risk of the men's lives, which was itself a sacrificial act, and David was, in effect, pouring out their blood as an offering to God.

David's offering may have been a thank-offering in gratitude for God's protecting and sparing the lives of the three soldiers. But his words and actions clearly acknowledge the connection between risk and sacrifice. It was the great risk taken by the three men that was recognized by the pouring out of the water on the altar, so to speak. The water became a symbol of the blood the men had risked. Their risk of death was a holy and blessed act in the face the enemy.

Missionaries and other Christians who face substantial risks for Christ are also willing to sacrifice their lives for the one they love. Some actually do make this sacrifice. I would argue that risking death in a situation where lives can be lost is itself a sacrifice. Risk becomes sacrificial, and as such is itself a hallowed state of being.

The true nature of suffering for God is that it is sacrificial. To put it another way, at the most profound level, being willing to accept persecution is sacrificial giving. Commitment to the sacrifice of life if necessary is of the same nature as the actual sacrifice of life. It is an all-invasive, deeply painful passion. It is facing the ultimate of our own cross and following Christ in spirit and in truth.

Following Christ in spirit and truth involves the sacrifice of our past lives and identities. We indeed become new creatures, with the old having passed away and the new forever before us (2 Cor 5:17). But there is no loss in this self-sacrifice. We give up the world and its material hope for hope in the Creator of all things. Sacrifice is eternal gain. We sacrifice the limited life of our infinitude to gain unbounded infinite being. We are returning to the infinite, from whence we came.

Risk as wisdom

> For Paul "God's foolishness is wiser than human wisdom" (1 Cor 1:25). God's wisdom is manifested in the incarnation, death and resurrection of the Son of God. To us, death, vulnerability, and risk seem utter folly . . . Yet the way of Jesus is the way of powerful love, a love that calls us to be reconciled with God, a love that raises us in resurrection life to share in the divine love. God has not chosen immunity from the suffering involved in a relationship with sinners.[12]

The way of love is the way of risk, and the way of love is the way of the cross. This is God's wisdom. We have arrived at risk for God not as folly but as wisdom. Most essentially we are saying that wisdom is love. Love necessitates risk, and therefore to enter risk, to take a leap of faith, to leave our home where we feel secure and accept radical vulnerability is wise. God's wisdom appears as foolish to worldly minds, but it remains wisdom.

Thinking of risk as wisdom or of risk as wise means that we think of it in an entirely different way to the world. But this wisdom is born of faith. This

---

12. Sanders, *God Who Risks*, 183.

faith-wisdom may seem foolish with respect to human reason. But God is not limited to puny human reason, although human reason is continuous with and compatible with faith. But we could call what we are talking of now "higher reason." This is reason with a faith priority. Risk is fundamental to such reason. In taking a risk, we leave behind our natural resources, our security base in the world, and step out in faith and into suffering.

Stepping out into total risk is a fearful thing. But we remind ourselves that "the fear of the LORD is the beginning of wisdom" (Prov 9:10). Therefore stepping out into risk is in reality stepping out into God. To risk all for God, to follow Jesus, is to arrive at the place of absolute security – our eternal heavenly home. In the light of the gospel, risk as faith in action is absolute certainty of sharing in the glory of God.

God's pain is grace in action. Our risk, which is our response to God's pain, is our own faith in action. In turn, faith in action is radical wisdom. In the light of this wisdom we can say that risk for God is absolute certainty. It is a foundation factor of the creation.

When Risk Overwhelms Us

Peter was so committed to Christ that he declared he was ready to die for him (Matt 26:35). But then Jesus was captured, and his proximity to Jesus put Peter at great risk. How would he handle the reality of risk, rather than the idea of risk? It turned out that when three different people asked Peter, "Were you with him?," Peter's nerve failed (Luke 22:55–62). He would not take the risk of acknowledging that he was a disciple. His faith had gone; or so it appeared. He disassociated himself from Christ and took refuge in a lie. To have confessed Christ at that point might have meant capture and death. In denying, and so betraying, Christ, Peter ensured his own safety.

Denial is equivalent to betrayal and is the antithesis of risk.[13] With betrayal faith dies. Betrayal is the suicide of faith, as enacted powerfully in the suicide of Judas Iscariot (Matt 27:5). The restoration of faith, and its dynamic essence risk, is forgiveness. We see Jesus's forgiveness in his restoration of Peter, symbolized by the three-fold question, "Do you love me?" Peter's answer was "Yes" (John 21:15–19). But Jesus says this love has to be evidenced through teaching the

---

13. We see a profound example of this in George Orwell's novel *Nineteen Eighty-Four*. The major character Winston's life begins with his love for Victoria and hers for him. Such love was forbidden by Big Brother. The tortures imposed on them with the purpose of destroying their love cause them to betray each other. Through this betrayal they lose both their love and the new faith which this love inspired.

gospel to those who believe in him. Peter has to step out in his restored faith in Christ.

We can say that Peter is converted through his betrayal and, unlike Judas, he goes on at great risk to build the church. With great courage he preaches to the Jews and ultimately is persecuted and dies as a martyr. Risk is the cost of love. It is what true love does. True love risks its life for the beloved now and always and utterly.

We can also learn more about the result of being overwhelmed by risk through the extended use of the parable of the talents (Matt 25:14–30). There the master gives different amounts of money to three servants. He clearly expects them to act in faith through taking risks with the money he has entrusted to them. They are to find ways to increase the master's investment in them. Two of them accept this risk and set to work, but the third does not. He seeks what he thinks of as maximum security. Rather than risk any of the money, he buries it in the ground where it will be safe.

Two of the servants stepped out, with urgency, in faith. Their faith in action yielded an increase. But there was no way the third servant's money could increase. His only fear was that he would lose what he had, and so he sought to secure it. The others might lose the money, but he would not – he acted wisely whereas they acted foolishly; or so he thought.

When the master returned, the two servants who had trusted him and taken a risk could report substantial gains, and they were complimented and rewarded. But the servant who had refused all risk was not praised. Rather, he was accused of being wicked and lazy. His actions showed that he did not know his master – he had no relationship with him and lacked even the wisdom to invest the money in a bank. This would still have involved risk, but only very limited risk. This servant was condemned to hell. He sought personal security through inactivity and protectionism but reaped disaster. And why? Because his concern was not the coming of the kingdom of God and the return of his master. He did not have faith in the master and did not know the master.

Faith in action always produces increase for both God and his true servants. Our eternal and real security lies in God himself. Living with and knowing God is fearful; it is risky. But this fear and this risk go together as the route to absolute and eternal security. That is the route to ultimate peace and fulfilment, the peace that passes human understanding. The one who avoids all risk will never know that peace.

Part 3

Trauma and Triumph

In this final portion of this book, we consider the roots of human conflict in terms of a metaphysical analysis of primal rebellion, the will to power, hatred and the hatred and threat of difference from within the concept of the dialectic of difference and similarity. The concluding chapter is a celebration of the transformation of pain and suffering into glory.

13

The Roots of Human Conflict

In this chapter we analyse the nature of human conflict, including the first conflict of Cain and Abel, and then progress to a metaphysical analysis of the roots of conflict in general. This section of the chapter can be read in conjunction with the section on angst in chapter 4. We also discuss terrorism as a current manifestation of conflict.

The world is full of conflicts both large and small. The Middle East, for example, is torn apart by bitter conflicts as Islamic terrorist groups conduct jihad against those whom they call "infidels," some of whom are Westerners while others are simply different factions within Islam. It is particularly poignant that terrorists are convinced that God is on their side, and so they murder, rape and pillage in the name of God.

The Israeli–Palestinian conflict continues to rage. Other conflicts engulf regions of Africa like Somalia, the Democratic Republic of Congo, and Northern Nigeria. There is ongoing tension in regions of Asia like Kashmir. Meanwhile Rwanda has to deal with the legacy of the Rwandan genocide, and South Africa with the lingering effects of apartheid. Tensions still simmer in parts of Northern Ireland. Corruption and violence are rife around the world.

The complexity of these conflicts produces a fog of confusion that we cannot even attempt to disperse here. But what we can do is reflect on the roots and nature of conflict in general, and on the suffering it engenders.

Conflict is highly destructive of persons, of identities and reputations, and of physical and cultural infrastructure. It attacks the unity and peace of life, physically, emotionally, and spiritually and is the antithesis of peace and harmony in human beings and communities. It the source of great suffering, especially for the weak and vulnerable. In extreme cases, it leads to the death of individuals, or of hundreds or thousands of individuals.

The Primal Rebellion

Any conflict must involve at least two parties. The parties may be individuals, families, communities, or even nations, and the conflict may manifest itself in personal attacks or all-out war. But regardless of the size of the parties involved, conflict usually produces acts of aggression and involves a long, bitter and painful struggle.

But our conflict is not only with our fellow human beings. Our human conflicts are a reflection of our primal rebellion against God, which began with the disobedience of our first parents Adam and Eve and continues to the present time. Before that rebellion, there was perfect unity between human beings and God, between man and woman, between humans and the environment, and between all animate and inanimate being. This complete creational unity afforded absolute ontological security and perfect peace and harmony.

The first act of rebellion and the fall into sin resulted in great disunity. The unity with God was broken and so was the potential unity of human society. Men and women would become disunited not only from each other but within their own being, within themselves. These disuniting forces all work to produce conflict in the world today.

The forces of disunity are evident in the curses pronounced by God on Adam and Eve in Genesis 3. The curse on Eve laid the groundwork for conflict between man and wife and so for conflict within and between communities. The curse on Adam heralded the alienation of the environment, now in opposition to human needs and requiring great struggle to subdue it and procure the fruit of land and sea. The scene was set for human conflict, which played out first in the case of Cain and Abel.

After Adam and Eve were expelled from the garden of Eden, they had two sons, whom they named Cain and Abel. Cain, the older brother, was a crop farmer while the younger, Abel, was a pastoralist who kept sheep. After a time, possibly a very long time, Cain brought an offering to God. So did Abel. But God rejected Cain's offering while accepting Abel's.

We are not told why Cain's offering was rejected and Abel's accepted, although in Hebrews 11:4 we read: "By faith Abel offered to God a more acceptable sacrifice than Cain, through which he was commended as righteous, God commending him by accepting his gifts." It appears that Abel's sacrifice was offered in deep sincerity. It may be that Abel was sacrificing a lamb for his sin. Cain, by contrast, must have been insincere in his offering. God challenged him to change his ways and make a sincere offering for sin, warning him that "sin is crouching at the door" (Gen 4:7). But Cain's heart was corrupted and full of hatred.

Rather than examining himself, Cain allowed himself to be consumed by furious anger and hatred. He may have been acting in response to God's acceptance of Abel and rejection of himself, but this rejection reflected God's knowledge of Cain's heart. We see his bitter hatred of Abel and of God as he murdered his own brother. Adam and Eve had passed on their fallen human nature to their children.

When God questioned Cain, saying "Where is Abel your brother?," Cain lied, saying "I do not know." He added the vile challenge, "am I my brother's keeper?" (Gen 4:9). This is the second great lie in Genesis: The first was uttered by Satan (in the form of a serpent) to Eve and the second by Cain to God. Cain, the first murderer recorded in the Bible, was then cursed by God as Adam his father had been before him.

In this story, we see the spread of evil and sin and also the roots of conflict between brothers, namely jealousy, hatred, and rebellion against God. Cain almost swears at God the creator in his deep disrespect of God's person while in the act of lying to God.

Speculating a little, it appears that Abel was a religious man who sacrificed for his sin to God, but Cain was a reprobate who had no love in his heart and no regard for God whatsoever. Implicit in the text is the great pride of Cain. He was deeply offended by his rejection, which was in effect a rejection of his sinful life. This was not a minor issue for him. He hated the righteousness of Abel who was so different from him. In Cain we see a man consumed with hubris and self-importance, corrupt, self-seeking and dangerous. In the person of Cain, we see conflict defined within human society and with God.

Inner Disunity and the Knowledge of Good and Evil

In the garden, Adam and Eve lived in in the immediate presence of God. They enjoyed blissful happiness with total knowledge of the good while submitting completely to God as Lord of their being. In this knowledge of the good they had dominion over all other created beings on this earth. They were free to remain in obedience or to leap into the abyss of the knowledge of good and evil by choosing to disobey. Satan tempted them to disobey, assuring them that if they ignored God's prohibition and ate of the fruit of the knowledge of good and evil, they would be equal with God in knowledge and power. Tragically they exercised their freedom and chose the abyss.

Through their disobedience, the knowledge of good and evil became accessible to all. In other words, the human race received the dialectical knowledge of good and evil into its consciousness. Let me remind you of the words of Bonhoeffer that I quoted in chapter 4: "Man at his origin knew only one thing: God. . . . He knows all things only in God and God in all things. The knowledge of good and evil shows that he is no longer at one with this origin."[1] Disunity with God means disunity with oneself and is the ground of inner conflict and profound moral disunity. Trying to balance the elements of good and evil knowledge always fails miserably. We thus live in a state of ontological division, which is a condition of perpetual inner conflict that contributes to angst.

The battle for good and evil is the human story. The objective battle in the world is, in reality, the extension and acting out of the inner battle of human persons. The nature of this never-ending battle is the nature of human conflict with its terrible suffering and agonies. Assertions of self-righteousness and self-justification along with the corrupting influence of power are the roots of war. In the end, humanity is left with war and pestilence. People seek the triumph of good over evil, even while holding that what is essentially evil is good.

Whereas Adam and Eve's relationships with each other and with God had once been governed by grace, that state of grace has been lost and replaced by a state of law. We now live in a world where any degree of social harmony among fallen human beings requires law. That is why the Old Covenant with God was grounded in law.[2] To put this another way, the profound disunity brought in by the knowledge of good and evil left no place for grace.

In the time of Moses, the Israelites were given the Decalogue as the law they must obey to remain in a covenant relationship with God. In the time of Jesus, the Pharisees functioned as the guardians and policemen of the law. Bonhoeffer speaks of the Pharisee as fixated on the disunity of the knowledge of good and evil and using this knowledge to condemn others and themselves.

Because we are all inclined to be Pharisees, we are all torn by guilt and shame and rush to hide in the delusion of our own greatness. But we do not find lasting peace but are the victims of self-conflict, burying our guilt and deeply concerned that we will be seen as we truly are, naked and shamed.

---

1. Bonhoeffer, *Ethics*, 18. I would recommend that you review the material on angst in chapters 4 and 6 of the present book when reading this chapter.

2. We must quickly state that both the law and the covenants in themselves were acts of grace from the gracious heart of God. The law pointing to and demonstrating the need for the Messiah. The covenants including the amazing grace in the promises. But there was little or no grace in the lives or hearts and being of fallen sinners in the world.

But if human beings have gained the ability to judge right and wrong, where does the sense of shame that generates such anger come from? After the disobedience in the garden of Eden. Adam and Eve's eyes were opened to see themselves and no longer God only, and they saw that that were naked. Shame, according to Bonhoeffer, is our recollection of our estrangement, our separation and alienation from our origin. "Man is ashamed because he has lost something which is essential to his original character, to himself as a whole; he is ashamed of his nakedness."[3] Shame is the loss of something. It is the evidence of disunity, enmity with God our origin, and the reality of sin in our life.

If the corruption of our human identity is discovered or alluded to by others, we react with anger. Yet it is not so much accusations of falsehood or attacks on our character that produce this reaction, although they are greatly threatening, but rather the uncovering of the deluded false identity which we regard as the solid ground of our self-righteousness. People have created their own good and their own law, which they cannot keep, and they have also become their own judge, and admonish themselves on a regular basis. With this self-creation comes the scourge of self-righteousness, which is the basis upon which they judge others. And so human beings' inner conflict is extended to society, which they must judge and condemn and seek pseudo-justice through some penalty that, if they can, they will impose on others.

The Radical Self: Being-for-Itself

Being-for-itself is a concept borrowed from Sartre,[4] who uses it when speaking of inauthentic life and bad faith. It is the state of self-sufficiency, a category of existence that simply is, like a tree from its roots to its leaves and flowers. A tree is a tree; it cannot transcend itself. It has no potentiality. There is no gap set before it. It has no choice and therefore no freedom. This kind of being is appropriate to inanimate objects that do not have consciousness. But human beings should not, but do, desire to be complete in themselves. Sartre describes this desire for completeness of being as the desire to be God, and terms it "bad faith." At heart, this desire is a longing for full control over one's own destiny and for absolute identity.

I would describe this type of being as that of the radical self, which desires to be complete apart from God, as Adam and Eve did. But their choice did not set them free from their finitude in relationship to the infinitude of God;

---

3. Bonhoeffer, *Ethics*, 20.
4. Sartre, *Being and Nothingness*, 97.

instead, it trapped them in a prison of a deeper finitude closer to that of inanimate being. They slipped into a life of lesser being, approaching thinghood or being inanimate. The great delusion here is finite being believing that its finitude is infinite. This, as we have said before, is in essence idolatry, bowing down to a finite being or some object that is worshipped as having infinite transcendent power.

Isaiah 44:14–20 is highly relevant here:

> He cuts down cedars, or he chooses a cypress tree or an oak and lets it grow strong among the trees of the forest. He plants a cedar and the rain nourishes it. Then it becomes fuel for a man. He takes a part of it and warms himself; he kindles a fire and bakes bread. Also he makes a god and worships it; he makes it an idol and falls down before it. Half of it he burns in the fire. Over the half he eats meat; he roasts it and is satisfied. Also he warms himself and says, "Aha, I am warm, I have seen the fire!" And the rest of it he makes into a god, his idol, and falls down to it and worships it. He prays to it and says, "Deliver me, for you are my god!" (Isa 44:14–17)

The absurdity of such behaviour is clear. Men and women seek God through the finite materialism of being-for-itself. Their life is inauthentic, resting on and hoping in an empty fruitless faith. In truth and reality, life apart from God is absurd. But the radical self is incomplete because it will end. Satan's lie to Eve, "you will not surely die" will be exposed when the man and the woman die.

This great human delusion that we discussed in chapter 3 is the terrible tragedy of the human race. The belief that we are complete in ourselves, needing no other (for marriage is held to be an addition to the self), means that we do not reach out to others as a part of us. Instead, we use others to advance our own agenda. Moreover, if our "self" is offended in any way, we feel that we have been robbed of our completeness and use whatever power we have to take revenge, which we seek to label as justice.

Taking and Giving Offence

In fallen human societies, human beings offend one another through behaviour that acts for the self against the other or at the expense of the other.[5] In so doing, we are acting in accordance with fallen human nature. We do not love

---

5. Note that I am talking here about the behaviour of human beings in general, not the behaviour of regenerate Christians.

the other but love the self. We judge the other and condemn them. We hate those who offend us or act in any way against us. We hate those who oppose us as individuals or as an ethnic group or nation. We seek revenge against those who caused offence. We cry out for justice but give little justice in return. We cry out against oppression but are ourselves oppressors.

All too often, the same charges can be levelled against Christians who fail to follow the teaching of Jesus. The universal fallen tendency is to judge and condemn. Jesus's command not to judge others is the first principle for peace and harmony in human society.

Everyone is a sinner; there are no exceptions even among Christians, and so everyone gives offence (some more often and more extensively than others). Offences are given through word and deed and are the existential trigger points and the motives for conflict. The world insists that the pain caused by an offence must be atoned for. Justice demands a penalty, although it cannot heal the hurt. We can see offence as the existential root of particular conflicts, even long-standing religious, political or ethnic conflicts.

The giving of offence and the taking of offence are of course different dynamics. Offence can be delivered in many ways and modalities. It can arise from deep hatred or jealousy or from a throw-away statement made without malicious intent. To be sinned against causes profound offence. The offence of false witness slanders our reputation, which can so easily be lost. All offences except the most minor have to be dealt with in some way. Either they are forgiven or they are propitiated through some act of revenge.

Individual offence

We have considered the disunity between human beings and between human beings and God, as well as the disunity within individuals. We saw this disunity at work in the conflict of Cain and Abel, the first conflict within human society. We now want to return to the offended self, for an offence is not an offence if no offence is taken. So we want to consider the psychological mechanism of taking offence.

Some people take offence very easily, so that anything with the slightest negative tone is reclassified as an attack on their person. Others do not take offence easily and can listen to creative criticism without being offended. But why do different persons take offence differently? What makes the difference?

The most immediate answer is that we all perceive things differently. But going beyond that, we can say that the answer is likely to be pride (hubris). Pride is part of the ego that is inflated with self-importance and drives each of us to want the top place at the table (see Jesus's parable in Luke 14:7–11). But the higher we rank in our own estimation, the further we have to fall and the greater the potential for pain. The old adage is, of course, "pride goes before a fall" or "what goes up must come down." The construction of a pseudo-status of high position is a delusion that most of us succumb to at some point, and consequently we endure the pain of threatened demotion. Even though such pain is grounded on a false premise, it is nevertheless real. It is like death because it is the death of a delusion. But that delusion is in reality a negative, so in this death, which Paul describes as "death to self"[6] we have the death of a negative, which is positive!

The Christian life of denying ourselves, taking up our cross, and following Jesus involves the death of the ego, which we must not seek to revive (Matt 16:24; Luke 9:23). Jesus dealt with non-assertion of the ego in the Sermon on the Mount when he spoke about turning the other cheek, giving the inner garment also, going the second mile, loving our enemies, doing good to those who do evil to us, and forgiving others (Matt 5:38–48).

What the denial of the ego communicates to Christians is that we should leave things to God. It is he who takes offence, not us, for all sin is ultimately against him. Christians are called to be holy as he is holy; that is, to be separate from the hamartia of the world. A dead or dying ego enables one to return to a balanced and measured view of the self. Humility is learned and loved as a virtue. With this new equanimity, offence is taken very sparingly, if at all. Some pain may remain in the form of hurt for the other or sorrow at a damaged relationship, but such pain is never really negative.

Corporate offence (war)

Communities can be offended by some public atrocity or public declaration, but it is difficult to gauge the precise quality of community offence. Mostly we understand offence in ourselves and through the behaviour and confession of other individuals. I want to pose that community offence is an aggregate offence of many individuals who have informal or formal access to each other through community infrastructure. Mass media such as TV and the Internet, more particularly Facebook and Twitter, offer an immediate and widespread network through which individual offence can be shared and so in some sense

---

6. See Gal 2:20. Many other texts in the New Testament also refer to the concept of the death of self (the ego).

can become corporate. The so-called Arab Spring[7] was facilitated by social media and resulted in mass conflict. The corporate offence in Egypt was the poverty of the people in contrast to the wealth of the leaders. This, of course, is no new thing, for poverty is an ancient source of offence. The mass of the offended poor rose up in revolution and expelled their president, and harsh and sometimes bloody conflict ensued.

A similar rebellion arose in Syria, although here the people were disunited and the result was civil war. The West, and particularly the USA, supported the rebels and Russia supported the establishment. The stage was set not only for civil war but also for the return of a cold war between two old enemies. To this conflict was added the invasion of the terrorist organization known as Daesh (also known as ISIS). The resultant disaster has shown that corporate conflict knows no boundaries and can explode to involve a vast number of persons, the majority of whom become victims who must flee for their lives. Today there are millions of refugees who are the responsibility of the states that will receive them.

The Will

We have discussed conflict as arising through the individual or corporate assertion of hubris. What is being asserted is the will, or what we, borrowing from Nietzsche, may call "the will to power."[8] Nietzsche includes knowledge as part of the will to power, and so propounds the relation of power and knowledge. He argues that to acknowledge and take up the will to power is to overcome the weakness and cowardliness in human nature.

Nietzsche's influence on Adolf Hitler, the leader of the National Socialist Party in Germany (the Nazis) is debated, but clearly Hitler had read his works and absorbed concepts like the will to power, master and slave mentalities, and the superman or overman. He incorporated them in Nazi ideology when he argued that the master race needed to take up the will to power and exterminate the so-called slave or inferior races. This taking up of the will to power led to murder on a vast scale.[9]

---

7. The Arab Spring was a revolutionary wave of demonstrations and protests (both non-violent and violent) and civil wars in the Arab world that began on 18 December 2010 in Tunisia with the Tunisian Revolution, and spread throughout the countries of the Arab League.

8. Nietzsche, *Will to Power*.

9. It must be said that, as far as I am aware, Nietzsche was concerned more with the power of individuals than with the power of corporate bodies or nations.

If we may return to Adam and Eve, they too manifested the will to power. They wanted the knowledge of good and evil because they believed it would make them "like God." So we could conceive of original sin as being linked to the will to power. However, in Nietzsche's thinking, Adam and Eve were noble in seeking to fully realize their potential. Nietzsche's teaching is thus the antithesis of the teaching of Jesus, and indeed of the Christian gospel as a whole. But it fits well with the idea of the survival of the fittest and Richard Dawkins' concept of the "selfish gene."[10] The will to power and fascist ideologies are simply the rebellion of finite being against the infinite being of God. The will to power in the heart of our first parents led them to seek to usurp the power of God, and the will to power of the Pharisees led them to murder the Son of God.

Nietzsche's philosophy is actually a brilliant interpretation of fallen human nature. His philosophy, and all fascist ideology, "is" conflict, and it is conflict involving untold depths of human suffering. Indeed this conflict almost defines evil. The will to power of human beings, nations and races, is the great rebellion against God. This is what the psalmist was speaking of when he wrote:

> Why do the nations rage,
> and the peoples plot in vain?
> The kings of the earth set themselves,
> and the rulers take counsel together,
> against the Lord and his Anointed, saying
> "Let us burst their bonds apart
> and cast away their cords from us." (Ps 2:1–3)

The will to power of national leaders is set against God. Human conflict is primarily sin against God, as King David recognized when he wrote, "Against you, you only, have I sinned" (Ps 51:4). Rebellion against God is futile, and further disunites human society. The casting aside of God's loving authority opens the way for pseudo-leadership with wrong and often evil motives, whose agenda causes untold suffering.

A dark satanic force with a deep hatred of God and his people can even permeate the spirit of nations. A prime example of this can be seen in the rise of the National Socialist Party in Germany that led to World War II. We see terrible hatred given free rein under Nazi rule, resulting in the murder of

---

10. Dawkins, *Selfish Gene*.

millions of those they regarded as inferior beings, including six million Jews and half a million Roma (Gypsies).[11]

Hatred

Hatred produces utopia. It purifies the strong and powerful by removing the corruption of the weak and cowardly. It gives the inner strength that underwrites the building of true character. It is also the ground of moral ethics and the cohesive force of an economy.

Clearly, all the above statements are false. Yet this is how fascists think. It is how the Nazis developed hatred to national proportions rarely seen on earth. In truth, hatred produces murder. It seeks power and it is overwhelmingly corrupting. Hatred along with hubris defines human conflict, for lying beneath the surface of fallen human nature is a propensity towards hatred. This hatred rejoices in the collapse of others, particularly their moral collapse, as it has the effect of establishing and raising the haters' self-esteem and status. As witness and assent to the collapse (and indeed extermination) of an entire ethnic group labelled "enemies of the state" thus raises the self-esteem and status of an entire nation. These attitudes lead to what we term nationalism. Nationalistic ideologies are premised on the believed superiority of a particular nation. But if there is to be a perceived superior nation, there must also be a perceived inferior nation. At a time when German nationalism was deeply frustrated by Germany's plight after the First World War and the Depression, the seeds of the Nazi ideology of the absolute superiority of the Aryan race fell on fertile ground.

The hatred that the fall installed in human hearts needs an object, and it seeks one around every corner. To establish that the object is worthy of hatred, the human heart constructs a network of lies and slander. It attacks reputations and standing. It destroys persons and the love between persons. All those who are not of its own tribe are the enemy.

Like jealousy and covetousness, hatred grows over time and has fatal potential. Shakespeare shows how it works in his play *Othello*, in which the hatred and jealousy spawned by Iago eventually lead the virtuous Othello to murder his once loved wife and commit suicide. Purity and virtue are converted into murderous tragedy through lies and deception.

---

11. Estimates of the number of Roma murdered range from 22,000 to 1.5 million. Other targeted groups included the mentally and physically disabled, homosexuals and freemasons.

We see a similar dynamic at work in the case of David's son Amnon, who lusted after his beautiful half-sister Tamar. His lust led him to rape the sister he claimed to love. Once his lust was satisfied, he turned on her: "Then Amnon hated her with very great hatred, so that the hatred with which he hated her was greater than the love with which he had loved her. And Amnon said to her, 'Get up! Go!'" (2 Sam 13:15). He discarded her like a soiled rag. His hatred justified his cruel treatment of her in his own eyes. Hatred then spread as Absalom, Tamar's full brother, hated Amnon for what he had done to Tamar and had him murdered. Hatred's travel companions are bloodshed and murder.

Hatred and terrorism

Terrorism is currently one of the most prolific forms of conflict in the world. In broad terms, it can be defined as

> the use of intentionally indiscriminate violence as a means to create terror among masses of people; or [to use] fear to achieve a religious or political aim. It is classified as fourth-generation warfare and as a violent crime. In modern times, terrorism is considered a major threat to society and therefore illegal under anti-terrorism laws in most jurisdictions. It is also considered a war crime under the laws of war when used to target non-combatants, such as civilians, neutral military personnel, or enemy prisoners of war.[12]

Terrorist leaders are essentially self-appointed and have no connection to a specific state. They adopt a cause that involves hatred of another group, people or country. In its manifestation in the Middle East and parts of Africa today, terrorism is inspired by Islamic fundamentalism, rooted in a literal reading of the Quran informed by terrorists' own biases and bigotry and has the following characteristics:

- It is waged in the name of God.
- It is in the general spirit of jihad (holy war), primarily against Christians but also against Jews in Israel and Muslims who interpret the Quran differently.
- It claims that it serves justice.
- It is based on a fundamentalist interpretation of the Quran and the Hadith.

---

12. Wikipedia definition, in 2017. The definition posted online has since changed.

- It aims to achieve universal submission to its particular interpretation.
- It involves conflict between different factions within Islam, primarily Sunni, Shia and Sufi.
- It seeks power and sovereignty, both religious and political.
- It uses extreme violence to meet its goals.
- It inflicts harsh suffering.
- It is widely regarded as criminal, guilty of both crimes against the state and war crimes.

Terrorist leaders have proved to be false prophets who seduce people with their passionate rhetoric. I would argue that both Hitler and Mussolini began as terrorist leaders who progressed by evil means to mislead a state.

Islamic terrorists perpetrate the worst and most evil form of conflict while calling it a holy war against infidels (unbelievers – really a term for Christians). The terrorist leader Osama bin Laden was especially hostile to America, which he deemed the enemy of Islam. He appeared to be completely convinced that he was a servant of God and that all he did was in the name of justice. His goal was to re-establish perceived justice through the sword, that is, by murdering the enemy. He justified the killing of Americans by referring to acts of violence by Americans, such as the bombings of Hiroshima and Nagasaki. Here his thinking on revenge was similar to that of some Old Testament dynamics.

But there was also another factor at play, for bin Laden regarded all Americans as Christians, and all Christians as blasphemers because they worship a man, Jesus. (The doctrine of the Trinity is highly offensive to Muslims.) The Quran declares that blasphemers are to be killed, and so this is what bin Laden set out to do.

Religious conflicts of this kind cannot easily be resolved because the doctrines of one faith are incompatible with those of another. However, it needs to be pointed out that while Muslims seek to kill Christians, Christians should seek to love Muslims in accordance with the will of God the Father, Son and Holy Spirit.

The current tragedy in Syria and Iraq that has sent floods of refugees into the surrounding nations and to the West is, in part, a highly complex conflict between the two great factions within Islam (Sunni and Shia). Some Sunni Muslims formed a militant group known as ISIS and set up an Islamic state, or caliphate, in Iraq and Syria. In so doing they took terrorism to a new level, executing all who would not immediately conform to their beliefs. They also orchestrated an international terrorist network, drawing in recruits from a number of Western countries.

Mixed in with the terrorist activity of ISIS in Syria is the complex conflict between rebels and the Syrian government. As already said, this conflict is a product of the Arab Spring. In Egypt, the government fell, but President Assad of Syria clung to power and launched what became a bloody civil war. Other powers were also drawn in, with Western nations siding with the rebels and Russia with Assad and the Syrian establishment.

The Suffering of the Trauma of Conflict

Conflict resolution is valuable, as is peace-making when wars threaten or have broken out. But all too often, once peace is restored, we forget about those who have endured the conflict and are still suffering in its aftermath. Yet they may have been exposed to violence, bombing, shooting and rape. They may have witnessed the execution of family members and friends and been forcibly dispossessed of their property and even of their country, leaving them completely in homelessness.

The resulting pain of both physical and psychological trauma can be very deep, particularly when children are involved. Trauma becomes part of the survivors' new life context. They continue to suffer in many different ways for they have experienced physical loss of property and possibly also of their health or even parts of their body. They have also experienced spiritual loss, the loss of value of being. Physical agony and the loss of meaning and purpose in life resulting in profound depression.

According to the American Psychiatric Association, trauma flows from

> direct personal experience of an event that involves actual or threatened death or serious injury, or other threat to one's physical integrity; or witnessing an event that involves death, injury, or a threat to another person; or learning about unexpected or violent death, serious harm, or threat of death or injury experienced by a family member or other close associate.[13]

They describe the traumatized person's response to the event as involving "intense fear, helplessness, or horror (or in children, ... disorganized or agitated behaviour)." Intense fear paralyses and produces utter helplessness. The word that may best sum up the whole experience of trauma is the word "horror," referring to something that goes far beyond our worst nightmares.

---

13. *The Diagnostic and Statistical Manual of Mental Disorders*, 4th ed. (DSM-IV-TR; American Psychiatric Association [APA], 2000), 463.

I would argue that Christians need not experience this utter helplessness because we can cry to God for help and trust in him. However, Christians have human emotions, and in terrible circumstances they too suffer trauma. Even great saints have feared martyrdom. But for Christians, their human fear does not affect their allegiance to Christ.

One of the greatest of traumas is the death of one's children. The Gospel of Matthew records the circumstances of one such traumatic loss and the tears that flowed from it:

> Then Herod, when he saw that he had been tricked by the wise men, became furious, and he sent and killed all the male children in Bethlehem and in all that region who were two years old or under, according to the time that he had ascertained from the wise men. Then was fulfilled what was spoken by the prophet Jeremiah:
>
> "A voice was heard in Ramah,
>   weeping and loud lamentation,
> Rachel weeping for her children;
>   she refused to be comforted, because they are no more."
>   (Matt 2:16–18)

The mothers in Bethlehem could not be comforted. The death of young children is a searing pain that parents cannot let go of. The trauma bites very deeply. But the Lord is with them in such suffering. It may also help to recognize that the verse Matthew quotes from Jeremiah 31:15 is followed by a promise of hope:

> "Keep your voice from weeping,
>   and your eyes from tears,
> for there is a reward for your work,"
>   declares the LORD,
>   "and they shall come back from the land of the enemy.
> There is hope for your future,"
>   declares the LORD,
>   "and your children shall come back to their own country."
>   (Jer 31:16–17)

The dead children are not lost they are in the protection of God and Christian mothers shall see them again in their own country of heaven.

14

The Dialectic of Difference and Similarity

In this chapter we consider conflict from the perspective of the dialectic of difference and similarity. We look at the persecution of difference, paying particular attention to its manifestations in segregation in apartheid South Africa and extermination in Nazi Germany.

Difference and similarity constitute a key dialectic when it comes to human relationships. In phenomenological terms, difference produces threat to being and threat to identity, whereas similarity reinforces being and identity.

The primary dialectic has to do with the creation of human beings as both absolutely different from and absolutely similar to God. It finds secondary expression in the creation of males and females as both absolutely different and absolutely similar. There is an authentic analogy between the primary dialectic and the secondary expression. It is in and through this analogy concerning persons that we are able to talk about and understand the Person of God.

Similarity and Difference

We understand the relation of finite being with infinite being through analogy. As finite beings we can know the transcendent infinite being of God and talk about this knowledge in theology because the absolute similarity of God and humankind is an essential element of creation. This is referred to as the *imago dei*, the image of God in men and women.[1] In other words, we are able to understand with authenticity because we are created with a similar nature. This similarity is also the ground for debates about our innate *a priori* knowledge of God. The difference, on the other hand, is the possibility, potential and actual, of human freedom, which is usually spoken of in existential terms as free will.

The secondary dialectic of difference and similarity between male and female, man and woman, arises essentially from the creation dynamic of human being. The man is created before the woman in the order of creation. He is taken from the earth and God breathes his spirit into the man's inanimate body. It is in the divine breath that the *imago dei* is installed in the man as his essential being in union with his physicality. We may thus say that man is a corporeal spirit.

Woman is taken from the body of the man, which means that she has an absolutely similar chemical composition to the man. She is made of the same material arranged differently in terms of her physicality. The differences between the male and female body profoundly influence the human spirit and identity, yet the capacity to know one another, male and female, is rooted exclusively in the similarity. As men and women were created in the *imago dei* they are equal persons, both physically and spiritually. In God's economy each completes the other.

Difference as a threat

Fallen human nature sees similarity as reassuring of our personal identity, but difference, that which cannot be known, is experienced as profoundly threatening. For children, difference is celebrated as an opportunity for fun and growth, but not so for adults. They perceive difference as having a potential for loss, which usurps our being, our status and our concept of ourselves. In short, because what is different cannot be known, it cannot be conquered and controlled in terms of our personal economy. Difference is perceived as a foreign being, that is, an enemy. Difference may hurt us, and so difference is taken to be the ground of conflict. It is frightening and presents itself to our psyche as a force of angst and so of inner pain.

Let us look at how this manifests itself in relation to common human differences.

---

1. The image and likeness may be regarded as different qualities, with "image" relating to essence and "likeness" being descriptive, but it is clear that the two qualities both indicate similarity.

Sexual difference

The creation of sexual difference reveals to us that difference is essential to human being and to healthy ontological balance. The balance of difference and similarity is the essence of holistic health. It defines creational normality in proper human being. The reality that we are both different from and similar to God defines our essential being and existence and is the basis for abundant, authentic, and even eternal, life. The creation order itself is our clear guide to an authentic lifestyle in God. Where precisely we are situated in the dialectical tension of difference and similarity is a statement of our own values and world view.

It is because the mystery of sexual difference is threatening to fallen human nature that there is conflict between men and women. Traditionally, this conflict seems to have been resolved by male domination and devaluing of women. The physical beating of women is now less common in the West, but it appears to be almost universal in the Middle East and Africa. This reflects the fact that one way to resolve the fear of difference is to seek to redefine the other by making them in some way less human, and so, inferior. At its worst, this approach to difference leads to slavery, when those who are defined as lesser humans are used to serve the needs of those who regard themselves as more human.

Looking again at the curse on Eve, we see that original sin disturbed the balance of difference and similarity and so the creation order. The dominance of the male sex is a direct result or product of the separation of humankind from God.

Racial difference

Racial difference shows up in what we may term symbols of difference. These symbols relate to bodily differences such as colour of skin and shape of face, most particularly as regards the nose and eyes. These attributes may also be associated with certain world views and religious beliefs.

When we stand a black man and a white man side by side, we are aware of differences in skin pigmentation. For many, the tendency is to ignore the similarities of their essential humanness and to impose on each of them the characteristics associated with their particular colour, and then to make judgement about their character even though there are no grounds for doing so. Both blacks and whites are guilty of this, just as both blacks and whites have been heard to say, "They all look alike to me." These words are evidence of false norms. What is perceived is a mystery arising from skin colour and other physical characteristics, and the mystery is perceived as threatening because, like all mysteries, it cannot be known.

Black and white are falsely taken to be opposites, but no such dialectic applies. Distinctions based on colour are false in that they focus solely on a surface attribute that does not correlate with any difference in essence. Yet this colour difference has been used as grounds for hatred, sometimes violent hatred, and the assertion that one colour is superior to the other. Groups like the Ku Klux Klan are composed of white supremacists who hate and seek to oppress blacks (as well as Roman Catholics and Jews). Such groups exalt racial purity. The Nazis are perhaps the supreme example of the evil that flows from such beliefs, with the former apartheid system in South Africa close behind.

Because of beliefs like these, racial differences and conflict seem to go together. The pain of racial conflict shouts out from the pages of history. We hear it in the cries of native Americans who suffered and still suffer at the hands of colonizers. We hear it in the cries of black Africans considered subhuman by white Europeans and Americans and forced into slavery. In this cruel denial of their human dignity, their great loss was freedom. Anything other than total submission to the will of their masters resulted in violence against them. They endured undeserved suffering, social and political persecution, injustice and great inner anguish. Their corporate suffering can be called the pain of racial difference or, more generally, the pain of difference.

The rejection of any human being on the grounds of alleged racial inferiority is a demonic attack on the Person of God himself. It shows up the true nature of fallenness. Being-for-itself, or for an aggregate of similar selves, is energized by the underlying hatred rising out of a great potential for hatred. This hatred murders at all levels. It is the essential motive of crime and ultimately of murder. Hatred and threat are expressions of deep-set racism.

Ethnic difference

Ethnicity is a characteristic associated with social groups that share a common and distinctive culture or language and a religion or ideology. While ethnicity can align with nationality, it does not necessarily do so. Ethnicity is also distinct from race in that it is social, whereas race may be understood more in genetic terms.[2] It is common to refer to ethnic groups in terms of religion, labelling

---

2. Although, in recent times, it is fair to say that anthropologists tend to reject the notion of race as there is so much blending of supposed races in the human genome.

them as Christians or Jews, Muslims or Hindus, etc. Or the label may be ideological, so that they are referred to as communists or capitalists. A common language such as Arabic or English is also an element of ethnicity. Cultural distinctions contribute to ethnicity, primarily when these concern world views and beliefs about what it means to be human and to live in this world. Such beliefs lead to particular patterns and styles of behaviour. In modern times sexual orientation, whether straight or gay or transgendered, has also taken on something of the nature of an ethnic distinction.

We can all identify major ethnic groups such as Jews, Arabs, Scots, Chinese and Americans, but when we seek to answer the question, "What is ethnicity?" with existential precision, we run into difficulty. Do Shia and Sunni Muslims constitute ethnic groups? What about evangelical Christians? Ethnicity is a loosely understood concept involving a diversity of groups with different characteristics. What stands out from all classifications of ethnic groups is the concept and reality of "perceived essential difference."

Ethnic groups judge other ethnic groups in terms of quality and even degree of what we may term "humanness." I have heard more than one Israeli Jew state that Arabs are subhuman, and I have heard Palestinian Arabs proclaim that Jews are pigs. The Nazis believed that all Jews, Roma, homosexuals and disabled people were subhuman, of no more value than animals. Colonial slave owners saw their African slaves in a similar light. In the same way, supporters of the apartheid regime in South Africa looked down on black people, and the Hutu despised the Tutsi in Rwanda. Such beliefs in ethnic superiority and inferiority lead to hatred, segregation, and murder.

The German philosopher Hegel talks of superior and inferior being in terms of a master/slave dialectic or a master/slave consciousness. He holds that human consciousness splits naturally into a master and slave consciousness and that the struggle for recognition results in two unequal social beings, yielding two ethnic groups, the masters and the slaves. The master recognizes the slave, and the slave the master. However, the master is his own being who owns the being of the slave, and so the slave does everything for the master but does not own anything. The master depends on the slave, who is reduced to being subhuman, for his recognition and therefore fulfilment. If there is a superior, there must be an inferior.[3] The slave, however, in Hegel's thinking, also needs the master in order to have a slave mentality. This master–slave distinction in Hegel is, I believe, influential in Western and especially European thinking.

---

3. Hegel, *Phenomenology of Mind*, 65.

When locked in a battle for superiority, ethnic differences pose a great threat to being in terms of identity and security, and fallen human nature must respond. The threat from certain ethnicities may be perceived as so great that it represents a crisis for certain other ethnicities. The sad reality is that where people of different ethnicities are in close contact, it is often felt that one group must either be subjugated by the more powerful ethnicities (enslaved) or in extreme cases exterminated (genocide).[4] Fairly recent examples of this dynamic are the struggles between the Hutu and the Tutsi in Rwanda and Burundi and between Palestinian Arabs and Israeli Jews in Israel and the Palestinian territories.[5]

Severe and intolerant persecution of those of different ethnicities is essentially a deep, corporate sin against God. The hatred of difference is hatred of God's creation. Freedom depends on difference, and extermination of difference and preservation and development only of similarity leads to captivity of the human soul. To enslave those who are different is to grossly devalue human personhood – not only the personhood of the one enslaved but also of the enslaver. The ultimate result is pain for both parties. The immediate result is the terrible pain of the slavery of the subjugated.

Too often racial and ethnic difference is perceived as impure, a degradation or corruption of what should be thoroughbred. To those who think like this, racial purity is perfection of human being. All deviation is at enmity with this perfection. Difference is seen as the enemy because it transcends racial or tribal similarity. An enemy cannot be assimilated and integrated into a social group. An enemy must be continually resisted as a potential destroyer. Enemies are perceived as the bringers of untold suffering. So it is amazing to remember that Jesus proclaimed that our enemies could be our own family members (Matt 10:36).

---

4. Western societies through democracy and "toleration" appear to have managed to integrate different ethnicities, forging a so called united equal society. However, protecting and allowing the continuing development of the harmony of disparate groups requires anti-race and hate speech laws. These societies have experienced great political and perhaps ideological division through which great bitterness and even death threats result.

5. The Jews and Palestinians are both Semites. But they have such radically different ethnicities with different world views, ethical norms and religious convictions that they are like oil and water, each group presenting itself as the antithesis of the other. They live in a constant and threatening tension.

Economic difference

Liberation theology arising from Latin America focuses on the difference between the rich and the poor, the "haves" and the "have-nots." The former are powerful; the latter powerless. The rich define themselves as "upper class" and look down on the so-called lower classes as dirty, uneducated, culturally illiterate and morally inferior. Some of the rich perceive the poor as little more than tools or commodities to be used to generate more wealth, with as little recompense as possible to the actual workers.

The rich want to exploit the poor and be served by them. So they feel threatened when they are confronted by the poor or by those who seek to reduce the power associated with wealth. Their fears may be justified, for at times the poor do rise up in bloody revolution. That was what happened in the French Revolution, the Marxist Revolution in Russia, and more recently the Arab Spring. In all these cases the poor revolted against the powerful classes in society.

The Bible, too, recognizes the disparity between rich and poor. The Old Testament repeatedly condemns exploitation of the poor and demands that it be replaced by loving care for them. The rich were to use their wealth to help the disadvantaged. Jesus told the rich young man to sell his possessions and give the proceeds to the poor (Matt 19:21). Giving away the treasure that maintains power in the world negates the difference between rich and poor, so that both recognize that their true treasure is in heaven.

The Angst That Sets Us Free

All perceived existential differences are profound sources of angst because they suggest that personal and ethnic identity may be overwhelmed or even destroyed. Difference is thus perceived as a root of inner pain. The reality is, however, that inner pain of this kind is the herald of freedom. It is a healthy part of the creation order. What fallen human consciousness perceives as destructive is the very means of setting us free. Difference sets us free from the bondage of similarity.

Similarity is the capacity and home of our knowledge, but it traps us in something like being-for-itself, which is delusional and therefore inauthentic. Through faith, Christians can overcome the angst of difference as we respond to Jesus's call to deny the comfort of what we perceive to be home and step out into the unfamiliar following him. In this breaking free from the delusion of self, we are embracing difference. Indeed, stepping out into difference is stepping into authentic and abundant life. Again, Paul exhorts us to die to self and live to Christ (Gal 2:20). This self-denial, denial of our old identity, is indeed a death, and death is always frightening, but Christianity is eternal life through the death of our old ego.

Stepping out into difference[6] is stepping out into the death of self. This is a great pain, but it is a necessary pain for the Christian's transformation from death and delusion to eternal life and truth. We die to be free. We need to die to our old spirit, our old radical self, to be reborn in the Spirit of God: "The old has passed away; behold, the new has come" (2 Cor 5:17).

Having said this, we have arrived at a new maxim. If we have to die to radical similarity, which we cling to, to be set free from the prison of our old nature, then difference is the medium of freedom. Our new nature is in the freedom of difference. The new creaturehood is difference. This is the difference of the kingdom of heaven. The kingdom of heaven is different even in the way it is different.[7] This difference is a goodness beyond human perception, a goodness of pure spirit that is holy.

Fallen human being is universally corrupt "for all have sinned and fall short of the glory of God" (Rom 3:23). But similarity hides the corruption and seeks to redefine it as good. It is the difference that exposes the corruption and defines it as bad. Thus the difference is felt to be of the essence of evil as it shines the light of truth into tortured souls. Human science, I believe, has the problem that it seeks the similarity, and in this it has a bias against the truth. The truth lies in the difference, but it balances the difference with the essential similarity.

Through the dynamic of the fall, God has become unrecognizably different from human beings. Human similarity with God, the *imago dei*, has been corrupted and dirtied, leaving only the difference that is mocked as irrelevant to the similarity and finitude of human life. If the difference is not marginalized, it brings great pain to the fallen human soul. The difference is synonymous with death of the corrupt ways of fallen human life. This knowledge elicits profoundly painful angst that cannot be dispelled. And so the way to freedom is misperceived as the way to death. Yet Paul summarized one aspect of Jesus's teaching with the words, "do not be anxious about anything" (Phil 4:6; see Matt 6:25). These words are a source of great comfort. Those who are on the Way are absolutely and infinitely secure.

---

6. I am not talking here about the existential metaphor of stepping out into the void.
7. Echoing Karl Rahner in *Hearers of the Word*.

The Persecution of Difference

The Jews provide a clear example of the persecution of difference. They are different from all other people groups or ethnicities in the world in that they are the primary chosen people of God. They were chosen with a purpose and given the law, to be a blessing to the nations. The tragic reality of their failure to fulfil this purpose does not detract from the reality of their chosenness. It set them apart from all others, so that the Bible categorizes people in terms of two great people groups, the Jews and the Gentiles. Their profound difference has led to their profound persecution.

Sadly, the pages of church history include much explicit anti-Semitic language, even from such great names as Augustine, Ambrose of Milan, and John Chrysostom. Martin Luther described the Jews as "venomous beasts, vipers, disgusting scum . . . devils incarnate."[8] Much Western literature also reveals how Jews were hated and despised. In Shakespeare's play *The Merchant of Venice* Shylock the Jew is treated by the other characters as the epitome of evil and all things vile. Shylock cries out in protest, reminding them of their similarity: "I am a Jew. Hath not a Jew eyes? Hath not a Jew hands . . . If you prick us, do we not bleed?"[9]

Nor is persecution of difference a thing of the past. We still see evidence of it in the backlash against refugees in Europe, in the hate speech directed at Muslims and Jews in the West, and in the callous killings of Blacks by Whites and vice versa.

Much of the persecution of difference takes place on the societal level, but it has at times been incorporated in state policy, where historically it took two radical and devastating forms, namely segregation and extermination.

Segregation

Both economic and physical segregation were often imposed on Jews in Europe who were prevented from entering certain professions and were forced to live in certain areas, which became known as ghettos. But segregation has been and still is used more widely, often against those with darker skin colours. A textbook example of extreme segregation in the twentieth century is the practice of apartheid in South Africa.

---

8. Luther, *On the Jews and their Lies*, 1543.
9. William Shakespeare, *The Merchant of Venice*, Act 3 Scene 1.

Apartheid is an Afrikaans word meaning "separation" or "segregation." In 1948 the South African government passed a law forbidding sexual relations and marriage between blacks and whites. This was the beginning of a policy that would categorize all South Africans as White, Black, Coloured (mixed race), or Asian. The category into which one fell determined one's eligibility to vote, where one was allowed to live and work, where one attended school and the curriculum studied.

To the so-called White people of South Africa, who were a minority, the prospect of those who were different (Black, Coloured and Asian South Africans) gaining political power was a great threat, and so the White minority worked to frustrate their access to power. The exclusively White government took up the will to power to remove the potential of Black power.

Here I am not concerned so much with the history of apartheid as with the profound human suffering it caused. Ethnic superiority necessarily demands that others be ethnically inferior, and so inevitably treats them as less than fully human. This applied to the situation between Jews and Gentiles in New Testament times, between "Aryans" and Jews in Nazi Germany, and between Whites and Blacks in South Africa. It extends beyond ethnic lines to all relationships, including the relationships between men and women. Superiority detracts from the humanity of those perceived as different.

To be a human being made in the image of God and treated as less than human cuts to the heart. It produces an agony of shame and nakedness in those who swallow this lie. One is judged and found guilty of being different, and so inferior. This subjugation of fellow members of the human race by those who believe they are their masters and so their judges, appointed as such by God, is a gross injustice. The effect of attempts to maintain superiority over others is that the oppressors forfeit their own humanity while those being brutally oppressed retain theirs.

As it has acknowledged, and deeply repented, the Dutch Reformed Church in South Africa was a key supporter of apartheid. In rejecting the wonderful diversity of God's human creation, it rejected fellow Christians, and fellow human beings. It sinned in supporting injustice and denying that in God's eyes all are equal.

The suffering of slaves and segregated peoples takes them to the depths of ultimate humanity, not the end of it. The edge of ultimate humanity is the place of heroes, as Nelson Mandela proved. He is rightly recognized and admired, but there were many other lesser known heroes in South Africa such as Steve Biko. These heroes were not flawless. Heroes remain sinners. But they are sinners who have acted against the sinful protection of self and have sacrificed their lives for others. They are the role models for humanity as a whole.

Extermination

History contains many accounts of attempts to eliminate groups who are different from the majority population or who are perceived as competitors. This was what has happened to tribal groups in the Amazon and in Rwanda and Burundi in the twentieth century. In the twenty-first century, it has happened to groups like the Rohingya in Myanmar and the Yazidi in Iraq. My focus here on the Holocaust in Europe should not be read as a statement that this evil exists only in the past.

The Holocaust is a classic example of the attempt to exterminate those who are different. Adolf Hitler regarded the Jews as a corrupt, subhuman people, deeply inferior to the Aryan race that populated Germany, Austria, Great Britain and North America. He taught that the Jews were a threat to the purity of Aryan blood and soil. When he came to power, he first sought to segregate the Jews in ghettos and work camps, and then he turned to his "final solution": mass genocide of Jews, Roma, homosexuals, disabled people, and all who bore an unacceptable difference of being. They were treated worse than animals – for animals pose no threat to human being. Hitler loved his dogs, but the hatred he directed at the Jews reached apocalyptic proportions as he set out to exterminate an entire people, men women and children.

Most of us have seen photographs of the concentration camps into which the Jews were herded. Names like Auschwitz/Birkenau, Belsen, Dachau, Treblinka and Chelmno evoke images of cattle trains filled with Jews, lines of terrified people being "assigned" to miserable life or immediate death by prison commanders and guards, gas chambers and Zyklon B containers, piles of bodies, and thin and starving prisoners in striped threadbare uniforms.

When faced with such atrocity, we find ourselves faced with a dilemma: Do we identify with the victims or the oppressors? Such is the enormity and depth of evil that we are compelled to identify with both of these groups. Both the perpetrators of great evil and the suffering victims of great evil represent essential human being. We see the spirit of the antichrist in the wanton destruction of those made in God's image, and in the utter despair, terror, and confusion of the oppressed we see the absence of God. The Holocaust is terrible evidence of the extent of human depravity. Adam and Eve's leap into the abyss of evil and fallenness was a leap into the reality of terrible holocausts to come in human history.

The Nazis, and particularly their special police force (the SS), were the perpetrators of this demonic evil, but we find ourselves asking, what about the ordinary German people? How was a whole nation persuaded to be complicit in the crimes of such a war and such a genocide? How was a nation with a long Christian tradition seduced by an evil ideology? This question fascinated the German Jewish philosopher Hannah Arendt. When she was sent to cover the trial of Adolf Eichmann, one of the major organizers of the Holocaust,

> she looked for a psychotic or sadistic personality, but what she found was a banal, mediocre, narrow-minded bureaucrat. She wrote a book about the trial entitled "The Banality of Evil." It was heavily criticized. She was accused of failing to convey the true nature of Nazi evil and of trivialising the Holocaust. But I believe she was right in pointing out an individual need not be a monster in order to commit monstrous deeds. The dividing line between good and evil is a thin one and quite ordinary people can be indoctrinated or brainwashed to cross it.[10]

In his book *Man's Search for Meaning*, Viktor Frankl, a Holocaust survivor, recalls his experience in the Nazi death camps and reflects on the awful suffering there. In his introduction to the book, Frankl says, "This story is not about the suffering and death of great heroes and martyrs . . . it is not so much concerned with the sufferings of the mighty but with the sacrifices, the crucifixion and the deaths of the great army of unknown and unrecorded victims."[11]

Today, visitors to the Auschwitz concentration camp walk along a corridor lined with the records of each prisoner's arrival date, their photograph, and the date on which they died. That date was usually three months to one year after the entry date. Women died after three to six months, and men within a year. Prisoners existed in filthy, sparse and cramped conditions enduring utter deprivation. Human persons were reduced to things or even beasts. Numbers were tattooed on their arms and sewn onto their filthy clothing. Their names were not used. "The authorities were interested only in the captives' numbers. These numbers were often tattooed on their skin, and also had to be sewn to a certain spot on the trousers, jacket, or coat."[12]

The prisoners were regarded as subhuman by their guards and were hated and despised. They lived knowing that death was imminent – if not today or

---

10. Ginsburg, "Why Did the Holocaust Take Place?"

11. Yad Vashem, the Holocaust Museum in Jerusalem carries out continuing research into the names and lives of victims.

12. Frankl, *Man's Search for Meaning*.

tomorrow, it would be the next day. Dead bodies surrounded them. Some hung on gallows in the camp, others on the electric fence that surrounded the camp, on which many prisoners committed suicide. At the adjoining death camp of Birkenau, two thousand people a day were dying in gas chambers by 1945. The massive crematorium where the bodies were burnt rained ash like snow across the camp.

Those who had not yet died lived in filth, clothed in rags, diseased and emaciated, yet forced to work for those who despised and murdered them. Their thinking was dominated by the need for food and the struggle to survive. For even in such appalling conditions, prisoners struggled for life. They hoped for the end of the war. They fantasized about good food. They lived an under-life in the shadows of the pain of their great suffering. To be was to suffer this overwhelming immediate pain every second. "Yet," says Frankl, "it is possible to practice the art of living even in a concentration camp, although suffering is omnipresent."[13]

Even in suffering of the greatest intensity, it is still possible to live and hope, even when there is no place for creativity or enjoyment, if one embraces suffering.

> If there is a meaning in life at all, then there must be a meaning in suffering. Suffering is an ineradicable part of life, even as fate and death. Without suffering and death human life cannot be complete.
>
> The way in which a man accepts his fate and all the suffering it entails, the way in which he takes up his cross, gives him ample opportunity – even under the most difficult circumstances – to add a deeper meaning to his life.[14]

Here there is an echo of Jesus's words, "If anyone would come after me, let him deny himself and take up his cross and follow me. For whoever would save his life will lose it, but whoever loses his life for my sake will find it. For what will it profit a man if he gains the whole world and forfeits his soul?" (Matt 16:24–26).

The denial of self is not the denial of personhood but the laying down of the delusion of pseudo-personhood. Taking up of one's cross – embracing one's own suffering – results in the destruction of false personhood and opens the way to abundant and eternal life.

Frankl, a Jew, applies the words of Jesus to his own plight and the plight of his fellow prisoners. He is inside suffering, so to speak, yet in and through

---

13. Frankl, 55.
14. Frankl, 79.

this suffering he comes to the position of seeing suffering as vital to gaining a more profound meaning to life.

> When a man finds that it is his destiny to suffer, he will have to accept his suffering as his task… He will have to acknowledge the fact that even in suffering he is unique and alone in the universe. No one can relieve him of his suffering or suffer in his place. His unique opportunity lies in the way in which he bears his burden.[15]

Frankl has reached a new world view in which worth based on material values and the enjoyment of a materialistic lifestyle has been found to be worthless. Meaning is not found in material things. Speaking of himself and his fellow prisoners, he writes:

> Once the meaning of suffering had been revealed to us, we refused to minimize or alleviate the camp's tortures by ignoring them or harbouring false illusions and entertaining artificial optimism. Suffering had become a task on which we did not want to turn our backs. We had realized its hidden opportunities for achievement, the opportunities which caused the poet Rilke to write, "*Wie viel ist aufzuleiden!*" (How much suffering there is to get through).[16]

The power of these words lies in the circumstances in which they were written. From such a terrible scenario comes a statement of great gravity and seriousness concerning the sufferers' view of the true value of their suffering.

"Life in a concentration camp tore open the human soul and exposed its depths."[17] The depths were the ultimate reality of good and evil. The prisoners could see unbounded evil in contrast with their hope for the good. For those who lost hope of the good and for those that committed suicide, there was only unbounded evil.

---

15. Frankl, 86.
16. Frankl, 86–87.
17. Frankl, 94.

15

The Triumph of Faith and Glory

> *We end by looking at the relationship between faith and meaning. Faith is the antithesis of our suffering, and the antidote for suffering is increased faith. Through the bonding of faith and meaning we gain total coherence in our lives. Meaning as a moral principle produces a new perspective on suffering until we ultimately arrive at the final destiny of faith, meaning, and suffering, which is seeing the majesty of the glory of God. This eternal and infinite glory transforms human pain into pearls of infinite value.*

Christians have taken the leap of faith into God and they seek to live completely in terms of this growing faith. They follow Christ on the way to heaven, where questions of meaning and purpose will be superfluous. Yet in the present their faith is confronted on all sides by the meaninglessness and apparent incoherence of human life and being. Faith itself, even strong resolute faith, is rarely constant. It has highs and lows, and the lows can take us into a sea of agonizing meaninglessness and pointlessness, leaving us cast down and even depressed, yet we are never in despair and never destroyed. It is this flux that makes it important that we end this book with consideration of the place of faith in relation to the meaning of our lives, and with a celebration of what God is doing in and through us.

The Place of Faith

The meaning of human life is God's meaning for it. We are commanded to love God with our whole heart and mind and our neighbours as ourselves (Mark 12:30–31), and this command to love is the ground of meaning. Our purpose is to live in the love of God, totally and absolutely, and in so doing glorify God.

More than all the heavens, all of God's visible creation, God's glory shines through his amazing grace.

But with what capacity are human beings to summon such love? The answer is through faith. Love and faith are a necessary marriage of spiritual reality, forged in heaven. Faith is thus the antithesis of suffering. The suffering of true and committed Christians (apart from deserved suffering) produces increased access to God, and increased access to God produces greater knowledge of God, and greater knowledge is evidenced through a greater capacity to love. Since this love of God and neighbour is the love born in human hearts through the gift of faith, faith is the medicine of suffering. It is not the cure for suffering but for the pain of suffering. Suffering continues, but the pain is reduced. The medicine of faith conquers the pain and renders it neutral.

The life of Jabez

Suffering is best understood as a process that increases being. We could even say that it increases our territory. Take, for example, the experience of Jabez:

> Jabez was more honourable than his brothers; and his mother called his name Jabez, saying, "Because I bore him in pain." Jabez called upon the God of Israel, saying, "Oh that you would bless me and enlarge my border, and that your hand might be with me, and that you would keep me from harm so that it might not bring me pain!" And God granted what he asked. (1 Chr 4:9–10)

Part of the curse of Eve was that she would bear children in pain. Jabez's mother endured that pain at his birth, and gave him a name that was a living memorial to her suffering. Similarly, Jesus in his reinterpretation of the Passover at the Last Supper commanded believers to remember his great pain and make it an essential part of their lives until he returns.

Jabez asked for the pain passed on from his mother's pain to be removed from him. He prayed for increased being and to be free from suffering. God blessed Jabez through granting his request. However, Jabez's fundamental request was that God would be with him and that he would undergo ontological increase through God's presence with him. It seems that Jabez was a great man of faith. The pain of fallen human being could not be removed from Jabez, but through his faith, the presence of God set him free from its pangs.

In the presence of God the pain of fallenness, in all its forms, is rendered impotent. Through faith, the pain of suffering is neutralized. In this respect suffering is cured, but it is not removed. It could be said that it is isolated, so that it has no negative effect on a believer and instead becomes a great privilege. The enduring of suffering is transformed so that the pain is no longer negative and destructive. This change comes with the recognition that the suffering of fallen human nature has a great purpose within the being of the love of God, for it renders its victim holy. Suffering is the pain of becoming holy or being sanctified.

Matthew Henry writes that Jabez's mother gave him his name:

> that it might likewise be a memorandum to him what this world is into which she bore him, a vale of tears, in which he must expect few days and full of trouble. The sorrow he carried in his name might help to put a seriousness upon his spirit. It might also remind him to love and honour his mother, and labour, in everything, to be a comfort to her who brought him into the world with so much sorrow.[1]

The increase Jabez asked for was an increase in faith, through which he would be freed from pain. Through faith, suffering changes from bondage and misery to freedom and privilege and even joy.

The suffering that is the existential reality of fallenness can have two outcomes. For unbelievers, who have no faith, it produces only misery and fear and ultimately the destruction of personhood. For believers, suffering increases both knowledge and the capacity to act with love through an increased faith that is able to receive and joyfully bear the presence of God. For believers, suffering is the way into the presence of God. It is a robe that must be donned to enter the fearful though joyful presence. Increased territory is increased faith.

Increased faith

Increased faith is the realm of certainty of the being of God, Father, Son and Holy Spirit. It is absolute surety of the truth of the Son, the Lord Jesus. It is utter commitment to the veracity and integrity of the perfection of the providence of a sovereign God. It is rejoicing in the inner heart that our personal identity and the personal identities of all of saved humanity – the new Jerusalem – are absolutely and eternally secure.

Increased faith is the realm of higher being reached through long suffering in Christ and with Christ. It is the fruit of inner ontological pain, undeserved suffering, suffering for others and suffering for God. Indeed, higher being is

---

1. Henry, *Commentary on the Whole Bible*.

built on a bed of suffering. Higher being is not a height but rather a depth in the valley of tears that has become a beautiful fragrant ointment of life. In this scenario, pain vanishes and suffering with Christ is the greatest joy.

Increased faith is the place of absolute healing of soul and spirit and mind. This place is the city of peace in the Son and in the neighbourhood of the people of God. It is in itself the absolute coherence of eternal being. It holds together redeemed being in God or, as Paul puts it, it is life "in" Christ. Faith is having our being in Christ. Greater faith is having all of our being in Christ, which is effectively all of our being in Father, Son and Holy Spirit.

Outside of saving faith human beings have their being in themselves and the image and perception they have of themselves. Their purpose is the security and elevation and ultimate glorification of themselves. Death and the thought of death threaten this delusion and prompt frantic effort to retain the self and its will to power. Yet self-sufficiency is termed being-for-itself by Sartre, who calls this mode of being bad faith, or inauthentic life.[2]

Jesus talks not of authentic life but of abundant life (John 10:10). We may say that real life or fruitful life is the life of, and in, increased faith. Yet Christ's dual commandment focuses not on faith but on love: we must "love" God with all of our heart, soul and mind and our neighbour as ourselves (Luke 10:27). This commandment, along with the commandment to forgive (Matt 18:23–35; Mark 11:25), is the essence of what we term human being and human life.

The essence of being then is love, but we have our being in faith. The most primary meaning of suffering is that it increases the faith in which we have our being. This faith when increased is the ground of abundant life. The ultimate purpose of suffering is thus abundant life.

Meaning and faith

One of the key ontological questions human beings ask, mostly to themselves, is "What is the meaning of human life?" More specifically we ask, "What is the meaning of my life?" We long for meaning to give coherence to human existence in general and to our own being. And because the Enlightenment has impressed on Western minds the presupposition that reason is the key element in gaining knowledge, we seek to use reason as we search for meaning.

In response to this search for meaning, the Dutch Christian philosopher Herman Dooyeweerd has said "Meaning is the being of all that has been

---

2. Sartre, *Being and Nothingness*, 95. (For more on this concept, see chapter 13.)

created," or more fully, "meaning is the mode of being of creation."[3] Whatever he means by this statement, and his meaning is obscure, he clearly treats "meaning" as synonymous with "being."

However, I would disagree with him and say that faith, rather than meaning, is our mode of being. It is in faith that we find ontological coherence, and indeed absolute ontological coherence. Faith is the glue that holds our being together, and all being together. It is synonymous with authentic being. Increased faith in Christ may be termed the authentic mode of being.

Meaning, however, is vital to fallen human being. In heaven, meaning is immediate; it requires no process of thought to be arrived at. But we are not yet in heaven, and so we need to use reasoning processes in order to find meaning. Indeed, God's creation appears to be structured in such a way that we may apply human logic to it in our search to understand it and acquire knowledge. To increased faith, however, faith is primary to reason and to the epistemological process.

The result of this is that those who have faith have a different value system, one in which knowledge and truth have moral value relating to the kingdom of God. When we are reborn of the Spirit we can "see" the kingdom of God.[4] Our eyes are opened to behold the transcendence and we receive faith as a gift of God. In this faith, which grows and increases through suffering, meaning takes on a moral dimension and becomes a higher principle.

We have said and can say then that through faith we can assent to the higher principle that the meaning of an object, or indeed of our own self, is the meaning that God gives it. There must, however, be continuity between the transcendent creation meaning and human meaning, logic and reason. If there were not, there would be no possibility of real analogy through which we could talk about God (theology) or even know God. Human meaning, then, is analogous to God's primordial meaning for creation. God speaks to us in human words; he engages us in human language. Human words have the capacity to receive and communicate the word of God. The hearing ear, however, can only be the ear of faith. It is only through faith that the word of God can be received in human words.[5]

---

3. Dooyeweerd, *New Critique of Theoretical Thought*, 4.

4. John 3:3. The beatitudes in Matt 5:2–11 give us insight into the value system of heaven. The kingdom of God means the rule of Christ in human hearts.

5. Echoing Karl Barth.

A New Perspective on Suffering

Karl Marx is often seen as attacking Christianity, and indeed all religions, with his famous dictum "religion is the opium of the people." But let us look at his statement in the context in which it was originally uttered:

> Religious suffering is, at one and the same time, the expression of real suffering and a protest against real suffering. Religion is the sigh of the oppressed creature, the heart of a heartless world, and the soul of soulless conditions. It is the opium of the people.[6]

According to humanist commentator Austin Cline:

> Marx is saying that religion's purpose is to create illusory fantasies for the poor. Economic realities prevent them from finding true happiness in this life, so religion tells them this is OK because they will find true happiness in the next life. Although this is a criticism of religion, Marx is not without sympathy: people are in distress and religion does provide solace, just as people who are physically injured receive relief from opiate-based drugs....
>
> The problem lies in the obvious fact that an opiate drug fails to fix a physical injury – it merely helps you forget pain and suffering. Relief from pain may be fine up to a point, but only as long as you are also trying to solve the underlying problems causing the pain. Similarly, religion does not fix the underlying causes of people's pain and suffering – instead, it helps them forget why they are suffering and causes them to look forward to an imaginary future when the pain will cease.
>
> Even worse, this "drug" is being administered by the oppressors who are responsible for the pain and suffering in the first place.[7]

Suffering in this scenario is understood to be a negative consequence of the evil behaviour of others.

Suffering may also be conceived of as karma, that is, a cosmic punishment for bad behaviour in this life or a previous life. What is almost universally true is that suffering is perceived as something to be avoided and escaped. Marxists

---

6. Marx, *Contribution to the Critique of Hegel's Philosophy of Right*.
7. Cline, "Karl Marx on Religion as the Opium of the People."

regard religion as a form of escapism, offering "pie in the sky when you die."[8] They regard the Bible as a kind of historical spiritual confidence trick.

If there were no God, such a view might be correct. But there is a God who is the sovereign creator of all being, and those who hold these views are tragically wrong. They are blind and cannot see the kingdom of heaven.

Those who through evil intent cause suffering, often terrible suffering, for others and particularly for the vulnerable will not escape judgement. According to the prophets, oppressors will not prosper. Their harshness, trickery and illusions through whatever means and in whatever form cannot prevail.

> May [God] defend the cause of the poor of the people,
> give deliverance to the children of the needy,
> and crush the oppressor! (Ps 72:4)

> I will make your oppressors eat their own flesh,
> and they shall be drunk with their own blood as with wine.
> Then all flesh shall know
> that I am the Lord your Saviour,
> and your Redeemer, the Mighty One of Jacob. (Isa 49:26)

True religion can never be an oppressor and a cruel and false master inflicting suffering on the already afflicted; rather, it is the means of restoration. Marxism, in the hands of Vladimir Lenin, Joseph Stalin and Communists in general is actually a cruel master. Part of the problem is that Marxists conceive of suffering as only a physical category, and understand it purely in economic and material terms. Tragically, many Christians appear to be conditioned to think in the same way. They think of suffering in economic terms, as something that destroys human resources and frustrates human fulfilment. They conceive of pain as the opposite of pleasure and as the enemy of abundant life, conceived of as a life of pleasure.

But, as I have argued in this book, suffering is not primarily physical; it is spiritual. Thus it must be understood not in economic terms but in spiritual terms. We need to recognize that suffering is itself the means of reaching not some utopia but eternal life in the presence of God the Father, Son and Holy Spirit. This suffering not only cannot be escaped from by Christian faith, it must not be escaped from. Following Christ is the way of taking up our cross. We must take up and accept our own suffering with Christ.

---

8. Original phrase from the song entitled *The Preacher and the Slave*, written by Joe Hill in 1911.

This is, I believe, the true perspective on suffering and its immense value. On this view, the suffering of Christians is wholly positive. It is inevitable and unavoidable for those of fallen human nature who are regenerate, for it is the force of sanctification and increased faith. Through increased faith we are able to embrace suffering, receive and grow in a greater knowledge of God, and so behold God's glory.

The Glory of God is the Transformation of Human Pain

The apostle Paul states: "I consider that the sufferings of this present time are not worth comparing with the glory about to be revealed to us" (Rom 8:18) and "I count everything as loss because of the surpassing worth of knowing Christ Jesus my Lord. For his sake I have suffered the loss of all things and count them as rubbish, in order that I may gain Christ" (Phil 3:8).

Increased faith takes away the pain of suffering not by delusion but in the utter weight of the love of God, received through beholding his glory. The glory of God wraps our pain with a wonderful cloak producing a valuable gem infinitely more valuable than diamonds, gold and silver.

The glory of God is the total consummation of the suffering of our souls. The consuming fire of God is the fire of infinite love and justice. This is the infinite weight of the glory of God which is made manifest through the dynamic and product of God's creation.

This infinite weight of glory is the appearance of God's *shekinah* glory as the infinity appears in the finite creation. It is what we read of in Exodus:

> Then Moses went up on the mountain, and the cloud covered the mountain. The glory of the Lord dwelt on Mount Sinai, and . . . he called to Moses out of the midst of the cloud. Now the appearance of the glory of the Lord was like a devouring fire on the top of the mountain in the sight of the people of Israel. (Exod 24:15–17)

God's glory is the manifestation of his being, which the people of Israel perceived as a consuming fire on Sinai. That fire also appeared to the Israelites at the tent of meeting (Num 14:10) and it will ultimately be revealed to all human beings (Isa 40:5).

Glory is the external manifestation of God to human perception. It is something that we can see, and therefore it exists in human consciousness, or rather, in the consciousness of all who behold it, including the angels. Glory is the visible manifestation of the greatness, goodness, love and grace of God.

The substance of the glory is God's nature, expressed through his creation and in relationship with his creation.

> Moses said, "Please show me your glory." And he said, "I will make all my goodness pass before you, and will proclaim before you my name 'The Lord.' And I will be gracious to whom I will be gracious, and will show mercy on whom I will show mercy. But," he said, "you cannot see my face, for man shall not see me and live." And the Lord said, "Behold, there is a place by me where you shall stand on the rock, and while my glory passes by I will put you in a cleft of the rock, and I will cover you with my hand until I have passed by. Then I will take away my hand, and you shall see my back, but my face shall not be seen." (Exod 33:18–23)

The face of the Lord is the infinite weight of the glory of God that cannot be revealed to a finite being. His "back" is that aspect of the infinite weight that is communicable to finite beings created in the image of infinite being.

Beholding the absolute beauty, veracity and goodness of the infinite and eternal holy Being through grace is the healing and, indeed, saving dynamic. This grace in its fullness of glory is beheld through the raising up of Christ on the cross. The beholding of this crucified Christ is the greatest glory witnessed and received by humankind. Those looking, however, may perceive two different realities: some will see the infinite grace of God while others see only a despised, humiliated and broken man enduring the most extreme Roman punishment for crime.

The concept of salvation through looking or gazing is glimpsed in the book of Numbers.

> From Mount Hor [the Israelites] set out by the way to the Red Sea, to go around the land of Edom. And the people became impatient on the way. And the people spoke against God and against Moses, "Why have you brought us up out of Egypt to die in the wilderness? For there is no food and no water, and we loathe this worthless food." Then the Lord sent fiery serpents among the people, and they bit the people, so that many people of Israel died. And the people came to Moses, and said, "We have sinned, for we have spoken against the Lord and against you. Pray to the Lord, that he take away the serpents from us." So Moses prayed for the people. And the Lord said to Moses, "Make a fiery serpent, and set it on a pole, and every one who is bitten, when he sees it, shall live." So Moses made a bronze serpent, and set it on a pole. And

if a serpent bit anyone, he would look at the bronze serpent and live. (Num 21:4–9)

We have already dealt fleetingly with the bronze serpent earlier in the book. Now I want to lay claim to the fact that the bronze serpent is mostly interpreted by Christians as an early representation of Christ.

When the Israelites who had been bitten looked to the bronzed serpent raised up on Moses's rod, they were saved from death. In the same way, God's wrath, his righteous judgement, is appeased when we look to Christ. Christ was raised up to be seen. The power of beholding both the abhorrence of his suffering and the glory of his body on the cross is revealed. The abhorrence is transformed into the glory of God in the consciousness of the beholder. In this act of beholding, the gift of faith is bestowed and the beholder sees the glory of the kingdom of God for the first time. The dialectic of good and evil is resolved for the beholder.

Jesus's prayer in the Gospel of John reveals this glory: "Now, Father, glorify me in your own presence with the glory that I had with you before the world existed" (John 17:5). This Trinitarian glory is beheld primarily by the Persons of the Trinity and secondarily by the angels. In this glory the passion of Christ is redefined as the greatest good, otherwise known as grace. This grace is the infinite glory of God flowing, or seeping, into human conscious awareness. The primary purpose of a human being is to live in and utterly assent to this glory, through the eyes of finite passion. Human suffering, then, is the preparation of the human heart to behold God's infinite and eternal glory.

The value of temporary suffering, as Paul recognized (Rom 8:18), cannot be compared with the value of the infinite glory of God revealed in the suffering of Christ. The value of our suffering lies in our increased capacity to behold this glory. This value is understood in terms of the meaning and purpose of human life.[9]

Through the pain of his great suffering, Job came to behold the glory of God. The revelation followed the suffering. The finite valley of tears makes the infinite glory of God accessible to human consciousness. Not to endure this pain, the pain suffered by Christ, is not to enter through the gate of this amazing revelation.

---

9. Compare the Westminster Confession of Faith, Shorter Catechism: "Q. 1. What is the chief end of man? A. Man's chief end is to glorify God, and to enjoy him forever."

Recommended Further Reading

For those who would like to get a further sense of Camus:

>Camus, Albert. *The Plague*. Translated by Stuart Gilbert. New York: Vintage Books, 1972.

An insightful reflection on the pain of aloneness:

>Ejsing, Anette. *The Power of One: Theological Reflections on Loneliness*. Eugene: Cascade Books (an imprint of Wipf & Stock), 2011.

I recommend this further central text of Hegel:

>Hegel, G. W. F. *Lectures on the Philosophy of Religion*. Edited by Peter C. Hodgson. Translated by R. F. Brown, Peter C. Hodgson and J. M. Stewart. Oxford: Clarendon, 2007.

Good for reviewing Augustine's theodicy and also Irenaeus:

>Hick, John. *Evil and the God of Love*. New York: Palgrave Macmillan, 2007.

>Irenaeus. *Adversus Haereses* (Against Heresies). Createspace. Amazon. Seattle, 2012.

For further reading in Kierkegaard, although difficult, this is a great insight into existential theology from the perspective of suffering of angst:

>Kierkegaard, Søren. *Fear and Trembling*. London: Penguin Great Ideas, 2005.

Here is Luther's apparently anti-semitic text cited often by Messianic believers (Christians) as an example of Christian anti-Semitism:

>Luther, Martin. *On the Jews and Their Lies*. Austin: Rivercrest Publishing, 2014.

For those who may want to look into Hegel's early biases:

> Marx, Karl. *Critique of Hegel's 'Philosophy of Right.'* Edited by J. O'Malley, translated by Annette Jolin and J. O'Malley, written 1843–44. Cambridge: Cambridge University Press, 1970.

This resource is an example of extreme racism and white supremacy, providing insight into profound bigotry and ignorance bent on wiping out difference:

> Ridgeway, James. *Blood in the Face.* New York: Thunder's Mouth Press, 1990.

Recommended reading on Surin:

> Surin, Kenneth. *Theology and the Problem of Evil.* Eugene, OR: Wipf & Stock, 2004.

Weinandy's book is well worth reading in full:

> Weinandy, Thomas G. *Does God Suffer?* Edinburgh: T&T Clark, 2000.

Bibliography

Anselm of Canterbury. *Cur Deus Homo* [Why God became a man] in *St. Anselm Basic Writings*. Chicago: Open Court Publishing, 1962.

Aquinas, Thomas. *Summa Theologica*. 1911 translation.

Arthur, James Bryson. *A Theology of Sexuality and Marriage*. Nairobi: Uzima Press, 1998.

Augustine of Hippo. *Confessions*. Translated by Henry Chadwick. Oxford: Oxford University Press, 2008.

Barth, Karl. *Church Dogmatics*, Vols. 3 and 4. Edinburgh: T&T Clark, 1962.

Berkhof, Louis. *Systematic Theology*. 4th ed. Grand Rapids: Eerdmans, 1976.

Bonhoeffer, Dietrich. *The Cost of Discipleship*. New York: Macmillan, 1963.

———. *Ethics*. London: SCM, 1955.

———. *Letters and Papers*. London: SCM Press, 1971.

Brand, Paul, and Phillip Yancey. *The Gift of Pain*. Grand Rapids: Zondervan, 1997.

Calvin, John. *Institutes of the Christian Religion*, Vol. 1. Grand Rapids: Eerdmans, 1981.

Camus, Albert. *The Myth of Sisyphus and Other Essays*. New York: Knopf, 1964.

———. *The Plague*. Translated by Stuart Gilbert. New York: Vintage Books, 1972.

Carstens, Kenneth N. *Article: Persecution of Churchmen and Other Religious Workers Oppressed by Apartheid*. South African History Online.

Cline, Austin. "Karl Marx on Religion as the Opium of the People." https://www.thoughtco.com/karl-marx-on-religion-251019.

Cosby, H. Brian. *Suffering and Sovereignty*. Grand Rapids: Reformation Heritage Books, 2012.

Cunningham, Scott. *Through Many Tribulations: The Theology of Persecution in Luke-Acts*. Sheffield: Sheffield Academic Press, 1997.

Davis, Stephen. *Encountering Evil: Live Options in Theodicy*. Louisville: John Knox Press, 1981.

Dawkins, Richard. *The Selfish Gene*. Oxford: Oxford University Press, 1976.

Dooyeweerd, Herman. *A New Critique of Theoretical Thought*, Vol. 1. Translated by David Freeman. New York: Edwin Mellen Press, 1997.

Dunn, James D. G. *The Theology of Paul the Apostle*. Grand Rapids: Eerdmans, 2006.

Erickson, Millard J. *Introducing Christian Theology*. 3rd ed. Grand Rapids: Baker Academic, 2015.

Eusebius. *Ecclesiastical History*. Book 11, chapter 23. Translated by C. F. Cruse. Peabody, MA: Hendrickson, 2008.

Frankl, Victor. *Man's Search for Meaning*. London: Random House, 2004.

Gerrish, B. A. *A Prince of the Church: Schleiermacher and the Beginnings of Modern Theology*. Philadelphia: Fortress, 1984.

Ginsburg, Val. "Why Did the Holocaust Take Place? The Personal View of Val Ginsburg." http://holocaustlearning.org/reflections/valginsburg1.
Guthrie, Donald. *New Testament Theology*. Downers Grove: IVP Academic, 2013.
Hegel, G. W. F. *Lectures on the Philosophy of Religion*. Edited by Peter C. Hodgson. Translated by R. F. Brown, Peter C. Hodgson and J. M. Stewart. Oxford: Clarendon, 2007.
———. *The Phenomenology of Mind*. Translated by J. B. Baillie. New York: Harper Torch, 1967.
Heidegger, Martin. *Being and Time*. Translated by John Macquarrie and Edwin Robinson. Oxford: Blackwell, 1967.
Hengel, Martin. *Crucifixion in the Ancient World and the Folly of the Message of the Cross*. Translated by John Bowden. London: SCM, 1977.
Henry, Matthew. *Commentary on the Whole Bible: Genesis to Revelation*. Edited by Leslie F. Church. Grand Rapids: Zondervan, 1978.
Hick, John. *Evil and the God of Love*. New York: Palgrave Macmillan, 2007.
Jung, Karl. "Definitions." In *Psychological Types*. Vol. 6 of *Collected Works of C. G. Jung*. Princeton: Princeton University Press, 2014.
Kelly, J. N. D. *Early Christian Doctrines*. London: A & C Black, 1985.
Kierkegaard, Søren. *The Concept of Anxiety*. Translated by Reidar Thomte in collaboration with Albert B. Anderson. Princeton: Princeton University Press, 1980.
———. "The Difference between Genius and an Apostle." In *Without Authority*, vol. 18 of *Kierkegaard's Writings*. Princeton: Princeton University Press, 2009.
———. *Fear and Trembling*. London: Penguin Great Ideas, 2005.
———. *The Gospel of Sufferings*. Translated by A. S. Aldworth and W. S. Ferrie. Cambridge: J. Clarke, 1982.
———. The *Sickness unto Death*. Translated by Alastair Hanny. London: Penguin Books, 2008.
Leftow, Brian. "Immutability." Article in *Stanford University Encyclopedia of Philosophy*, posted 5 August 2014. https://plato.stanford.edu/entries/immutability/.
Longman, Tremper, III. *Job*. Grand Rapids: Baker Academic, 2012.
Luther, Martin. *On the Jews and Their Lies*. Austin: Rivercrest Publishing, 2014.
Macquarrie, John. *Principles of Christian Theology*. London: SCM, 1977.
Mandela, Nelson. *Long Walk To Freedom*. London: Abacus, 1995.
Marshall, Taylor. *The Catholic Perspective on Paul: Paul and Origins of Catholic Christianity*. Dallas: Saint John Press, 2010.
———. *In Search of Deity*. London: SCM Press, 1984.
———. *In Search of Humanity*. London: SCM Press, 1982.
More, Thomas. *The Sadness of Christ*. Oxford: Benediction Classics, 2010. Also available online at https://www.thomasmorestudies.org/docs/Sadness%20Christ%201.pdf.
Morris, Henry et al. *Creation Basics & Beyond*. Dallas: Institute for Creation Research, 2013.

Munza, Kasongo. *A Letter to Africa about Africa.* Kempton Park, SA: TWR Africa Region, 2008.

Murphy-O'Connor, Jerome. *Paul: A Critical Life.* Oxford: Clarendon, 1996.

Nietzsche, Friedrich. *The Will to Power.* London: Penguin, 1968.

O'Brien, Peter. *Colossians Philemon.* In Word Biblical Commentary. Nashville: Thomas Nelson, 1982.

Otto, Rudolf. *The Idea of the Holy.* Translated by John Harvey. Oxford: Oxford University Press, 1958.

Penner, Glen. *In the Shadow of the Cross: A Biblical Theology of Persecution and Discipleship.* Bartlesville: Living Sacrifice Books, 2004.

Pizzalato, Brian. *St Paul Explains the Meaning of Suffering.* Catholic News Agency CNA. 8 July 2010.

Plank, Karl. *Paul and the Irony of Affliction.* Atlanta: Scholars Press, 1987.

Rahner, Karl. *Hearers of the Word.* London: Sheed & Ward, 1969.

———. *Theological Investigations.* New York: Herder & Herder, 1972.

———. *The Trinity.* London: Herder & Herder, 1970.

Rice, Richard. *Suffering and the Search for Meaning.* Downers Grove: IVP Academic, 2014.

Ridgeway, James. *Blood in the Face.* New York: Thunder's Mouth Press, 1990.

Samson, Anthony. *Mandela.* London: Harper Collins, 1999.

Sanders, John. *The God Who Risks: A Theology of Divine Providence.* Downers Grove: InterVarsity Press, 2007.

Sartre, Jean-Paul. *Being and Nothingness.* Translated by Hazel E. Barnes. Abingdon: Routledge, 2003.

———. *Nausea.* Translated by Robert Baldrick. London: Penguin, 1963.

Saunders, Fr. William. "The Passion of Jesus Christ." Article posted by Catholic Education Resource Centre. www.catholiceducation.org.

Schleiermacher, Friedrich. *The Christian Faith.* Louisville, KY: Westminster John Knox, 2016. Originally published in German in 1830.

———. *On Religion: Speeches to Its Cultured Despisers.* Translated by Richard Crouter. Cambridge: Cambridge University Press, 1996. Originally published in German in 1799.

Schreiner, Thomas. *Paul – Apostle of God's Glory in Christ: A Pauline Theology.* Downers Grove: IVP Academic, 2001.

Shimmel, Solomon. *Wounds Not Healed by Time: The Power of Repentance and Forgiveness.* Oxford: Oxford University Press, 2002.

Stott, John. *The Message of Acts.* The Bible Speaks Today Series. Leicester: Inter-Varsity Press. Previously Nottingham, 1994.

Surin, Kenneth. *Theology and the Problem of Evil.* Eugene, OR: Wipf & Stock, 2004.

Tiesze, Charles L. "Striving Towards a Theology of Persecution." *Global Missiology* 2, no. 4 (2007). http://ojs.globalmissiology.org/index.php/english/article/viewFile/295/825.

Tillich, Paul. *Ultimate Concern.* London: SCM Press, 1965.
Vanstone, W. H. *The Risk of Love.* New York: Oxford University Press, 1978.
Wall, Robert. *Colossians and Philemon.* Leicester: Inter-Varsity Press, 1993.
Weinandy, Thomas G. *Does God Suffer?* Edinburgh: T&T Clark, 2000.

Index

A
abandonment, Jesus's sufferings 107
Adam and Eve 5
   conscience 16
   disobedience 24
   image of God 24
   physical pain 15
adoption 75
agape love 23
alienation, cause of suffering 7
aloneness 17, 65
   and adoption 75
angst 4, 22
   and blessing 76
   and freedom 201
   awareness of our finitude 59
   das Nichtige 36
   inner suffering 35
   knowledge of evil 37
   return to non-being 58
   solution 69
Aquinas, Thomas 120
Arendt, Hannah 206
aseity 128
atheism 59
attributes
   God's communicable 130
   God's incommunicable 130
Augustine 26

B
Barth, Karl 54
being-for-itself 20, 183, 184, 201, 212
Bonhoeffer, Dietrich 38, 182

C
Camus, Albert 18, 57
community, our need 65
conflict, its roots 179
conscience 16

Council of Chalcedon 118
Council of Ephesus 118
creation love 23
cross
   of Christ 25
   revelation of grace 138
crucifixion 109
curse
   on Adam 6
   on Eve 7

D
death 7, 149
   the great problem 56
delusion 11
dialectic, difference and similarity 195
difference
   as threat 196
   economic 201
   ethnic 198
   racial 197
   sexual 197
disobedience 6
Dooyeweerd, Herman 212
Dunn, James 1
dying to self 37

E
Ecclesiastes, on meaninglessness 18
extermination 205

F
faith, the antithesis of suffering 210
fall, the 14
fear 22
finitude 20
foreknowledge 122
forgiveness
   definition 49
   of God 51

Frankl, Viktor 206
free choice 6
freedom 5, 27
   and responsibility 62
   and security 74

G
God, fear of 138
GodMan 115
God's essential nature 121

H
hatred 189
   and terrorism 190
Heidegger, Martin 6
Heilsgeschichte 121
Hick, John 55
Hitler, Adolf 147
human body, pre-fall 15

I
immanence 123
   of God in creation 25, 124
immutability 119
   doctrine of 123
   of God 120
impassibility 117
   and God's activity 124
   of God 119
impotence
   and atonement 72
   our sense of 60
incarnation 127
individuation 6
   original sin 8
   self-determination. *See* self-determination
   type of 8
Irenaeus 27

J
Job
   counsellors 98
   God's providence 95
   God's voice 96
   his lament 87
   ignorant of God's law 83, 85
   reaching to transcendance 87
   staring at death 88
   suffering 79, 81, 83
judgement 6
Jung, Karl 8

K
kenosis 118
Kierkegaard, Søren 140
knowledge
   innate 133
   of good and evil 6

L
Leftow, Brian 121
love 123

M
Marx, Karl 214
meaning, of life 212

N
natural theology 132
Nestorius 117
Nichtige, das 54
Nietzsche, Friedrich 9, 147, 187
nothingness 54

O
offence(s)
   corporate or community 186
   individual 185
offences, against one's personhood 48
omnipotence 128
omniscience 121
original sin 6, 132
   moral evil 28
   root of suffering 13
Otto, Rudolf 132

P
pain
   before the fall 16
   of aloneness 66
   of God 23

physical 14
spiritual 14
passibility 117
persecution 156
   and mission 165
   and the triumph of God 164
   as risk 167
   divine providence 162
   dying for Christ 160
   its character 164
   its nature 156
   of difference 203
   suffering for righteousness 158
Plank, Karl 137
providence 122

R
Rahner, Karl 123
responsibility and inability 60
resurrection 70
revelation, limits of 128
risk
   and betrayal 174
   as faith in action 169
   as inner suffering 167
   as leap of faith 171
   as potential loss 170
   as sacrifice 173
   as vulnerability 168
   as wisdom 173

S
sacrifice, Son of God 25
Sartre, Jean-Paul 11, 20, 56, 64, 183
segregation 203
self-determination 7, 8, 9, 147
self-forgiveness 51
self-love 23
shame 51
silence, divine, as abandonment 93
spiritual pain, aloneness 17
Stephen (first Christian martyr) 160
suffering
   and comfort 145
   Apostle Paul 137
   atonement for sin 101

   author of 1
   cause 3
   deserved 31
   for God 40
   for others 39
   freedom from evil 102
   healing 45
   inner or ontological 139
   intrinsic to creation? 13
   meaning of 43
   mystery of 139
   nature and origins of 2
   nature of 3
   nature of Christ's suffering 102
   of biblical figures 79
   offences against our personhood 47
   offences by ourselves against
      ourselves 50
   of God 2
   of Jesus 101, 103, 114
   Paul 34
   product of evil 27
   quality of 1
   servant's, vicarious nature 113
   trauma of conflict 192
   types 31
   undeserved 3, 34, 44
   undeserved, divine silence 92
suicide 57

T
theodicy 26
transcendence 120, 123
transformation, of human pain 216
tree, knowledge of good and evil 5
Trinity, immanent or ontological 128
truth and transcendence 90

W
Weinandy, Thomas G. 127
Westminster Confession 120
will to power 9, 187

Langham

Langham Literature and its imprints are a ministry of Langham Partnership.

Langham Partnership is a global fellowship working in pursuit of the vision God entrusted to its founder John Stott –

> *to facilitate the growth of the church in maturity and Christ-likeness through raising the standards of biblical preaching and teaching.*

Our vision is to see churches in the majority world equipped for mission and growing to maturity in Christ through the ministry of pastors and leaders who believe, teach and live by the Word of God.

Our mission is to strengthen the ministry of the Word of God through:
- nurturing national movements for biblical preaching
- fostering the creation and distribution of evangelical literature
- enhancing evangelical theological education

especially in countries where churches are under-resourced.

Our ministry

Langham Preaching partners with national leaders to nurture indigenous biblical preaching movements for pastors and lay preachers all around the world. With the support of a team of trainers from many countries, a multi-level programme of seminars provides practical training, and is followed by a programme for training local facilitators. Local preachers' groups and national and regional networks ensure continuity and ongoing development, seeking to build vigorous movements committed to Bible exposition.

Langham Literature provides majority world preachers, scholars and seminary libraries with evangelical books and electronic resources through publishing and distribution, grants and discounts. The programme also fosters the creation of indigenous evangelical books in many languages, through writer's grants, strengthening local evangelical publishing houses, and investment in major regional literature projects, such as one volume Bible commentaries like *The Africa Bible Commentary* and *The South Asia Bible Commentary*.

Langham Scholars provides financial support for evangelical doctoral students from the majority world so that, when they return home, they may train pastors and other Christian leaders with sound, biblical and theological teaching. This programme equips those who equip others. Langham Scholars also works in partnership with majority world seminaries in strengthening evangelical theological education. A growing number of Langham Scholars study in high quality doctoral programmes in the majority world itself. As well as teaching the next generation of pastors, graduated Langham Scholars exercise significant influence through their writing and leadership.

To learn more about Langham Partnership and the work we do visit **langham.org**